# The Lectionary 2007

SPCK

First published in Great Britain in 2006

Society for Promoting Christian Knowledge
36 Causton Street
London SW1P 4ST



British Library Cataloguing-in-Publication Data
A catalogue record for this book is available from the British Library

ISBN-13: 978–0–281–05819–8
ISBN-10: 0–281–05819–9

1 3 5 7 9 10 8 6 4 2

Typeset by Northern Phototypesetting Co. Ltd, Bolton
Printed in Great Britain by Creative Print and Design (Wales), Ebbw Vale

# CONTENTS

# UNDERSTANDING THE

*Column 3 (Common Worship)*
**On Principal Feasts, Principal Holy Days, Sundays and Festivals** this gives the Principal Service Lectionary, intended for use at the maiin service of the day (in most churches the mid-morning service), whether or not it is a Eucharist.

**On other weekdays** this gives the Daily Eucharistic Lectionary for those wanting a semi-continuous pattern of readings and a psalm for Holy Communion. It is most useful in a church where there is a daily celebration and a core community that worships together day by day, though its use is not restricted to that.

*Column 4 (Common Worship)*
**On Principal Feasts, Principal Holy Days, Sundays and Festivals** this gives the Third Service Lectionary. Many churches will have no need of it, for it comes into use only if the Principal and Second Service Lectionaries have been used. Its most likely use is at Morning Prayer (when this is not the Principal Service). Where psalms are recommended for use in the morning, these also appear in this column.

**On other weekdays** this provides the psalmody and readings for Morning Prayer. Where two or more psalms are appointed, the psalm in bold italic may be used as the only psalm. Psalms printed in round brackets ( ) may be omitted if they are used as an opening canticle at Morning Prayer. Where † is printed after the psalm number, the psalm may be shortened if desired. For those wishing to follow the Ordinary Time psalm cycle throughout the year (except for the period between 19 December and the Epiphany and from the Monday of Holy Week to the Saturday of Easter Week), this is printed as an alternative to the seasonal provision.

*Column 1*
The date

**COMMON WORSHIP**

| **July 2007** | | | **Sunday Principal Service**<br>**Weekday Eucharist** | **Third Service**<br>**Morning Prayer** |
|---|---|---|---|---|
| **14** | Sa<br>**Gw** | **John Keble, Priest, Tractarian, Poet, 1866**<br>Com. Pastor *or*<br>*also* Lam. 3. 19–26<br>Matt. 5. 1–8 | Gen. 49. 29–end; 50. 15–25<br>Ps. 105. 1–7<br>Matt. 10. 24–33 | Ps. 120; ***121***; 122<br>Esther ch. 3<br>2 Cor. ch. 5 |
| **15** | **S**<br>**G** | **THE SIXTH SUNDAY AFTER TRINITY (Proper 10)**<br>*Track 1*<br>Amos 7. 7–end<br>Ps. 82<br>Col. 1. 1–14<br>Luke 10. 25–37 | *Track 2*<br>Deut. 30. 9–14<br>Ps. 25. 1–10<br>Col. 1. 1–14<br>Luke 10. 25–37 | Ps. 76<br>Deut. 28. 1–14<br>Acts 28. 17–end |
| **16**<br>DEL 15 | M<br>**G** | *Osmund, Bishop of Salisbury, 1099* | Exod. 1. 8–14, 22<br>Ps. 124<br>Matt. 10.34 – 11.1 | Ps. 123; 124; 125; ***126***<br>Esther ch. 4<br>2 Cor. 6.1 – 7.1 |

Week number of Daily Eucharistic Lectionary

*Column 2 provides for Common Worship:*

- the name of the Principal Holy Day, Sunday, Festival or Lesser Festival;
- a note of other Commemorations for mention in prayers;
- any general note that applies to the whole *Common Worship* provision for the day;
- one of the options where there are two options for readings at the Eucharist or Principal Service;
- an indication of the liturgical colour.

*Readings:* Readings occur in this column only in two circumstances. On Sundays after Trinity where ther are two 'tracks' for the Principal Service readings (where there is a choice of first reading and psalm, but the second reading and Gospel are the same in both tracks), Track 1 appears in this column. On Lesser Festivals throughout the year, where there are readings for that festival that are alternative to the semi-continuous Daily Eucharistic Lectionary, these also appear in this column.

*Colour:* An upper-case letter indicates the liturgical colour of the day. A lower-case second colour indicates the colour for a Lesser Festival while the upper-case letter indicates the continuing seasonal colour.

# LECTIONARY

*Column 5 (Common Worship)*
**On Principal Feasts, Principal Holy Days, Sundays and Festivals** this gives the Second Service Lectionary, intended for use when a second set of readings is required. Its most likely use is in the evening, when the Principal Service Lectionary has been used in the morning. Sometimes it might be used at an evening Eucharist. Where the second reading is not a Gospel reading, an alternative to meet this need is provided. Where psalms are recommended for use in the evening, these also appear in this column.

**On other weekdays** this provides the psalmody and readings for Evening Prayer. Where two or more psalms are provided, the psalm in bold italic may be used as the only psalm. Psalms printed in round brackets ( ) may be omitted if they are used as an opening canticle at Evening Prayer. Where † is printed after the psalm number, the psalm may be shortened if desired. For those wishing to follow the Ordinary Time psalm cycle throughout the year (except for the period between 19 December and the Epiphany and from the Monday of Holy Week to the Saturday of Easter Week), this is printed as an alternative to the seasonal provision.

*Column 7 (Book of Common Prayer)*
This provides the readings for Morning Prayer, together with psalm provision where it varies from the BCP monthly cycle.

A letter to indicate liturgical colour in this column indicates a change of colour before Evening Prayer. The symbol in bold lower case, **ct**, indicates that the Collect at Evening Prayer should be that of the following day.

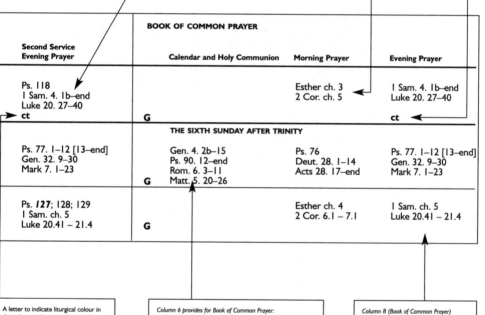

| Second Service Evening Prayer | | BOOK OF COMMON PRAYER<br>Calendar and Holy Communion | Morning Prayer | Evening Prayer |
|---|---|---|---|---|
| Ps. 118<br>I Sam. 4. 1b–end<br>Luke 20. 27–40<br>**ct** | **G** | | Esther ch. 3<br>2 Cor. ch. 5 | I Sam. 4. 1b–end<br>Luke 20. 27–40<br>**ct** |
| | | **THE SIXTH SUNDAY AFTER TRINITY** | | |
| Ps. 77. 1–12 [13–end]<br>Gen. 32. 9–30<br>Mark 7. 1–23 | **G** | Gen. 4. 2b–15<br>Ps. 90. 12–end<br>Rom. 6. 3–11<br>Matt. 5. 20–26 | Ps. 76<br>Deut. 28. 1–14<br>Acts 28. 17–end | Ps. 77. 1–12 [13–end]<br>Gen. 32. 9–30<br>Mark 7. 1–23 |
| Ps. ***127***; 128; 129<br>I Sam. ch. 5<br>Luke 20.41 – 21.4 | **G** | | Esther ch. 4<br>2 Cor. 6.1 – 7.1 | I Sam. ch. 5<br>Luke 20.41 – 21.4 |

A letter to indicate liturgical colour in this column indicates a change of colour before Evening Prayer. The symbol in bold lower case, **ct**, indicates that the Collect at Evening Prayer should be that of the following day.

*Column 6 provides for Book of Common Prayer:*
- the name of the Principal Holy Day, Sunday, Festival or Lesser Festival;
- any general note that applies to the whole Prayer Book provision for the day and an indication of points at which users may wish to draw on *Common Worship* material on the opposite page where the BCP has no provision;
- the lectionary for the Eucharist on any day for which provision is made;
- an indication of liturgical colour (see column 2).

*Column 8 (Book of Common Prayer)*
This provides the readings for Evening Prayer, together with psalm provision where it varies from the BCP monthly cycle.

## Making Choices in *Common Worship*

*Common Worship* makes provision for a variety of pastoral and liturgical circumstances. It needs to, for it has to serve some church communities where Morning Prayer, Holy Communion and Evening Prayer are all celebrated every day, and yet be useful also in a church with only one service a week, and that service varying in form and time from week to week.

At the beginning of the year, some decisions in principle need to be taken.

In relation to the Calendar, a decision needs to be taken whether to keep The Epiphany on Saturday 6 January or on Sunday 7 January, the Presentation of Christ (Candlemas) on Friday 2 February or on Sunday 28 January, and whether to keep the Feast of All Saints on Thursday 1 November or on Sunday 4 November.

In relation to the Lectionary, the initial choices every year to decide in relation to Sundays are:

- which of the services on a Principal Feast, Principal Holy Day, Sunday or Festival constitutes the 'Principal Service'; then use the Principal Service Lectionary (column 3) consistently for that service through the year;
- during the Sundays after Trinity, whether to use Track 1 of the Principal Service Lectionary (column 2), where the first reading stays over several weeks with one Old Testament book read semi-continuously, or Track 2 (column 3), where the first reading is chosen for its relationship to the Gospel reading of the day;
- which, if any, service on a Principal Feast, Principal Holy Day, Sunday or Festival constitutes the 'Second Service'; then use the Second Service Lectionary (column 5) consistently for that service through the year;
- which, if any, service on a Principal Feast, Principal Holy Day, Sunday or Festival constitutes the 'Third Service'; then use the Third Service Lectionary (column 4) consistently for that service through the year.

And in relation to weekdays:

- whether to use the Daily Eucharistic Lectionary (column 3) consistently for weekday celebrations of Holy Communion (with the exception of Principal Feasts, Principal Holy Days and Festivals) or to make some use of the Lesser Festival provision;
- whether to follow the first psalm provision in column 4 (morning) and column 5 (evening), where psalms during the seasons have a seasonal flavour but in ordinary time follow a sequential pattern; or to follow the alternative provision in the same columns, where psalms follow the sequential pattern throughout the year, except for the period between 19 December and The Epiphany and from the Monday of Holy Week to the Saturday of Easter Week; or to follow the psalm cycle in the Book of Common Prayer, where they are nearly always used 'in course'.

The flexibility of *Common Worship* is intended to enable the church and the minister to find the most helpful provision for them. But once a decision is made, it is advisable to stay with that decision through the year or at the very least through a complete season.

## Book of Common Prayer

A separate Lectionary for the Book of Common Prayer is no longer issued. Provision is made on the right-hand pages of this Lectionary for BCP worship on all Sundays in the year, for the major festivals and for Morning and Evening Prayer. The Epistles and Gospels for Holy Communion are those of 1662, with the additions and variations of 1928, now authorized under the *Common Worship* overall provision. The Old Testament readings and psalms for these services, formerly appended to the Series One Holy Communion service, may be used but are not mandatory with the 1662 order.

Readings for Morning and Evening Prayer, which are the same as those for *Common Worship*, are set out in the BCP section for Sundays and weekdays. The special psalm provision of the BCP is given. Otherwise the Psalter is read in course daily through each month.

The Calendar observes BCP dates when these differ from those of *Common Worship*, for example, St Thomas on 21 December. Additional commemorations in the *Common Worship* Calendar are not included, but those who wish to observe them may use the *Collects and Post Communions in Traditional Language: Lesser Festivals, Common of the Saints, Special Occasions* (Church House Publishing).

The Lectionaries of 1871 and 1922, to be found in many copies of the BCP, are still authorized and may be used, but (with the exception of the psalms and readings for Holy Communion mentioned above) the Additional Alternative Lectionary (1961) is no longer authorized for public worship.

Although those who use the BCP, for private or public worship or both, are free to follow any of the authorized lectionaries, there is much to be said for common usage across the Church of England, so that the same passages are being read by all. It is of course appropriate that BCP readings should be taken from the Authorized or King James Version for harmony of style, with the daily recitation of the BCP Psalter.

The integrity of the BCP as the traditional source of worship in the Church of England is not in any way affected by the use of a common lectionary for the daily offices.

## CERTAIN DAYS AND OCCASIONS COMMONLY OBSERVED

**Plough Sunday** may be observed on 7 January 2007.
**The Week of Prayer for Christian Unity** may be observed from 18 to 25 January 2007.
**Education Sunday** may be observed on 4 February 2007.
**Rogation Sunday** may be observed on 13 May 2007.
**The Feast of Dedication** is observed on the anniversary of the dedication or consecration of a church, or, when the actual date is unknown, on 7 October 2007. In CW 28 October 2007 is an alternative date.
**Ember Days.** CW encourages the bishop to set the Ember Days in each diocese in the week before the ordinations whereas in BCP the dates are fixed.
**Days of Discipline and Self-Denial** in CW are the weekdays of Lent and all Fridays in the year, except all Principal Feasts and festivals outside Lent and Fridays between Easter Day and Pentecost. The eves of Principal Feasts are also appropriately kept as days of discipline and self-denial in preparation for the feast.
**Days of Fasting and Abstinence** according to the BCP are the forty days of Lent, the Ember Days at the four seasons, the three Rogation Days, and all Fridays in the year except Christmas Day. The BCP also orders the observance of the Evens or Vigils before The Nativity of our Lord, The Purification of the Blessed Virgin Mary, The Annunciation of the Blessed Virgin Mary, Easter Day, Ascension Day, Pentecost, and before the following saints' days: Matthias, John the Baptist, Peter, James, Bartholomew, Matthew, Simon and Jude, Andrew, Thomas, and All Saints. (If any of these days falls on Monday, the Vigil is to be kept on the previous Saturday.)

## KEY TO LITURGICAL COLOURS

*Common Worship* suggests appropriate liturgical colours. They are not mandatory and traditional or local use may be followed.

For a detailed discussion of when colours may be used see *Common Worship: Services and Prayers for the Church of England* (Church House Publishing), *New Handbook of Pastoral Liturgy* (SPCK) or *A Companion to Common Worship: Volume 1* (SPCK).

| | |
|---|---|
| W | White |
| 𝔚 | Gold or white |
| R | Red |
| P | Purple (may vary from 'Roman purple' to violet, with blue as an alternative; a Lent array of sackcloth may be used in Lent, and rose pink on The Third Sunday of Advent and Fourth Sunday of Lent. |
| G | Green |

When a lower-case letter accompanies an upper-case letter, the lower-case letter indicates the liturgical colour appropriate to the Lesser Festival of that day, while the upper-case letter indicates the continuing seasonal colour.

## PRINCIPAL FEASTS, HOLY DAYS AND FESTIVALS

Principal Feasts, and other principal Holy Days (Ash Wednesday, Maundy Thursday, Good Friday), are printed in **LARGE BOLD CAPITALS** in the Lectionary.

The Epiphany may, for pastoral reasons, be celebrated on The Second Sunday of Christmas. All Saints' Day is celebrated on either 1 November or the Sunday between 30 October and 5 November.

There are no longer proper readings relating to the Holy Spirit on the six days after Pentecost. Instead they have been located on the nine days before Pentecost.

When Patronal and Dedication Festivals are kept as Principal Feasts, they may be transferred to the nearest Sunday, unless that day is already either a Principal Feast or The First Sunday of Advent, The Baptism of Christ, The First Sunday of Lent or Palm Sunday.

Festivals are printed in the Lectionary in **SMALL BOLD CAPITALS**.

For each day there is a full liturgical provision for the Holy Communion and for Morning and Evening Prayer. Most holy days that are in the category 'Festival' are provided with an optional First Evening Prayer. Its use is entirely at the discretion of the minister. Where it is used, the liturgical colour for the next day should be used at that First Evening Prayer and this has been indicated in the provision on the following pages.

## LESSER FESTIVALS AND COMMEMORATIONS

Lesser Festivals (printed in **bold roman** typeface) are observed at the level appropriate to a particular church. The readings and psalms for The Common of the Saints are listed on page 11. In addition, there are special readings appropriate to the Festival listed in the first column. The daily psalms and readings at Morning and Evening Prayer are not usually superseded by those for Lesser Festivals, but the readings and psalms for Holy Communion may on occasion be used at Morning or Evening Prayer.

Commemorations are printed in the Lectionary in *italic* typeface. They do not have collect, psalm or readings, but may be observed by mention in prayers of intercession and thanksgiving. For local reasons, or where there is an established tradition in the wider Church, they may be kept as Lesser Festivals using the appropriate material from The Common of the Saints. Equally, it may be desirable to observe some Lesser Festivals as Commemorations.

If a Lesser Festival or a Commemoration falls on a Principal Feast, Principal Holy Day, Sunday or Festival, it is not normally observed that year, although it may be celebrated, where there is sufficient reason, on the nearest available day. Lesser Festivals and Commemorations which, for this reason, would not be celebrated in 2006–07 are listed on pages 9–10, so that, if desired, they may be mentioned in prayer of intercession and thanksgiving.

## LESSER FESTIVALS AND COMMEMORATIONS NOT OBSERVED IN 2006–07

**The Lesser Festivals and Commemorations (shown in italics) listed below fall on a Sunday or during Holy Week or Easter Week this year, and are thus not observed in this lectionary.**

### Common Worship

### 2006

**December**

| | |
|---|---|
| 3 | *Francis Xavier, Missionary, Apostle of the Indies, 1552* |
| 17 | *Eglantyne Jebb, Social Reformer, Founder of 'Save the Children', 1928* |

### 2007

**January**

| | |
|---|---|
| 21 | Agnes, Child Martyr at Rome, 304 |
| 28 | Thomas Aquinas, Priest, Philosopher, Teacher, 1274 |

**February**

| | |
|---|---|
| 4 | *Gilbert of Sempringham, Founder of the Gilbertine Order, 1189* |

**March**

| | |
|---|---|
| 18 | *Cyril, Bishop of Jerusalem, Teacher, 386* |
| 26 | *Harriet Monsell, Founder of the Community of St John the Baptist, Clewer, 1883* |

**April**

| | |
|---|---|
| 1 | *Frederick Denison Maurice, Priest, Teacher, 1872* |
| 9 | *Dietrich Bonhoeffer, Lutheran Pastor, Martyr, 1945* |
| 10 | William Law, Priest, Spiritual Writer, 1761 |
| | *William of Ockham, Friar, Philosopher, Teacher, 1347* |
| 11 | *George Augustus Selwyn, first Bishop of New Zealand, 1878* |
| 29 | Catherine of Siena, Teacher, 1380 |

**May**

| | |
|---|---|
| 20 | Alcuin of York, Deacon, Abbot of Tours, 804 |

**June**

| | |
|---|---|
| 3 | *The Martyrs of Uganda, 1885–7 and 1977* |
| 17 | *Samuel and Henrietta Barnett, Social Reformers, 1913 and 1936* |

**July**

| | |
|---|---|
| 1 | *Henry, John and Henry Venn the Younger, Priests, Evangelical Divines, 1797, 1813 and 1873* |
| 15 | Swithun, Bishop of Winchester, c. 862 |
| | *Bonaventure, Friar, Bishop, Teacher, 1274* |
| 29 | Mary, Martha and Lazarus, Companions of our Lord |

**August**

| | |
|---|---|
| 5 | Oswald, King of Northumbria, Martyr, 642 |

**September**

2 *The Martyrs of Papua New Guinea, 1901 and 1942*
9 *Charles Fuge Lowder, Priest, 1880*
16 Ninian, Bishop of Galloway, Apostle of the Picts, *c.* 432
*Edward Bouverie Pusey, Priest, Tractarian, 1882*
30 *Jerome, Translator of the Scriptures, Teacher, 420*

**November**

11 Martin, Bishop of Tours, *c.* 397
18 Elizabeth of Hungary, Princess of Thuringia, Philanthropist, 1231
25 *Catherine of Alexandria, Martyr, 4th century; Isaac Watts, Hymn Writer, 1748*

## Book of Common Prayer
## 2006

**December**

31 Silvester, Bishop of Rome, 335

## 2007

**January**

21 Agnes, Child Martyr at Rome, 304

**March**

18 Edward, King of the W. Saxons, 978

**April**

3 Richard, Bishop of Chichester, 1253
4 Ambrose, Bishop of Milan, 397

**May**

6 John the Evangelist, ante Portam Latinam

**June**

17 Alban, first Martyr of Britain, *c.* 250

**July**

15 Swithun, Bishop of Winchester, *c.* 862

**November**

11 Martin, Bishop of Tours, *c.* 397
25 Catherine of Alexandria, Martyr, 4th century

## THE COMMON OF THE SAINTS

### The Blessed Virgin Mary

Genesis 3. 8–15, 20; Isaiah 7. 10–14; Micah 5. 1–4

Acts 1. 12–14; Romans 8. 18–30; Galatians 4. 4–7

Psalms 45. 10–17; 113; 131

Luke 1. 26–38; Luke 1. 39–47; John 19. 25–27

### Martyrs

2 Chronicles 24. 17–21; Isaiah 43. 1–7; Jeremiah 11. 18–20; Wisdom 4. 10–15

Romans 8. 35–39; 2 Corinthians 4. 7–15; 2 Timothy 2. 3–7 [8–13]; Hebrews 11. 32–40; 1 Peter 4. 12–19; Revelation 12. 10–12a

Psalms 3; 11; 31. 1–5; 44. 19–24; 126

Matthew 10. 16–22; Matthew 10. 28–39; Matthew 16. 24–26; John 12. 24–26; John 15. 18–21

### Teachers of the Faith and Spiritual Writers

1 Kings 3. [6–10] 11–14; Proverbs 4. 1–9; Wisdom 7. 7–10, 15–16; Ecclesiasticus 39. 1–10

1 Corinthians 1. 18–25; 1 Corinthians 2. 1–10; 1 Corinthians 2. 9–16;

Ephesians 3. 8–12; 2 Timothy 4. 1–8; Titus 2. 1–8

Psalms 19. 7–10; 34. 11–17; 37. 30–35; 119. 89–96; 119. 97–104

Matthew 5. 13–19; Matthew 13. 52–58; Matthew 23. 8–12; Mark 4. 1–9; John 16. 12–15

### Bishops and Other Pastors

1 Samuel 16. 1, 6–13; Isaiah 6. 1–8; Jeremiah 1. 4–10; Ezekiel 3. 16–21; Malachi 2. 5–7

Acts 20. 28–35; 1 Corinthians 4. 1–5; 2 Corinthians 4. 1–10 (*or* 1, 2, 5–7); 2 Corinthians 5. 14–20; 1 Peter 5. 1–4

Psalms 1; 15; 16. 5–11; 96; 110

Matthew 11. 25–30; Matthew 24. 42–46; John 10. 11–16; John 15. 9–17; John 21. 15–17

### Members of Religious Communities

1 Kings 19. 9–18; Proverbs 10. 27–32; Song of Solomon 8. 6–7; Isaiah 61.10 – 62.5; Hosea 2. 14–15, 19–20

Acts 4. 32–35; 2 Corinthians 10.17 – 11.2; Philippians 3. 7–14; 1 John 2. 15–17; Revelation 19. 1, 5–9

Psalms 34. 1–8; 112. 1–9; 119. 57–64; 123; 131

Matthew 11. 25–30; Matthew 19. 3–12; Matthew 19. 23–30; Luke 9. 57–62; Luke 12. 32–37

### Missionaries

Isaiah 52. 7–10; Isaiah 61. 1–3a; Ezekiel 34. 11–16; Jonah 3. 1–5

Acts 2. 14, 22–36; Acts 13. 46–49; Acts 16. 6–10; Acts 26. 19–23; Romans 15. 17–21; 2 Corinthians 5.11 – 6.2

Psalms 67; 87; 97; 100; 117

Matthew 9. 35–38; Matthew 28. 16–20; Mark 16. 15–20; Luke 5. 1–11; Luke 10. 1–9

### Any Saint

Genesis 12. 1–4; Proverbs 8. 1–11; Micah 6. 6–8; Ecclesiasticus 2. 7–13 [14–17]

Ephesians 3. 14–19; Ephesians 6. 11–18; Hebrews 13. 7–8, 15–16; James 2. 14–17; 1 John 4, 7–16; Revelation 21. [1–4] 5–7

Psalms 32; 33. 1–5; 119. 1–8; 139. 1–4 [5–12]; 145. 8–14

Matthew 19. 16–21; Matthew 25. 1–13; Matthew 25. 14–30; John 15. 1–8; John 17. 20–26

# SPECIAL OCCASIONS

## The Guidance of the Holy Spirit

Proverbs 24. 3–7; Isaiah 30. 15–21; Wisdom 9. 13–17
Acts 15. 23–29; Romans 8. 22–27; 1 Corinthians 12. 4–13
Psalms 25. 1–9; 104. 26–33; 143. 8–10
Luke 14. 27–33; John 14. 23–26; John 16. 13–15

## The Commemoration of the Faithful Departed

Lamentations 3. 17–26, 31–3 *or* Wisdom 3. 1–9
Psalm 23 *or* Psalm 27. 1–6, 16–17
Romans 5. 5–11 *or* 1 Peter 1. 3–9
John 5. 19–25 *or* John 6. 37–40

## Rogation Days

Deuteronomy 8. 1–10; 1 Kings 8. 35–40; Job 28. 1–11
Philippians 4. 4–7; 2 Thessalonians 3. 6–13; 1 John 5. 12–15
Psalms 104. 21–30; 107. 1–9; 121
Matthew 6. 1–15; Mark 11. 22–24; Luke 11. 5–13

## Harvest Thanksgiving

**Year A**
Deuteronomy 8. 7–18 *or* Deuteronomy 28. 1–14
Psalm 65
2 Corinthians 9. 6–15
Luke 12. 16–30 *or* Luke 17. 11–19

**Year B**
Joel 2. 21–27
Psalm 126
1 Timothy 2. 1–7 *or* 1 Timothy 6. 6–10
Matthew 6. 25–33

**Year C**
Deuteronomy 26. 1–11
Psalm 100
Philippians 4. 4–9 *or* Revelation 14. 14–18
John 6. 25–35

## Mission and Evangelism

Isaiah 49. 1–6; Isaiah 52. 7–10; Micah 4. 1–5
Acts 17. 12–34; 2 Corinthians 5.14 – 6.2; Ephesians 2. 13–22
Psalms 2; 46; 67
Matthew 5. 13–16; Matthew 28. 16–20; John 17. 20–26

## The Unity of the Church

Jeremiah 33. 6–9a; Ezekiel 36. 23–28; Zephaniah 3. 16–20
Ephesians 4. 1–6; Colossians 3. 9–17; 1 John 4. 9–15
Psalms 100; 122; 133
Matthew 18. 19–22; John 11. 45–52; John 17. 11b–23

### The Peace of the World

Isaiah 9. 1–6; Isaiah 57. 15–19; Micah 4. 1–5
Philippians 4. 6–9; 1 Timothy 2. 1–6; James 3. 13–18
Psalms 40. 14–17; 72. 1–7; 85. 8–13
Matthew 5. 43–48; John 14. 23–29; John 15. 9–17

### Social Justice and Responsibility

Isaiah 32. 15–20; Amos 5. 21–24; Amos 8. 4–7; Acts 5. 1–11
Colossians 3. 12–15; James 2. 1–4
Psalms 31. 21–24; 85. 1–7; 146. 5–10
Matthew 5. 1–12; Matthew 25. 31–46; Luke 16. 19–31

### Ministry (including Ember Days)

Numbers 11. 16–17, 24–29; Numbers 27. 15–23; 1 Samuel 16. 1–13a
Isaiah 6. 1–8; Isaiah 61. 1–3; Jeremiah 1. 4–10
Acts 20. 28–35; 1 Corinthians 3. 3–11; Ephesians 4. 4–16; Philippians 3. 7–14
Psalms 40. 8–13; 84. 8–12; 89. 19–25; 101. 1–5, 7; 122
Luke 4. 16–21; Luke 12. 35–43; Luke 22. 24–27; John 4. 31–38; John 15. 5–17

### In Time of Trouble

Genesis 9. 8–17; Job 1. 13–22; Isaiah 38. 6–11
Romans 3. 21–26; Romans 8. 18–25; 2 Corinthians 8. 1–5, 9
Psalms 86. 1–7; 107. 4–15; 142. 1–7
Mark 4. 35–41; Luke 12. 1–7; John 16. 31–33

### For the Sovereign

Joshua 1. 1–9; Proverbs 8. 1–16
Romans 13. 1–10; Revelation 21.22 – 22.4
Psalms 20; 101; 121
Matthew 22. 16–22; Luke 22. 24–30

# December 2006

| Date | Day | Colour | Observance | Sunday Principal Service / Weekday Eucharist | Third Service / Morning Prayer |
|---|---|---|---|---|---|
| 3 | S | P | THE FIRST SUNDAY OF ADVENT<br>CW Year C begins | Jer. 33. 14–16<br>Ps. 25. 1–9<br>1 Thess. 3. 9–end<br>Luke 21. 25–36 | Ps. 44<br>Isa. 51. 4–11<br>Rom. 13. 11–end |
| 4 | M | P | *John of Damascus, Monk, Teacher, c. 749; Nicholas Ferrar, Deacon, Founder of the Little Gidding Community, 1637*<br>Daily Eucharistic Lectionary Year 2 begins | Isa. 2. 1–5<br>Ps. 122<br>Matt. 8. 5–11 | Ps. ***50***; 54<br>*alt.* Ps. ***1***; 2; 3<br>Isa. 42. 18–end<br>Rev. ch. 19 |
| 5 | Tu | P | | Isa. 11. 1–10<br>Ps. 72. 1–4, 18–19<br>Luke 10. 21–24 | Ps. ***80***; 82<br>*alt.* Ps. ***5***; 6 (8)<br>Isa. 43. 1–13<br>Rev. ch. 20 |
| 6 | W | Pw | **Nicholas, Bishop of Myra, c. 326**<br>Com. Bishop *or*<br>*also* Isa. 61. 1–3<br>1 Tim. 6. 6–11<br>Mark 10. 13–16 | Isa. 25. 6–10a<br>Ps. 23<br>Matt. 15. 29–37 | Ps. 5; ***7***<br>*alt.* Ps. 119. 1–32<br>Isa. 43. 14–end<br>Rev. 21. 1–8 |
| 7 | Th | Pw | **Ambrose, Bishop of Milan, Teacher, 397**<br>Com. Teacher *or*<br>*also* Isa. 41. 9b–13<br>Luke 22. 24–30 | Isa. 26. 1–6<br>Ps. 118. 18–27a<br>Matt. 7. 21, 24–27 | Ps. ***42***; 43<br>*alt.* Ps. 14; ***15***; 16<br>Isa. 44. 1–8<br>Rev. 21. 9–21 |
| 8 | F | Pw | **The Conception of the Blessed Virgin Mary**<br>Com. BVM *or* | Isa. 29. 17–end<br>Ps. 27. 1–4, 16–17<br>Matt. 9. 27–31 | Ps. ***25***; 26<br>*alt.* Ps. 17; ***19***<br>Isa. 44. 9–23<br>Rev. 21.22 – 22.5 |
| 9 | Sa | P | | Isa. 30. 19–21, 23–26<br>Ps. 146. 4–9<br>Matt. 9.35 – 10.1, 6–8 | Ps. ***9*** (10)<br>*alt.* Ps. 20; 21; ***23***<br>Isa. 44.24 – 45.13<br>Rev. 22. 6–end |
| 10 | S | P | THE SECOND SUNDAY OF ADVENT | Baruch ch. 5<br>*or* Mal. 3. 1–4<br>*Canticle:* Benedictus<br>Phil. 1. 3–11<br>Luke 3. 1–6 | Ps. 80<br>Isa. 64. 1–7<br>Matt. 11. 2–11 |
| 11 | M | P | | Isa. ch. 35<br>Ps. 85. 7–end<br>Luke 5. 17–26 | Ps. 44<br>*alt.* Ps. 27; ***30***<br>Isa. 45. 14–end<br>1 Thess. ch. 1 |
| 12 | Tu | P | | Isa. 40. 1–11<br>Ps. 96. 1, 10–end<br>Matt. 18. 12–14 | Ps. ***56***; 57<br>*alt.* Ps. 32; ***36***<br>Isa. ch. 46<br>1 Thess. 2. 1–12 |
| 13 | W | Pr | **Lucy, Martyr at Syracuse, 304**<br>Ember Day*<br>*Samuel Johnson, Moralist, 1784*<br>Com. Martyr *or*<br>*also* Wisd. 3. 1–7<br>2 Cor. 4. 6–15 | Isa. 40. 25–end<br>Ps. 103. 8–13<br>Matt. 11. 28–end | Ps. ***62***; 63<br>*alt.* Ps. 34<br>Isa. ch. 47<br>1 Thess. 2. 13–end |

*For Ember Day provision, see p. 13.

| Second Service Evening Prayer | | Calendar and Holy Communion | Morning Prayer | Evening Prayer |
|---|---|---|---|---|
| Ps. 9. 1–8 [9–end]<br>Joel 3. 9–end<br>Rev. 14.13 – 15.4<br>*Gospel:* John 3. 1–17 | **P** | **THE FIRST SUNDAY IN ADVENT**<br>Advent 1 Collect until Christmas Eve<br>Mic. 4. 1–4, 6–7<br>Ps. 25. 1–9<br>Rom. 13. 8–14<br>Matt. 21. 1–13 | Ps. 44<br>Isa. 51. 4–11<br>Rom. 13. 11–end | Ps. 9. 1–8 [9–end]<br>Joel 3. 9–end<br>Rev. 14.13 – 15.4 |
| Ps. 70; ***71***<br>*alt.* Ps. ***4***; 7<br>Isa. 25. 1–9<br>Matt. 12. 1–21 | **P** | | Isa. 42. 18–end<br>Rev. ch. 19 | Isa. 25. 1–9<br>Matt. 12. 1–21 |
| Ps. ***74***; 75<br>*alt.* Ps. ***9***; 10†<br>Isa. 26. 1–13<br>Matt. 12. 22–37 | **P** | | Isa. 43. 1–13<br>Rev. ch. 20 | Isa. 26. 1–13<br>Matt. 12. 22–37 |
| Ps. 76; ***77***<br>*alt.* Ps. ***11***; 12; 13<br>Isa. 28. 1–13<br>Matt. 12. 38–end | **Pw** | **Nicholas, Bishop of Myra, *c.* 326**<br>Com. Bishop | Isa. 43. 14–end<br>Rev. 21. 1–8 | Isa. 28. 1–13<br>Matt. 12. 38–end |
| Ps. ***40***; 46<br>*alt.* Ps. 18†<br>Isa. 28. 14–end<br>Matt. 13. 1–23 | **P** | | Isa. 44. 1–8<br>Rev. 21. 9–21 | Isa. 28. 14–end<br>Matt. 13. 1–23 |
| Ps. 16; ***17***<br>*alt.* Ps. 22<br>Isa. 29. 1–14<br>Matt. 13. 24–43 | **Pw** | **The Conception of the Blessed Virgin Mary** | Isa. 44. 9–23<br>Rev. 21.22 – 22.5 | Isa. 29. 1–14<br>Matt. 13. 24–43 |
| Ps. 27; ***28***<br>*alt.* Ps. ***24***; 25<br>Isa. 29. 15–end<br>Matt. 13. 44–end<br>**ct** | **P** | | Isa. 44.24 – 45.13<br>Rev. 22. 6–end | Isa. 29. 15–end<br>Matt. 13. 44–end<br>**ct** |
| Ps. 75 [76]<br>Isa. 40. 1–11<br>Luke 1. 1–25 | **P** | **THE SECOND SUNDAY IN ADVENT**<br>2 Kings 22. 8–10; 23. 1–3<br>Ps. 50. 1–6<br>Rom. 15. 4–13<br>Luke 21. 25–33 | Ps. 40<br>Isa. 64. 1–7<br>Luke 3. 1–6 | Ps. 75 [76]<br>Mal. 3. 1–4<br>Luke 1. 1–25 |
| Ps. ***144***; 146<br>*alt.* Ps. 26; ***28***; 29<br>Isa. 30. 1–18<br>Matt. 14. 1–12 | **P** | | Isa. 45. 14–end<br>1 Thess. ch. 1 | Isa. 30. 1–18<br>Matt. 14. 1–12 |
| Ps. ***11***; 12; 13<br>*alt.* Ps. 33<br>Isa. 30. 19–end<br>Matt. 14. 13–end | **P** | | Isa. ch. 46<br>1 Thess. 2. 1–12 | Isa. 30. 19–end<br>Matt. 14. 13–end |
| Ps. ***10***; 14<br>*alt.* Ps. 119. 33–56<br>Isa. ch. 31<br>Matt. 15. 1–20 | **Pr** | **Lucy, Martyr at Syracuse, 304**<br>Com. Virgin Martyr | Isa. ch. 47<br>1 Thess. 2. 13–end | Isa. ch. 31<br>Matt. 15. 1–20 |

# December 2006

| | | | Sunday Principal Service<br>Weekday Eucharist | Third Service<br>Morning Prayer |
|---|---|---|---|---|
| **14** | Th<br>**Pw** | **John of the Cross, Poet, Teacher, 1591**<br>Com. Teacher<br>*esp.* 1 Cor. 2. 1–10<br>*also* John 14. 18–23 | *or* Isa. 41. 13–20<br>Ps. 145. 1, 8–13<br>Matt. 11. 11–15 | Ps. 53; ***54***; 60<br>*alt.* Ps. 37†<br>Isa. 48. 1–11<br>1 Thess. ch. 3 |
| **15** | F<br>**P** | Ember Day* | Isa. 48. 17–19<br>Ps. 1<br>Matt. 11. 16–19 | Ps. 85; ***86***<br>*alt.* Ps. 31<br>Isa. 48. 12–end<br>1 Thess. 4. 1–12 |
| **16** | Sa<br>**P** | Ember Day* | Ecclus. 48. 1–4, 9–11<br>*or* 2 Kings 2. 9–12<br>Ps. 80. 1–4, 18–19<br>Matt. 17. 10–13 | Ps. 145<br>*alt.* Ps. 41; **42**; 43<br>Isa. 49. 1–13<br>1 Thess. 4. 13–end |
| **17** | **S**<br>**P** | **THE THIRD SUNDAY OF ADVENT**<br>O Sapientia | Zeph. 3. 14–end<br>*Canticle*: Isa. 12.2–end<br>*or* Ps. 146. 4–end<br>Phil. 4. 4–7<br>Luke 3. 7–18 | Ps. 12; 14<br>Isa. 25. 1–9<br>1 Cor. 4. 1–5 |
| **18** | M<br>**P** | | Jer. 23. 5–8<br>Ps. 72. 1–2, 12–13, 18–end<br>Matt. 1. 18–24 | Ps. 40<br>*alt.* Ps. 44<br>Isa. 49. 14–25<br>1 Thess. 5. 1–11 |
| **19** | Tu<br>**P** | | Judg. 13. 2–7, 24–end<br>Ps. 71. 3–8<br>Luke 1. 5–25 | Ps. 144; ***146***<br>Isa. ch. 50<br>1 Thess. 5. 12–end |
| **20** | W<br>**P** | | Isa. 7. 10–14<br>Ps. 24. 1–6<br>Luke 1. 26–38 | Ps. **46**; 95<br>Isa. 51. 1–8<br>2 Thess. ch. 1 |
| **21** | Th**<br>**P** | | Zeph. 3. 14–18<br>Ps. 33. 1–4, 11–12, 19–end<br>Luke 1. 39–45 | Ps. ***121***; 122; 123<br>Isa. 51. 9–16<br>2 Thess. ch. 2 |
| **22** | F<br>**P** | | 1 Sam. 1. 24–end<br>Ps. 113<br>Luke 1. 46–56 | Ps. ***124***; 125; 126; 127<br>Isa. 51. 17–end<br>2 Thess. ch. 3 |
| **23** | Sa<br>**P** | | Mal. 3. 1–4; 4. 5–end<br>Ps. 25. 3–9<br>Luke 1. 57–66 | Ps. 128; 129; ***130***; 131<br>Isa. 52. 1–12<br>Jude |
| **24** | **S**<br>**P** | **THE FOURTH SUNDAY OF ADVENT**<br>**CHRISTMAS EVE** | Mic. 5. 2–5a<br>*Canticle:* Magnificat<br>*or* Ps. 80.1–8<br>Heb. 10.5–10<br>Luke 1. 39–45 [46–55] | Ps. 144<br>Isa. 32. 1–8<br>Rev. 22. 6–end |

*For Ember Day provision, see p. 13.
**Thomas the Apostle may be celebrated on 21 December instead of 3 July.

| Second Service Evening Prayer | | Calendar and Holy Communion | Morning Prayer | Evening Prayer |
|---|---|---|---|---|
| Ps. 73<br>*alt*. Ps. 39; ***40***<br>Isa. ch. 32<br>Matt. 15. 21–28 | **P** | | Isa. 48. 1–11<br>1 Thess. ch. 3 | Isa. ch. 32<br>Matt. 15. 21–28 |
| Ps. 82; ***90***<br>*alt*. Ps. 35<br>Isa. 33. 1–22<br>Matt. 15. 29–end | **P** | | Isa. 48. 12–end<br>1 Thess. 4. 1–12 | Isa. 33. 1–22<br>Matt. 15. 29–end |
| Ps. 93; ***94***<br>*alt*. Ps. 45; ***46***<br>Isa. ch. 35<br>Matt. 16. 1–12<br>**ct** | **P** | **O Sapientia** | Isa. 49. 1–13<br>1 Thess. 4. 13–end | Isa. ch. 35<br>Matt. 16. 1–12<br>**ct** |
| Ps. 50. 1–6 [62]<br>Isa. ch. 35<br>Luke 1. 57–66 [67–end] | **P** | **THE THIRD SUNDAY IN ADVENT**<br>Isa. 35. 1–10<br>Ps. 80. 1–7<br>1 Cor. 4. 1–5<br>Matt. 11. 2–10 | Ps. 12; 14<br>Isa. 25. 1–9<br>Luke 3. 7–18 | Ps. 62<br>Zeph. 3. 14–end<br>Luke 1. 57–66<br>[67–end] |
| Ps. 25; ***26***<br>*alt*. Ps. ***47***; 49<br>Isa. 38. 1–8, 21–22<br>Matt. 16. 13–end | **P** | | Isa. 49. 14–25<br>1 Thess. 5. 1–11 | Isa. 38. 1–8, 21–22<br>Matt. 16. 13–end |
| Ps. 10; ***57***<br>Isa. 38. 9–20<br>Matt. 17. 1–13 | **P** | | Isa. ch. 50<br>1 Thess. 5. 12–end | Isa. 38. 9–20<br>Matt. 17. 1–13 |
| Ps. ***4***; 9<br>Isa. ch. 39<br>Matt. 17. 14–21 | **P** | Ember Day<br>Ember CEG | Isa. 51. 1–8<br>2 Thess. ch. 1 | Isa. ch. 39<br>Matt. 17. 14–21<br>*or First EP of Thomas the Apostle*<br>(Ps. 27)<br>Isa. ch. 35<br>Heb. 10.35 – 11.1<br>**R ct** |
| Ps. 80; ***84***<br>Zeph. 1.1 – 2.3<br>Matt. 17. 22–end | **R** | **THOMAS THE APOSTLE**<br>Job 42. 1–6<br>Ps. 139. 1–11<br>Eph. 2. 19–end<br>John 20. 24–end | (Ps. 92; 146)<br>2 Sam. 15. 17–21<br>*or* Ecclus. ch. 2<br>John 11. 1–16 | (Ps. 139)<br>Hab. 2. 1–4<br>1 Pet. 1. 3–12 |
| Ps. 24; ***48***<br>Zeph. 3. 1–13<br>Matt. 18. 1–20 | **P** | Ember Day<br>Ember CEG | Isa. 51. 17–end<br>2 Thess. ch. 3 | Zeph. 3. 1–13<br>Matt. 18. 1–20 |
| Ps. 89. 1–37<br>Zeph. 3. 14–end<br>Matt. 18. 21–end<br>**ct** | **P** | Ember Day<br>Ember CEG | Isa. 52. 1–12<br>Jude | Zeph. 3. 14–end<br>Matt. 18. 21–end<br>**ct** |
| *EP*: Ps. 85<br>Zech. ch. 2<br>Rev. 1. 1–8 | **P** | **THE FOURTH SUNDAY IN ADVENT**<br>**CHRISTMAS EVE**<br>Isa. 40. 1–9<br>Ps. 145. 17–end<br>Phil. 4. 4–7<br>John 1. 19–28 | Ps. 144<br>Isa. 32. 1–8<br>Rev. 22. 6–end | Ps. 85<br>Zech. ch. 2<br>Rev. 1. 1–8 |

# December 2006

| Date | Day | Observance | Sunday Principal Service / Weekday Eucharist | Third Service / Morning Prayer |
|---|---|---|---|---|
| **25** | M<br>W | **CHRISTMAS DAY**<br>*Any of the following sets of readings may be used on the evening of Christmas Eve and on Christmas Day.*<br>*Set III should be used at some service during the celebration.* | *I*<br>Isa. 9. 2–7<br>Ps. 96<br>Titus 2. 11–14<br>Luke 2. 1–14 [15–20]<br>*II*<br>Isa. 62. 6–end<br>Ps. 97<br>Titus 3. 4–7<br>Luke 2. [1–7] 8–20<br>*III*<br>Isa. 52. 7–10<br>Ps. 98<br>Heb. 1. 1–4 [5–12]<br>John 1. 1–14 | *MP*: Ps. ***110***; 117<br>Isa. 62. 1–5<br>Matt. 1. 18–end |
| **26** | Tu<br>**R** | **STEPHEN, DEACON, FIRST MARTYR**<br>*The reading from Acts must be used as either the first or second reading at the Eucharist.* | 2 Chron. 24. 20–22<br>*or* Acts 7. 51–end<br>Ps. 119. 161–168<br>Acts 7. 51–60<br>*or* Gal. 2. 16b–20<br>Matt. 10 17–22 | *MP*: Ps. ***13***; 31. 1–8; 150<br>Jer. 26. 12–15<br>Acts ch. 6 |
| **27** | W<br>**W** | **JOHN, APOSTLE AND EVANGELIST** | Exod. 33. 7–11a<br>Ps. 117<br>1 John ch. 1<br>John 21. 19b–end | *MP*: Ps. ***21***; 147. 13–end<br>Exod. 33.12–end<br>1 John 2. 1–11 |
| **28** | Th<br>**R** | **THE HOLY INNOCENTS** | Jer. 31. 15–17<br>Ps. 124<br>1 Cor. 1. 26–29<br>Matt. 2. 13–18 | *MP*: Ps. ***36***; 146<br>Baruch 4. 21–27<br>*or* Gen. 37. 13–20<br>Matt. 18. 1–10 |
| **29** | F<br>**Wr** | **Thomas Becket, Archbishop of Canterbury, Martyr, 1170***<br>Com. Martyr<br>*esp*. Matt. 10. 28–33<br>*also* Ecclus. 51. 1–8 | *or* 1 John 2. 3–11<br>Ps. 96. 1–4<br>Luke 2. 22–35 | Ps. ***19***; 20<br>Isa. 57. 15–end<br>John 1. 1–18 |
| **30** | Sa<br>**W** | | 1 John 2. 12–17<br>Ps. 96. 7–10<br>Luke 2. 36–40 | Ps. 111; 112; ***113***<br>Isa. 59. 1–15a<br>John 1. 19–28 |
| **31** | **S**<br>**W** | **THE FIRST SUNDAY OF CHRISTMAS** | 1 Sam. 2. 18–20, 26<br>Ps. 148. 1–6 [7–end]<br>Col. 3. 12–17<br>Luke 2. 41–end | Ps. 105. 1–11<br>Isa. 41.21 – 42.1<br>1 John 1. 1–7 |

*Thomas Becket may be celebrated on 7 July instead of 29 December.

| Second Service Evening Prayer | | Calendar and Holy Communion | Morning Prayer | Evening Prayer |
|---|---|---|---|---|
| *EP*: Ps. 8<br>Isa. 65. 17–25<br>Phil. 2. 5–11<br>*or* Luke 2. 1–20<br>*if it has not been used at the Principal Service of the day* | W | **CHRISTMAS DAY**<br>Isa. 9. 2–7<br>Ps. 98<br>Heb. 1. 1–12<br>John 1. 1–14 | Ps. 110; 117<br>Isa. 62. 1–5<br>Matt. 1. 18–end | Ps. 8<br>Isa. 65. 17–25<br>Phil. 2. 5–11<br>*or* Luke 2. 1–20 |
| *EP*: Ps. 57; ***86***<br>Gen. 4. 1–10<br>Matt. 23. 34–end | R | **STEPHEN, DEACON, FIRST MARTYR**<br>Collect<br>(1) Stephen<br>(2) Christmas<br>2 Chron. 24. 20–22<br>Ps. 119. 161–168<br>Acts 7. 55–end<br>Matt. 23. 34–end | (Ps. 13; 31. 1–8; 150)<br>Jer. 26. 12–15<br>Acts ch. 6 | (Ps. 57; 86)<br>Gen. 4. 1–10<br>Matt. 10. 17–22 |
| *EP*: Ps. 97<br>Isa. 6. 1–8<br>1 John 5. 1–12 | W | **JOHN, APOSTLE AND EVANGELIST**<br>Collect<br>(1) John<br>(2) Christmas<br>Exod. 33. 18–end<br>Ps. 92. 11–end<br>1 John ch. 1<br>John 21. 19b–end | (Ps. 21; 147. 13–end)<br>Exod. 33. 7–11a<br>1 John 2. 1–11 | (Ps. 97)<br>Isa. 6. 1–8<br>1 John 5. 1–12 |
| *EP*: Ps. 124; ***128***<br>Isa. 49. 14–25<br>Mark 10. 13–16 | R | **THE HOLY INNOCENTS**<br>Collect<br>(1) Innocents<br>(2) Christmas<br>Jer. 31. 10–17<br>Ps. 123<br>Rev. 14. 1–5<br>Matt. 2. 13–18 | (Ps. 36; 146)<br>Baruch 4. 21–27<br>*or* Gen. 37. 13–20<br>Matt. 18. 1–10 | (Ps. 123; ***128***)<br>Isa. 49. 14–25<br>Mark 10. 13–16 |
| Ps. 131; ***132***<br>Jonah ch. 1<br>Col. 1. 1–14 | W | **CEG of Christmas** | Isa. 57. 15–end<br>John 1. 1–18 | Jonah ch. 1<br>Col. 1. 1–14 |
| Ps. ***65***; 84<br>Jonah ch. 2<br>Col. 1. 15–23<br>**ct** | W | **CEG of Christmas** | Isa. 59. 1–15a<br>John 1. 19–28 | Jonah ch. 2<br>Col. 1. 15–23<br>**ct** |
| Ps. 132<br>Isa. ch. 61<br>Gal. 3.27 – 4.7<br>*or* Luke 2. 15–21 | W | **THE SUNDAY AFTER CHRISTMAS DAY**<br>Isa. 62. 10–12<br>Ps. 45. 1–7<br>Gal. 4. 1–7<br>Matt. 1. 18–end | Ps. 105. 1–11<br>Isa. 41.2 – 42.1<br>1 John 1. 1–7 | Ps. 132<br>Isa. ch. 61<br>Luke 2. 15–21 |

# January 2007

| | | | Sunday Principal Service / Weekday Eucharist | Third Service / Morning Prayer |
|---|---|---|---|---|
| **1** | M | **THE NAMING AND CIRCUMCISION OF JESUS** | | |
| | | | Num. 6. 22–end<br>Ps. 8<br>Gal. 4. 4–7<br>Luke 2.15–21 | *MP:* Ps. ***103***; 150<br>Gen. 17.1–13<br>Rom. 2. 17–end |
| | **W** | | | |
| **2** | Tu | **Basil the Great and Gregory of Nazianzus, Bishops, Teachers, 379 and 389**<br>*Seraphim, Monk of Sarov, Spiritual Guide, 1833; Vedanayagam Samuel Azariah, Bishop in South India, Evangelist, 1945* | | |
| | **W** | Com. Teacher<br>*esp.* 2 Tim. 4. 1–8<br>Matt. 5. 13–19 | *or* 1 John 2. 22–28<br>Ps. 98. 1–4<br>John 1. 19–28 | Ps. 18. 1–30<br>Isa. 60. 1–12<br>John 1. 35–42 |
| **3** | W<br>**W** | | 1 John 2.29 – 3.6<br>Ps. 98. 2–7<br>John 1. 29–34 | Ps. ***127***; 128; 131<br>Isa. 60. 13–end<br>John 1. 43–end |
| **4** | Th<br>**W** | | 1 John 3. 7–10<br>Ps. 98. 1, 8–end<br>John 1. 35–42 | Ps. 89. 1–37<br>Isa. ch. 61<br>John 2. 1–12 |
| **5** | F<br>**W** | | 1 John 3. 11–21<br>Ps. 100<br>John 1. 43–end | Ps. 8; ***48***<br>Isa. ch. 62<br>John 2. 13–end |
| **6** | Sa | **THE EPIPHANY** | | |
| | **𝔚** | | Isa. 60. 1–6<br>Ps. 72. [1–9] 10–15<br>Eph. 3. 1–12<br>Matt. 2. 1–12 | *MP:* Ps. ***132***; 113<br>Jer. 31. 7–14<br>John 1. 29–34 |
| | | *or, if The Epiphany is celebrated on 7 January:* | | |
| | **W** | | 1 John 5. 5–13<br>Ps. 147. 13–end<br>Mark 1. 7–11 | Ps. ***99***; 147. 1–12<br>Isa. 63. 7–end<br>1 John ch. 3 |
| **7** | **S** | **THE BAPTISM OF CHRIST (The First Sunday of Epiphany)**<br>*(or transferred to 8 January if The Epiphany is celebrated today. For The Epiphany, see provision on the 6th.)* | | |
| | **𝔚** | | Isa. 43. 1–7<br>Ps. 29<br>Acts 8. 14–17<br>Luke 3. 15–17, 21–22 | Ps. 89. 19–29<br>Isa. 42. 1–9<br>Acts 19. 1–7 |
| **8**<br>DEL 1 | M<br>**W** | For The Baptism, see provision on the 7th. | Heb. 1. 1–6<br>Ps. 97. 1–2, 6–10<br>Mark 1. 14–20 | Ps. **2**; 110<br>*alt.* Ps. 71<br>Amos ch. 1<br>1 Cor. 1. 1–17 |
| **9** | Tu<br>**W** | | Heb. 2. 5–12<br>Ps. 8<br>Mark 1. 21–28 | Ps. 8; **9**<br>*alt.* Ps. 73<br>Amos ch. 2<br>1 Cor. 1. 18–end |
| **10** | W<br>**W** | *William Laud, Archbishop of Canterbury, 1645* | Heb. 2. 14–end<br>Ps. 105. 1–9<br>Mark 1. 29–39 | Ps. 19; **20**<br>*alt.* Ps. 77<br>Amos ch. 3<br>1 Cor. ch. 2 |

| Second Service<br>Evening Prayer | | Calendar and Holy Communion | Morning Prayer | Evening Prayer |
|---|---|---|---|---|
| *EP*: Ps. 115<br>Deut. 30. [1–10] 11–end<br>Acts 3. 1–16 | W | **THE CIRCUMCISION OF CHRIST**<br>Additional collect<br>Gen. 17. 3b–10<br>Ps. 98<br>Rom. 4. 8–13<br>*or* Eph. 2. 11–18<br>Luke 2. 15–21 | Ps. 103; 150<br>Gen. 17. 1–13<br>Rom. 2. 17–end | Ps. 115<br>Deut. 30. [1–10]<br>11–end<br>Acts 3. 1–16 |
| Ps. 45; ***46***<br>Ruth ch. 1<br>Col. 2. 8–end | W | | Isa. 60. 1–12<br>John 1. 35–42 | Ruth ch. 1<br>Col. 2. 8–end |
| Ps. **2**; 110<br>Ruth ch. 2<br>Col. 3. 1–11 | W | | Isa. 60. 13–end<br>John 1. 43–end | Ruth ch. 2<br>Col. 3. 1–11 |
| Ps. 85; ***87***<br>Ruth ch. 3<br>Col 3.12 – 4.1 | W | | Isa. ch. 61<br>John 2. 1–12 | Ruth ch. 3<br>Col 3.12 – 4.1 |
| *First EP of The Epiphany*<br>Ps. 96; **97**<br>Isa. 49. 1–13<br>John 4. 7–26<br>**𝔚 ct**<br>*or, if The Epiphany is celebrated on 7 January:*<br>Ps. 118<br>Ruth 4. 1–17<br>Col. 4. 2–end | W | | Isa. ch. 62<br>John 2. 13–end | *First EP of The Epiphany*<br>Ps. 96; **97**<br>Isa. 49. 1–13<br>John 4. 7–26<br>**𝔚 ct** |
| *EP*: Ps. ***98***; 100<br>Baruch 4.36 – 5.end<br>*or* Isa. 60. 1–9<br>John 2. 1–11 | | **THE EPIPHANY**<br>Isa. 60. 1–9<br>Ps. 100<br>Eph. 3. 1–12<br>Matt. 2. 1–12 | Ps. 132; 113<br>Jer. 31. 7–14<br>John 1. 29–34 | Ps. 72; 98<br>Baruch 4.36 – 5.end<br>*or* Isa. 60. 1–9<br>John 2. 1–11 |
| Ps. 96; **97**<br>Isa. 49. 1–13<br>John 4.7–26<br>**𝔚 ct** | 𝔚 | | | |
| Ps. 46; 47<br>Isa. 55. 1–11<br>Rom. 6. 1–11<br>*Gospel:* Mark 1. 4–11 | **W** *or* **G** | **THE FIRST SUNDAY AFTER EPIPHANY**<br>To celebrate The Baptism of Christ, see *Common Worship* provision.<br>Zech. 8. 1–8<br>Ps. 72. 1–8<br>Rom. 12. 1–5<br>Luke 2. 41–end | Ps. 89. 19–29<br>Isa. 42. 1–9<br>Acts 19. 1–7 | Ps. 46; 47<br>Isa. 55. 1–11<br>Rom. 6. 1–11 |
| Ps. ***34***; 36<br>*alt.* Ps. ***72***; 75<br>Gen. 1. 1–19<br>Matt. 21. 1–17 | **Wr** *or* **Gr** | **Lucian, Priest and Martyr, 290**<br>Com. Martyr | Amos ch. 1<br>1 Cor. 1. 1–17 | Gen. 1. 1–19<br>Matt. 21. 1–17 |
| Ps. ***45***; 46<br>*alt.* Ps. 74<br>Gen. 1.20 – 2.3<br>Matt. 21. 18–32 | **W** *or* **G** | | Amos ch. 2<br>1 Cor. 1. 18–end | Gen. 1.20 – 2.3<br>Matt. 21. 18–32 |
| Ps. ***47***; 48<br>*alt.* Ps. 119. 81–104<br>Gen. 2. 4–end<br>Matt. 21. 33–end | **W** *or* **G** | | Amos ch. 3<br>1 Cor. ch. 2 | Gen. 2. 4–end<br>Matt. 21. 33–end |

# January 2007

| Date | Day | | Sunday Principal Service<br>Weekday Eucharist | Third Service<br>Morning Prayer | Colour |
|---|---|---|---|---|---|
| **11** | Th | *Mary Slessor, Missionary in West Africa, 1915* | Heb. 3. 7–14<br>Ps. 95. 1, 8–end<br>Mark 1. 40–end | Ps. ***21***; 24<br>*alt*. Ps. 78. 1–39†<br>Amos ch. 4<br>1 Cor. ch. 3 | **W** |
| **12** | F | **Aelred of Hexham, Abbot of Rievaulx, 1167**<br>*Benedict Biscop, Abbot of Wearmouth, Scholar, 689*<br>Com. Religious<br>*also* Ecclus. 15. 1–6 | *or* Heb. 4. 1–5, 11<br>Ps. 78. 3–8<br>Mark 2. 1–12 | Ps. ***67***; 72<br>*alt*. Ps. 55<br>Amos 5. 1–17<br>1 Cor. ch. 4 | **W** |
| **13** | Sa | **Hilary, Bishop of Poitiers, Teacher, 367**<br>*Kentigern (Mungo), Missionary Bishop in Strathclyde and Cumbria, 603; George Fox, Founder of the Society of Friends (the Quakers), 1691*<br>Com. Teacher<br>*also* 1 John 2. 18–25<br>John 8. 25–32 | *or* Heb. 4. 12–16<br>Ps. 19. 7–end<br>Mark 2. 13–17 | Ps. 29; ***33***<br>*alt*. Ps. ***76***; 79<br>Amos 5. 18–end<br>1 Cor. ch. 5 | **W** |
| **14** | **S** | **THE SECOND SUNDAY OF EPIPHANY** | Isa. 62. 1–5<br>Ps. 36. 5–10<br>1 Cor. 12. 1–11<br>John 2. 1–11 | Ps. 145. 1–13<br>Isa. 49. 1–7<br>Acts 16. 11–15 | **W** |
| **15**<br>DEL 2 | M | | Heb. 5. 1–10<br>Ps. 110. 1–4<br>Mark 2. 18–22 | Ps. 145; ***146***<br>*alt*. Ps. ***80***; 82<br>Amos ch. 6<br>1 Cor. 6. 1–11 | **W** |
| **16** | Tu | | Heb. 6. 10–end<br>Ps. 111<br>Mark 2. 23–end | Ps. ***132***; 147. 1–12<br>*alt*. Ps. 87; ***89. 1–18***<br>Amos ch. 7<br>1 Cor. 6. 12–end | **W** |
| **17** | W | **Antony of Egypt, Hermit, Abbot, 356**<br>*Charles Gore, Bishop, Founder of the Community of the Resurrection, 1932*<br>Com. Religious<br>*esp*. Phil. 3. 7–14<br>*also* Matt. 19. 16–26 | *or* Heb. 7. 1–3, 15–17<br>Ps. 110. 1–4<br>Mark 3. 1–6 | Ps. ***81***; 147. 13–end<br>*alt*. Ps. 119. 105–128<br>Amos ch. 8<br>1 Cor. 7. 1–24 | **W** |
| **18** | Th | The Week of Prayer for Christian Unity until 25th | Heb. 7.25 – 8.6<br>Ps. 40. 7–10, 17–end<br>Mark 3. 7–12 | Ps. ***76***; 148<br>*alt*. Ps. 90; ***92***<br>Amos ch. 9<br>1 Cor. 7. 25–end | **W** |
| **19** | F | **Wulfstan, Bishop of Worcester, 1095**<br>Com. Bishop<br>*esp*. Matt. 24. 42–46 | *or* Heb. 8. 6–end<br>Ps. 85. 7–end<br>Mark 3. 13–19 | Ps. ***27***; 149<br>*alt*. Ps. ***88*** (95)<br>Hos. 1.1 – 2.1<br>1 Cor. ch. 8 | **W** |
| **20** | Sa | *Richard Rolle of Hampole, Spiritual Writer, 1349* | Heb. 9. 2–3, 11–14<br>Ps. 47. 1–8<br>Mark 3. 20–21 | Ps. ***122***; 128; 150<br>*alt*. Ps. 96; ***97***; 100<br>Hos. 2. 2–17<br>1 Cor. 9. 1–14 | **W** |

| Second Service Evening Prayer | Calendar and Holy Communion | Morning Prayer | Evening Prayer |
|---|---|---|---|
| Ps. ***61***; 65<br>*alt.* Ps. 78. 40–end†<br>Gen. ch. 3<br>Matt. 22. 1–14 | **W** *or* **G** | Amos ch. 4<br>1 Cor. ch. 3 | Gen. ch. 3<br>Matt. 22. 1–14 |
| Ps. 68<br>*alt.* Ps. 69<br>Gen. 4. 1–16, 25–26<br>Matt. 22. 15–33 | **W** *or* **G** | Amos 5. 1–17<br>1 Cor. ch. 4 | Gen. 4. 1–16, 25–26<br>Matt. 22. 15–33 |
| Ps. 84; ***85***<br>*alt.* Ps. 81; ***84***<br>Gen. 6. 1–10<br>Matt. 22. 34–end<br>**ct** | **Hilary, Bishop of Poitiers, Teacher, 367**<br>Com. Doctor<br>**W** *or* **Gw** | Amos 5. 18–end<br>1 Cor. ch. 5 | Gen. 6. 1–10<br>Matt. 22. 34–end<br>**ct** |
| Ps. 96<br>1 Sam. 3. 1–20<br>Eph. 4. 1–16<br>*Gospel:* John 1. 29–42 | **THE SECOND SUNDAY AFTER EPIPHANY**<br>2 Kings 4. 1–17<br>Ps. 107. 13–22<br>Rom. 12. 6–16a<br>John 2. 1–11<br>**W** *or* **G** | Ps. 145. 1–13<br>Isa. 49. 1–7<br>Acts 16. 11–15 | Ps. 96<br>1 Sam. 3. 1–20<br>Eph. 4. 1–16 |
| Ps. 71<br>*alt.* Ps. ***85***; 86<br>Gen. 6.11 – 7.10<br>Matt. 24. 1–14 | **W** *or* **G** | Amos ch. 6<br>1 Cor. 6. 1–11 | Gen. 6.11 – 7.10<br>Matt. 24. 1–14 |
| Ps. 89. 1–37<br>*alt.* Ps. 89. 19–end<br>Gen. 7. 11–end<br>Matt. 24. 15–28 | **W** *or* **G** | Amos ch. 7<br>1 Cor. 6. 12–end | Gen. 7. 11–end<br>Matt. 24. 15–28 |
| Ps. ***97***; 98<br>*alt.* Ps. ***91***; 93<br>Gen. 8. 1–14<br>Matt. 24. 29–end | **W** *or* **G** | Amos ch. 8<br>1 Cor. 7. 1–24 | Gen. 8. 1–14<br>Matt. 24. 29–end |
| Ps. 99; 100; ***111***<br>*alt.* Ps. 94<br>Gen. 8.15 – 9.7<br>Matt. 25. 1–13 | **Prisca, Martyr at Rome, c. 265**<br>Com. Virgin Martyr<br>**Wr** *or* **Gr** | Amos ch. 9<br>1 Cor. 7. 25–end | Gen. 8.15 – 9.7<br>Matt. 25. 1–13 |
| Ps. 73<br>*alt.* Ps. 102<br>Gen. 9. 8–19<br>Matt. 25. 14–30 | **W** *or* **G** | Hos. 1.1 – 2.1<br>1 Cor. ch. 8 | Gen. 9. 8–19<br>Matt. 25. 14–30 |
| Ps. ***61***; 66<br>*alt.* Ps. 104<br>Gen. 11. 1–9<br>Matt. 25. 31–end<br>**ct** | **Fabian, Bishop of Rome, Martyr, 250**<br>Com. Martyr<br>**Wr** *or* **Gr** | Hos. 2. 2–17<br>1 Cor. 9. 1–14 | Gen. 11. 1–9<br>Matt. 25. 31–end<br>**ct** |

# January 2007

| Date | Day | | Sunday Principal Service / Weekday Eucharist | Third Service / Morning Prayer |
|---|---|---|---|---|
| **21** | **S** / **W** | **THE THIRD SUNDAY OF EPIPHANY** | Neh. 8. 1–3, 5–6, 8–10<br>Ps. 19. 1–6 [7–end]<br>1 Cor. 12. 12–31a<br>Luke 4. 14–21 | Ps. 113<br>Deut. 30. 11–15<br>3 John 1, 5–8 |
| **22** DEL 3 | M / **W** | *Vincent of Saragossa, Deacon, first Martyr of Spain, 304* | Heb. 9. 15, 24–end<br>Ps. 98. 1–7<br>Mark 3. 22–30 | Ps. 40; ***108***<br>*alt.* Ps. ***98***; 99; 101<br>Hos. 2.18 – 3.end<br>1 Cor. 9. 15–end |
| **23** | Tu / **W** | | Heb. 10. 1–10<br>Ps. 40. 1–4, 7–10<br>Mark 3. 31–35 | Ps. 34; ***36***<br>*alt.* Ps. 106† (*or* Ps. 103)<br>Hos. 4. 1–16<br>1 Cor. 10. 1–13 |
| **24** | W / **W** | **Francis de Sales, Bishop of Geneva, Teacher, 1274**<br>Com. Teacher<br>*also* Prov. 3. 13–18<br>John 3. 17–21 | *or* Heb. 10. 11–18<br>Ps. 110. 1–4<br>Mark 4. 1–20 | Ps. 45; ***46***<br>*alt.* Ps. 110; ***111***; 112<br>Hos. 5. 1–7<br>1 Cor. 10.14 – 11.1 |
| **25** | Th / **W** | **THE CONVERSION OF PAUL**<br>*The reading from Acts must be used as either the first or second reading at the Eucharist.* | Jer. 1. 4–10<br>*or* Acts 9. 1–22<br>Ps. 67<br>Acts 9. 1–22<br>*or* Gal. 1. 11–16a<br>Matt. 19. 27–end | *MP:* Ps. 66; 147. 13–end<br>Ezek. 3. 22–end<br>Phil. 3. 1–14 |
| **26** | F / **W** | **Timothy and Titus, Companions of Paul**<br>Isa. 61. 1–3a<br>Ps. 100<br>2 Tim. 2. 1–8<br>*or* Titus 1. 1–5<br>Luke 10. 1–9 | *or* Heb. 10. 32–39<br>Ps. 37. 3–6, 40–end<br>Mark 4. 26–34 | Ps. 61; ***65***<br>*alt.* Ps. 139<br>Hos. 6.7 – 7.2<br>1 Cor. 11. 17–end |
| **27** | Sa / **W** | | Heb. 11. 1–2, 8–19<br>*Canticle:* Luke 1. 69–73<br>Mark 4. 35–end | Ps. 68<br>*alt.* Ps. 120; ***121***; 122<br>Hos. ch. 8<br>1 Cor. 12. 1–11 |
| **28** | **S** / **W** | **THE FOURTH SUNDAY OF EPIPHANY**<br>*or The Presentation of Christ in the Temple*** | Ezek. 43.27 – 44.4<br>Ps. 48<br>1 Cor. ch. 13<br>Luke 2. 22–40 | Ps. 71. 1–6, 15–17<br>Mic. 6. 1–8<br>1 Cor. 6. 12–end |
| **29** DEL 4 | M / **W [G]**** | | Heb. 11. 32–end<br>Ps. 31. 19–end<br>Mark 5. 1–20 | Ps. **57**; 96***<br>*alt.* Ps. 123; 124; 125; ***126***<br>Hos. ch. 9<br>1 Cor. 12. 12–end |

*See provision for First EP on 1 February and throughout the day for The Presentation on 2 February.
**Ordinary Time begins today if The Presentation was observed on 28th.
***If The Presentation was observed on 28th, the alternative psalms are used.

| Second Service Evening Prayer | | Calendar and Holy Communion | Morning Prayer | Evening Prayer |
|---|---|---|---|---|
| Ps. 33. 1–12 [13–end]<br>Num. 9. 15–end<br>1 Cor. 7. 17–24<br>*Gospel:* Mark 1. 21–28 | **W** *or* **G** | **THE THIRD SUNDAY AFTER EPIPHANY**<br>2 Kings 6. 14b–23<br>Ps. 102. 15–22<br>Rom. 12. 16b–end<br>Matt. 8. 1–13 | Ps. 113<br>Deut. 30. 11–15<br>3 John 1, 5–8 | Ps. 33. 1–12 [13–end]<br>Num. 9. 15–end<br>1 Cor. 7. 17–24 |
| Ps. ***138***; 144<br>*alt.* Ps. 105† (*or* Ps. 103)<br>Gen. 11.27 – 12.9<br>Matt. 26. 1–16 | **Wr** *or* **Gr** | **Vincent of Saragossa, Deacon, first Martyr of Spain, 304**<br>Com. Martyr | Hos. 2.18 – 3.end<br>1 Cor. 9. 15–end | Gen. 11.27 – 12.9<br>Matt. 26. 1–16 |
| Ps. 145<br>*alt.* Ps. 107†<br>Gen. 13. 2–end<br>Matt. 26. 17–35 | **W** *or* **G** | | Hos. 4. 1–16<br>1 Cor. 10. 1–13 | Gen. 13. 2–end<br>Matt. 26. 17–35 |
| Ps. 21; ***29***<br>*alt.* Ps. 119. 129–152<br>Gen. ch. 14<br>Matt. 26. 36–46<br>*or First EP of The Conversion of Paul*<br>Ps. 149<br>Isa. 49. 1–13<br>Acts 22. 3–16<br>**ct** | **W** *or* **G** | | Hos. 5. 1–7<br>1 Cor. 10.14 – 11.1 | Gen. ch. 14<br>Matt. 26. 36–46<br>*or First EP of The Conversion of Paul*<br>(Ps. 149)<br>Isa. 49. 1–13<br>Acts 22. 3–16<br>**W ct** |
| *EP:* Ps. 119. 41–56<br>Ecclus. 39. 1–10<br>*or* Isa. 56. 1–8<br>Col. 1.24 – 2.7 | **W** | **THE CONVERSION OF PAUL**<br>Josh. 5. 13–end<br>Ps. 67<br>Acts 9. 1–22<br>Matt. 19. 27–end | (Ps. 66; 147. 13–end)<br>Ezek. 3. 22–end<br>Phil. 3. 1–14 | (Ps. 119. 41–56)<br>Ecclus. 39. 1–10<br>*or* Isa. 56. 1–8<br>Col. 1.24 – 2.7 |
| Ps. ***67***; 77<br>*alt.* Ps. ***130***; 131; 137<br>Gen. ch. 16<br>Matt. 26. 57–end | **W** *or* **G** | | Hos. 6.7 – 7.2<br>1 Cor. 11. 17–end | Gen. ch. 16<br>Matt. 26. 57–end |
| Ps. ***72***; 76<br>*alt.* Ps. 118<br>Gen. 17. 1–22<br>Matt. 27. 1–10<br>**ct** | **W** *or* **G** | | Hos. ch. 8<br>1 Cor. 12. 1–11 | Gen. 17. 1–22<br>Matt. 27. 1–10<br>**ct** |
| Ps. 34. 1–10 [11–end]<br>1 Chron. 29. 6–19<br>Acts 7. 44–50<br>*Gospel:* John 4. 19–29a | **W** *or* **G** | **THE FOURTH SUNDAY AFTER EPIPHANY**<br>1 Sam. 10. 17–24<br>Ps. 97<br>Rom. 13. 1–7<br>Matt. 8. 23–34 | Ps. 71. 1–6, 15–17<br>Mic. 6. 1–8<br>1 Cor. 6. 12–end | Ps. 34. 1–10 [11–end]<br>1 Chron. 29. 6–19<br>Acts 7. 44–50 |
| Ps. 2; ***20******<br>*alt.* Ps. ***127***; 128; 129<br>Gen. 18. 1–15<br>Matt. 27. 11–26 | **W** *or* **G** | | Hos. ch. 9<br>1 Cor. 12. 12–end | Gen. 18. 1–15<br>Matt. 27. 11–26 |

# January 2007

| Date | Day | | Sunday Principal Service<br>Weekday Eucharist | Third Service<br>Morning Prayer |
|---|---|---|---|---|
| **30** | Tu<br>**Wr [Gr]** | **Charles, King and Martyr, 1649**<br>Com. Martyr *or*<br>*also* Ecclus. 2. 12–17<br>1 Tim. 6. 12–16 | Heb. 12. 1–4<br>Ps. 22. 25b–end<br>Mark 5. 21–43 | Ps. ***93***; 97*<br>*alt.* Ps. ***132***; 133<br>Hos. ch. 10<br>1 Cor. ch. 13 |
| **31** | W<br>**W [G]** | *John Bosco, Priest, Founder of the Salesian Teaching Order, 1888* | Heb. 12. 4–7, 11–15<br>Ps. 103. 1–2, 13–18<br>Mark 6. 1–6 | Ps. ***95***; 98*<br>*alt.* Ps. 119. 153–end<br>Hos. 11. 1–11<br>1 Cor. 14. 1–19 |

# February 2007

| Date | Day | | Sunday Principal Service<br>Weekday Eucharist | Third Service<br>Morning Prayer |
|---|---|---|---|---|
| **1** | Th<br>**W [G]** | *Brigid, Abbess of Kildare, c. 525* | Heb. 12. 18–19, 21–24<br>Ps. 48. 1–3, 8–10<br>Mark 6. 7–13 | Ps. 99; ***110****<br>*alt.* Ps. ***143***; 146<br>Hos. 11.12 – 12.end<br>1 Cor. 14. 20–end |
| **2** | F<br>𝔚 | **THE PRESENTATION OF CHRIST IN THE TEMPLE (CANDLEMAS)** | Mal. 3. 1–5<br>Ps. 24. [1–6] 7–end<br>Heb. 2. 14–end<br>Luke 2. 22–40 | *MP:* Ps. ***48***; 146<br>Exod. 13. 1–16<br>Rom. 12. 1–5 |
| | **G** | *or, if The Presentation is observed on 28 January:* | Heb. 13. 1–8<br>Ps. 27. 1–6, 9–12<br>Mark 6. 14–29 | Ps. 142; ***144***<br>Hos. 13. 1–14<br>1 Cor. 16. 1–9 |
| **3** | Sa<br>**Gw** | **Anskar, Archbishop of Hamburg, Missionary in Denmark and Sweden, 865**<br>Ordinary Time starts today (or on 29 January if The Presentation is observed on 28 January)<br>Com. Missionary *or*<br>*esp.* Isa. 52. 7–10<br>*also* Rom. 10. 11–15 | Heb. 13. 15–17, 20–21<br>Ps. 23<br>Mark 6. 30–34 | Ps. 147<br>Hos. ch. 14<br>1 Cor. 16. 10–end |
| **4** | **S**<br>**G** | **THE THIRD SUNDAY BEFORE LENT (Proper 1)** | Isa. 6. 1–8 [9–end]<br>Ps. 138<br>1 Cor. 15. 1–11<br>Luke 5. 1–11 | Ps. 3; 4<br>Jer. 26. 1–16<br>Acts 3. 1–10 |
| **5**<br>DEL 5 | M<br>**G** | | Gen. 1. 1–19<br>Ps. 104. 1–2, 6–13, 26<br>Mark 6. 53–end | Ps. ***1***; 2; 3<br>2 Chron. 2. 1–16<br>John 17. 1–5 |
| **6** | Tu<br>**G** | *The Martyrs of Japan, 1597*<br>(The Accession of Queen Elizabeth II may be observed on 6 February, and Collect, Readings and Post-Communion for the sovereign used.) | Gen. 1.20 – 2.4a<br>Ps. 8<br>Mark 7. 1–13 | Ps. ***5***; 6 (8)<br>2 Chron. ch. 3<br>John 17. 6–19 |
| **7** | W<br>**G** | | Gen. 2. 4b–9, 15–17<br>Ps. 104. 12, 29–32<br>Mark 7. 14–23 | Ps. 119. 1–32<br>2 Chron. ch. 5<br>John 17. 20–end |

*If The Presentation was observed on 28 January, the alternative psalms are used.

| Second Service Evening Prayer | | Calendar and Holy Communion | Morning Prayer | Evening Prayer |
|---|---|---|---|---|
| Ps. ***93***; 97*<br>*alt.* Ps. (134) ***135***<br>Gen. 18. 16–end<br>Matt. 27. 27–44 | **Wr** *or* **Gr** | **Charles, King and Martyr, 1649**<br>Com. Martyr | Hos. ch. 10<br>1 Cor. ch. 13 | Gen. 18. 16–end<br>Matt. 27. 27–44 |
| Ps. ***81***; 111*<br>*alt.* Ps. 136<br>Gen. 19. 1–3, 12–29<br>Matt. 27. 45–56 | **W** *or* **G** | | Hos. 11. 1–11<br>1 Cor. 14. 1–19 | Gen. 19. 1–3, 12–29<br>Matt. 27. 45–56 |
| | | | | |
| *First EP of The Presentation*<br>Ps. 118<br>1 Sam. 1. 19b–end<br>Heb. 4. 11–end<br>**𝔚 ct**<br>*or, if The Presentation was kept on 28th:*<br>Ps. ***138***; 140; 141<br>Gen. 21. 1–21<br>Matt. 27. 57–end | **W** *or* **G** | | Hos. 11.12 – 12.end<br>1 Cor. 14. 20–end | *First EP of The Presentation*<br>Ps. 118<br>1 Sam. 1. 19b–end<br>Heb. 4. 11–end<br>**𝔚 ct** |
| *EP*: Ps. 122; ***132***<br>Hag. 2. 1–9<br>John 2. 18–22<br><br>Ps. 145<br>Gen. 22. 1–19<br>Matt. 28. 1–15 | **𝔚** | **THE PRESENTATION OF CHRIST IN THE TEMPLE**<br>Mal. 3. 1–5<br>Ps. 48. 1–7<br>Gal. 4. 1–7<br>Luke 2. 22–40 | Ps. 48; 146<br>Exod. 13. 1–16<br>Rom. 12. 1–5 | Ps. 122; 132<br>Hag. 2. 1–9<br>John 2. 18–22 |
| Ps. ***148***; 149; 150<br>Gen. ch. 23<br>Matt. 28. 16–end<br>**ct** | **Gr** | **Blasius, Bishop of Sebastopol, Martyr, c. 316**<br>Com. Martyr | Hos. ch. 14<br>1 Cor. 16. 10–end | Gen. ch. 23<br>Matt. 28. 16–end<br>**ct** |
| Ps. [1] 2<br>Wisd. 6. 1–21<br>*or* Hos. ch. 1<br>Col. 3. 1–22<br>*Gospel*: Matt. 5. 13–20 | **G** | **SEPTUAGESIMA**<br>Gen. 1. 1–5<br>Ps. 9. 10–20<br>1 Cor. 9. 24–end<br>Matt. 20. 1–16 | Ps. 3; 4<br>Jer. 26. 1–16<br>Acts 3. 1–10 | Ps. [1] 2<br>Wisd. 6. 1–21<br>*or* Hos. ch. 1<br>Col. 3. 1–22 |
| Ps. ***4***; 7<br>Gen. 24. 1–28<br>1 Tim. 6. 1–10 | **Gr** | **Agatha, Martyr in Sicily, 251**<br>Com. Virgin Martyr | 2 Chron. 2. 1–16<br>John 17. 1–5 | Gen. 24. 1–28<br>1 Tim. 6. 1–10 |
| Ps. ***9***; 10<br>Gen. 24. 29–end<br>1 Tim. 6. 11–end | **G** | **The Accession of Queen Elizabeth II, 1952**<br>*For Accession Service:* Ps. 20; 101; 121; Josh. 1. 1–9; Prov. 8. 1–16; Rom. 13. 1–10; Rev. 21.22 – 22.4<br>*For The Accession:*<br>1 Pet. 2. 11–17<br>Matt. 22. 16–22 | 2 Chron. ch. 3<br>John 17. 6–19 | Gen. 24. 29–end<br>1 Tim. 6. 11–end |
| Ps. ***11***; 12; 13<br>Gen. 25. 7–11, 19–end<br>2 Tim. 1. 1–14 | **G** | | 2 Chron. ch. 5<br>John 17. 20–end | Gen. 25. 7–11, 19–end<br>2 Tim. 1. 1–14 |

# February 2007

| Date | Day / Colour | | Sunday Principal Service<br>Weekday Eucharist | Third Service<br>Morning Prayer |
|---|---|---|---|---|
| **8** | Th<br>**G** | | Gen. 2. 18–end<br>Ps. 128<br>Mark 7. 24–30 | Ps. 14; ***15***; 16<br>2 Chron. 6. 1–21<br>John 18. 1–11 |
| **9** | F<br>**G** | | Gen. 3. 1–8<br>Ps. 32. 1–8<br>Mark 7. 31–end | Ps. 17; ***19***<br>2 Chron. 6. 22–end<br>John 18. 12–27 |
| **10** | Sa<br>**G** | *Scholastica, sister of Benedict, Abbess of Plombariola, c. 543* | Gen. 3. 9–end<br>Ps. 90. 1–12<br>Mark 8. 1–10 | Ps. 20; 21; ***23***<br>2 Chron. ch. 7<br>John 18. 28–end |
| **11** | **S**<br>**G** | **THE SECOND SUNDAY BEFORE LENT** | Gen. 2. 4b–9, 15–end<br>Ps. 65<br>Rev. ch. 4<br>Luke 8. 22–25 | Ps. 104. 1–26<br>Job 28. 1–11<br>Acts 14. 8–17 |
| **12**<br>DEL 6 | M<br>**G** | | Gen. 4. 1–15, 25<br>Ps. 50. 1, 8, 16–end<br>Mark 8. 11–13 | Ps. 27; ***30***<br>2 Chron. 9. 1–12<br>John 19. 1–16 |
| **13** | Tu<br>**G** | | Gen. 6. 5–8; 7. 1–5, 10<br>Ps. 29<br>Mark 8. 14–21 | Ps. 32; ***36***<br>2 Chron. 10.1 – 11.4<br>John 19. 17–30 |
| **14** | W<br>**Gw** | **Cyril and Methodius, Missionaries to the Slavs, 869 and 885**<br>*Valentine, Martyr at Rome, c. 269*<br>Com. Missionaries<br>*esp.* Isa. 52. 7–10<br>*also* Rom. 10. 11–15 | *or* Gen. 8. 6–13, 20–end<br>Ps. 116. 10–end<br>Mark 8. 22–26 | Ps. 34<br>2 Chron. ch. 12<br>John 19. 31–end |
| **15** | Th<br>**G** | *Sigfrid, Bishop, Apostle of Sweden, 1045; Thomas Bray, Priest, Founder of the SPCK and the SPG, 1730* | Gen. 9. 1–13<br>Ps. 102. 16–23<br>Mark 8. 27–33 | Ps. 37†<br>2 Chron. 13.1 – 14.1<br>John 20. 1–10 |
| **16** | F<br>**G** | | Gen. 11. 1–9<br>Ps. 33. 10–15<br>Mark 8.34 – 9.1 | Ps. 31<br>2 Chron. 14. 2–end<br>John 20. 11–18 |
| **17** | Sa<br>**Gr** | **Janani Luwum, Archbishop of Uganda, Martyr, 1977**<br>Com. Martyr<br>*also* Ecclus. 4. 20–28<br>John 12. 24–32 | *or* Heb. 11. 1–7<br>Ps. 145. 1–10<br>Mark 9. 2–13 | Ps. 41; ***42***; 43<br>2 Chron. 15. 1–15<br>John 20. 19–end |
| **18** | **S**<br>**G** | **THE SUNDAY NEXT BEFORE LENT** | Exod. 34. 29–end<br>Ps. 99<br>2 Cor. 3.12 – 4.2<br>Luke 9. 28–36 [37–43a] | Ps. 2<br>Exod. 33. 17–end<br>1 John 3. 1–3 |
| **19**<br>DEL 7 | M<br>**G** | | Ecclus. 1. 1–10<br>*or* James 1. 1–11<br>Ps. 93<br>*or* Ps. 119. 65–72<br>Mark 9. 14–29 | Ps. 44<br>Jer. ch. 1<br>John 3. 1–21 |
| **20** | Tu<br>**G** | | Ecclus. 2. 1–11<br>*or* James 1. 12–18<br>Ps. 37. 3–6, 27–28<br>*or* Ps. 94. 12–18<br>Mark 9. 30–37 | Ps. ***48***; 52<br>Jer. 2. 1–13<br>John 3. 22–end |
| **21** | W<br>**P** | **ASH WEDNESDAY** | Joel 2. 1–2, 12–17<br>*or* Isa. 58. 1–12<br>Ps. 51. 1–18<br>2 Cor. 5.20b – 6.10<br>Matt. 6. 1–6, 16–21<br>*or* John 8. 1–11 | *MP:* Ps. 38<br>Dan. 9. 3–6, 17–19<br>1 Tim. 6. 6–19 |

| Second Service Evening Prayer | | Calendar and Holy Communion | Morning Prayer | Evening Prayer |
|---|---|---|---|---|
| Ps. 18†<br>Gen. 26.34 – 27.40<br>2 Tim. 1.15 – 2.13 | **G** | | 2 Chron. 6. 1–21<br>John 18. 1–11 | Gen. 26.34 – 27.40<br>2 Tim. 1.15 – 2.13 |
| Ps. 22<br>Gen. 27.41 – 28.end<br>2 Tim. 2. 14–end | **G** | | 2 Chron. 6. 22–end<br>John 18. 12–27 | Gen. 27.41 – 28.end<br>2 Tim. 2. 14–end |
| Ps. ***24***; 25<br>Gen. 29. 1–30<br>2 Tim. ch. 3<br>**ct** | **G** | | 2 Chron. ch. 7<br>John 18. 28–end | Gen. 29. 1–30<br>2 Tim. ch. 3<br>**ct** |
| Ps. 147. [1–12] 13–end<br>Gen. 1.1 – 2.3<br>Matt. 6. 25–end | **G** | **SEXAGESIMA**<br>Gen. 3. 9–19<br>Ps. 83. 1–2, 13–end<br>2 Cor. 11. 19–31<br>Luke 8. 4–15 | Ps. 104. 1–26<br>Job 28. 1–11<br>Acts 14. 8–17 | Ps. 147. [1–12] 13–end<br>Gen. 1.1 – 2.3<br>Matt. 6. 25–end |
| Ps. 26; ***28***; 29<br>Gen. 29.31 – 30.24<br>2 Tim. 4. 1–8 | **G** | | 2 Chron. 9. 1–12<br>John 19. 1–16 | Gen. 29.31 – 30.24<br>2 Tim. 4. 1–8 |
| Ps. 33<br>Gen. 31. 1–24<br>2 Tim. 4. 9–end | **G** | | 2 Chron. 10.1 – 11.4<br>John 19. 17–30 | Gen. 31. 1–24<br>2 Tim. 4. 9–end |
| Ps. 119. 33–56<br>Gen. 31.25 – 32.2<br>Titus ch. 1 | **Gr** | **Valentine, Martyr at Rome, c. 269**<br>Com. Martyr | 2 Chron. ch. 12<br>John 19. 31–end | Gen. 31.25 – 32.2<br>Titus ch. 1 |
| Ps. 39; ***40***<br>Gen. 32. 3–30<br>Titus ch. 2 | **G** | | 2 Chron. 13.1 – 14.1<br>John 20. 1–10 | Gen. 32. 3–30<br>Titus ch. 2 |
| Ps. 35<br>Gen. 33. 1–17<br>Titus ch. 3 | **G** | | 2 Chron. 14. 2–end<br>John 20. 11–18 | Gen. 33. 1–17<br>Titus ch. 3 |
| Ps. 45; ***46***<br>Gen. ch. 35<br>Philemon<br>**ct** | **G** | | 2 Chron. 15. 1–15<br>John 20. 19–end | Gen. ch. 35<br>Philemon<br>**ct** |
| Ps. 89. [1–4] 5–12 [13–18]<br>Exod. 3. 1–6<br>John 12. 27–36a | **G** | **QUINQUAGESIMA**<br>Gen. 9. 8–17<br>Ps. 77. 11–end<br>1 Cor. ch. 13<br>Luke 18. 31–43 | Ps. 2<br>Exod. 33. 17–end<br>Luke 9. 28–43 | Ps. 89. [1–4] 5–12 [13–18]<br>Exod. 3. 1–6<br>John 12. 27–36a |
| Ps. ***47***; 49<br>Gen. 37. 1–11<br>Gal. ch. 1 | **G** | | Jer. ch. 1<br>John 3. 1–21 | Gen. 37. 1–11<br>Gal. ch. 1 |
| Ps. 50<br>Gen. 37. 12–end<br>Gal. 2. 1–10 | **G** | | Jer. 2. 1–13<br>John 3. 22–end | Gen. 37. 12–end<br>Gal. 2. 1–10 |
| *EP*: Ps. ***51*** *or* Ps. 102. 1–18 [19–end]<br>Isa. 1. 10–18<br>Luke 15. 11–end | **P** | **ASH WEDNESDAY**<br>Ash Wed. Coll. until 7 April<br>Commination<br>Joel 2. 12–17<br>Ps. 57<br>James 4. 1–10<br>Matt. 6. 16–21 | Ps. 38<br>Dan. 9. 3–6, 17–19<br>1 Tim. 6. 6–19 | Ps. 51 *or* Ps. 102. 1–18 [19–end]<br>Isa. 1. 10–18<br>Luke 15. 11–end |

# February 2007

| Date | Day | Commemoration | Sunday Principal Service<br>Weekday Eucharist | Third Service<br>Morning Prayer |
|---|---|---|---|---|
| **22** | Th<br>**P** | | Deut. 30. 15–end<br>Ps. 1<br>Luke 9. 22–25 | Ps. 77<br>*alt*. Ps. 56; **57** (63†)<br>Jer. 2. 14–32<br>John 4. 1–26 |
| **23** | F<br>**Pr** | **Polycarp, Bishop of Smyrna, Martyr, c. 155**<br>Com. Martyr<br>*also* Rev. 2. 8–11 | *or* Isa. 58. 1–9a<br>Ps. 51. 1–5, 17–18<br>Matt. 9. 14–15 | Ps. **3**; 7<br>*alt*. Ps. ***51***; 54<br>Jer. 3. 6–22<br>John 4. 27–42 |
| **24** | Sa *<br>**P** | | Isa. 58. 9b–end<br>Ps. 86. 1–7<br>Luke 5. 27–32 | Ps. 71<br>*alt*. Ps. 68<br>Jer. 4. 1–18<br>John 4. 43–end |
| **25** | **S**<br>**P** | **THE FIRST SUNDAY OF LENT** | Deut. 26. 1–11<br>Ps. 91. 1–2, 9–end (*or* 1–11)<br>Rom. 10. 8b–13<br>Luke 4. 1–13 | Ps. 50. 1–15<br>Mic. 6. 1–8<br>Luke 5. 27–end |
| **26** | M<br>**P** | | Lev. 19. 1–2, 11–18<br>Ps. 19. 7–end<br>Matt. 25. 31–end | Ps. 10; ***11***<br>*alt*. Ps. 71<br>Jer. 4. 19–end<br>John 5. 1–18 |
| **27** | T<br>**Pw** | **George Herbert, Priest, Poet, 1633**<br>Com. Pastor<br>*esp*. Mal. 2. 5–7<br>Matt. 11. 25–30<br>*also* Rev. 19. 5–9 | *or* Isa. 55. 10–11<br>Ps. 34. 4–6, 21–22<br>Matt. 6. 7–15 | Ps. 44<br>*alt*. Ps. 73<br>Jer. 5. 1–19<br>John 5. 19–29 |
| **28** | W<br>**P** | Ember Day** | Jonah ch. 3<br>Ps. 51. 1–5, 17–18<br>Luke 11. 29–32 | Ps. **6**; 17<br>*alt*. Ps. 77<br>Jer. 5. 20–end<br>John 5. 30–end |

# March 2007

| Date | Day | Commemoration | Sunday Principal Service<br>Weekday Eucharist | Third Service<br>Morning Prayer |
|---|---|---|---|---|
| **1** | Th<br>**Pw** | **David, Bishop of Menevia, Patron of Wales, c. 601**<br>Com. Bishop<br>*also* 2 Sam. 23. 1–4<br>Ps. 89. 19–23, 25 | *or* Esther 14. 1–5, 12–14<br>*or* Isa. 55. 6–9<br>Ps. 138<br>Matt. 7. 7–12 | Ps. **42**; 43<br>*alt*. Ps. 78. 1–39†<br>Jer. 6. 9–21<br>John 6. 1–15 |
| **2** | F<br>**Pw** | **Chad, Bishop of Lichfield, Missionary, 672*****<br>Ember Day**<br>Com. Missionary<br>*also* 1 Tim. 6. 11b–16 | *or* Ezek. 18. 21–28<br>Ps. 130<br>Matt. 5. 20–26 | Ps. 22<br>*alt*. Ps. 55<br>Jer. 6. 22–end<br>John 6. 16–27 |

*Matthias may be celebrated on 24 February instead of 14 May.

**For Ember Day provision, see p. 13.

***Chad may be celebrated with Cedd on 26 October instead of 2 March.

| Second Service Evening Prayer | | Calendar and Holy Communion | Morning Prayer | Evening Prayer |
|---|---|---|---|---|
| Ps. 74<br>*alt*. Ps. 61; ***62***; 64<br>Gen. ch. 39<br>Gal. 2. 11–end | **P** | Exod. 24. 12–end<br>Matt. 8. 5–13 | Jer. 2. 14–32<br>John 4. 1–26 | Gen. ch. 39<br>Gal. 2. 11–end |
| Ps. 31<br>*alt*. Ps. 38<br>Gen. ch. 40<br>Gal. 3. 1–14 | **P** | 1 Kings 19. 3b–8<br>Matt. 5. 43 – 6.6 | Jer. 3. 6–22<br>John 4. 27–42 | Gen. ch. 40<br>Gal. 3. 1–14<br>*or First EP of Matthias*<br>(Ps. 147)<br>Isa. 22. 15–22<br>Phil. 3.13b – 4.1<br>**R ct** |
| Ps. 73<br>*alt*. Ps. 65; ***66***<br>Gen. 41. 1–24<br>Gal. 3. 15–22<br>**ct** | **R** | **MATTHIAS THE APOSTLE**<br>1 Sam. 2. 27–35<br>Ps. 16. 1–7<br>Acts 1. 15–end<br>Matt. 1. 25–end | (Ps. 15)<br>Jonah 1. 1–9<br>Acts 2. 37–end | (Ps. 80)<br>1 Sam. 16. 1–13a<br>Matt. 7. 15–27 |
| Ps. 119. 73–88<br>Jonah ch. 3<br>Luke 18. 9–14 | **P** | **THE FIRST SUNDAY IN LENT**<br>Coll.<br>(1) Lent 1<br>(2) Ash Wednesday<br>Ember until 3 March<br>Gen. 3. 1–6<br>Ps. 91. 1–12<br>2 Cor. 6. 1–10<br>Matt. 4. 1–11 | Ps. 50. 1–15<br>Mic. 6. 1–8<br>Luke 5. 27–end | Ps. 119. 73–88<br>Jonah ch. 3<br>Luke 18. 9–14 |
| Ps. 12; ***13***; 14<br>*alt*. Ps. ***72***; 75<br>Gen. 41. 25–45<br>Gal. 3.23 – 4.7 | **P** | Ezek. 34. 11–16a<br>Matt. 25. 31–end | Jer. 4. 19–end<br>John 5. 1–18 | Gen. 41. 25–45<br>Gal. 3.23 – 4.7 |
| Ps. 46; ***49***<br>*alt*. Ps. 74<br>Gen. 41.46 – 42.5<br>Gal. 4. 8–20 | **P** | Isa. 55. 6–11<br>Matt. 21. 10–16 | Jer. 5. 1–19<br>John 5. 19–29 | Gen. 41.46 – 42.5<br>Gal. 4. 8–20 |
| Ps. 9; ***28***<br>*alt*. Ps. 119. 81–104<br>Gen. 42. 6–17<br>Gal. 4.21 – 5.1 | **P** | Ember Day<br>Ember CEG *or*<br>Isa. 58. 1–9a<br>Matt. 12. 38–end | Jer. 5. 20–end<br>John 5. 30–end | Gen. 42. 6–17<br>Gal. 4.21 – 5.1 |
| | | | | |
| Ps. 137; 138; ***142***<br>*alt*. Ps. 78. 40–end†<br>Gen. 42. 18–28<br>Gal. 5. 2–15 | **Pw** | **David, Bishop of Menevia, Patron of Wales, c. 601**<br>Com. Bishop *or*<br>Isa. 58. 9b–end<br>John 8. 31–45 | Jer. 6. 9–21<br>John 6. 1–15 | Gen. 42. 18–28<br>Gal. 5. 2–15 |
| Ps. 54; ***55***<br>*alt*. Ps. 69<br>Gen. 42. 29–end<br>Gal. 5. 16–end | **Pw** | **Chad, Bishop of Lichfield, Missionary, 672**<br>Ember Day<br>Ember CEG *or*<br>Com. Bishop *or*<br>Ezek. 18. 20–25<br>John 5. 2–15 | Jer. 6. 22–end<br>John 6. 16–27 | Gen. 42. 29–end<br>Gal. 5. 16–end |

# March 2007

| Date | Day | Observance | Sunday Principal Service<br>Weekday Eucharist | Third Service<br>Morning Prayer | Colour |
|---|---|---|---|---|---|
| **3** | Sa | Ember Day* | Deut. 26. 16–end<br>Ps. 119. 1–8<br>Matt. 5. 43–end | Ps. 59; ***63***<br>*alt.* Ps. ***76***; 79<br>Jer. 7. 1–20<br>John 6. 27–40 | **P** |
| **4** | **S** | **THE SECOND SUNDAY OF LENT** | Gen. 15. 1–12, 17–18<br>Ps. 27<br>Phil. 3.17 – 4.1<br>Luke 13. 31–end | Ps. 119. 161–end<br>Gen. 17. 1–7, 15–16<br>Rom. 11. 13–24 | **P** |
| **5** | M | | Dan. 9. 4–10<br>Ps. 79. 8–9, 12, 14<br>Luke 6. 36–38 | Ps. 26; ***32***<br>*alt.* Ps. ***80***; 82<br>Jer. 7. 21–end<br>John 6. 41–51 | **P** |
| **6** | Tu | | Isa. 1. 10, 16–20<br>Ps. 50. 8, 16–end<br>Matt. 23. 1–12 | Ps. 50<br>*alt.* Ps. 87; ***89. 1–18***<br>Jer. 8. 1–15<br>John 6. 52–59 | **P** |
| **7** | W | **Perpetua, Felicity and their Companions, Martyrs at Carthage, 203**<br>Com. Martyr<br>*esp.* Rev. 12. 10–12a<br>*also* Wisd. 3. 1–7 | *or* Jer. 18. 18–20<br>Ps. 31. 4–5, 14–18<br>Matt. 20. 17–28 | Ps. 35<br>*alt.* Ps. 119. 105–128<br>Jer. 8.18 – 9.11<br>John 6. 60–end | **Pr** |
| **8** | Th | **Edward King, Bishop of Lincoln, 1910**<br>*Felix, Bishop, Apostle to the East Angles, 647; Geoffrey Studdert Kennedy, Priest, Poet, 1929*<br>Com. Bishop<br>*also* Heb. 13. 1–8 | *or* Jer. 17. 5–10<br>Ps. 1<br>Luke 16. 19–end | Ps. 34<br>*alt.* Ps. 90; ***92***<br>Jer. 9. 12–24<br>John 7. 1–13 | **Pw** |
| **9** | F | | Gen. 37. 3–4, 12–13, 17–28<br>Ps. 105. 16–22<br>Matt. 21. 33–43, 45–46 | Ps. 40; ***41***<br>*alt.* Ps. ***88*** (95)<br>Jer. 10. 1–16<br>John 7. 14–24 | **P** |
| **10** | Sa | | Mic. 7. 4–15, 18–20<br>Ps. 103. 1–4, 9–12<br>Luke 15. 1–3, 11–end | Ps. 3; ***25***<br>*alt.* Ps. 96; ***97***; 100<br>Jer. 10. 17–24<br>John 7. 25–36 | **P** |
| **11** | **S** | **THE THIRD SUNDAY OF LENT** | Isa. 55. 1–9<br>Ps. 63. 1–9<br>1 Cor. 10. 1–13<br>Luke 13. 1–9 | Ps. 26; 28<br>Deut. 6. 4–9<br>John 17. 1a, 11b–19 | **P** |
| **12** | M** | | 2 Kings 5. 1–15<br>Ps. 42. 1–2; 43. 1–4<br>Luke 4. 24–30 | Ps. ***5***; 7<br>*alt.* Ps. ***98***; 99; 101<br>Jer. 11. 1–17<br>John 7. 37–52 | **P** |
| **13** | Tu | | Song of the Three 2, 11–20<br>*or* Dan. 2. 20–23<br>Ps. 25. 3–10<br>Matt. 18. 21–25 | Ps. 6; ***9***<br>*alt.* Ps. ***106***† (*or* 103)<br>Jer. 11.18 – 12.6<br>John 7.53 – 8.11 | **P** |
| **14** | W | | Deut. 4. 1, 5–9<br>Ps. 147. 13–end<br>Matt. 5. 17–19 | Ps. 38<br>*alt.* Ps. 110; ***111***; 112<br>Jer. 13. 1–11<br>John 8. 12–30 | **P** |

*For Ember Day provision, see p. 13.

**The following readings may replace those provided for Holy Communion on any day during the Third Week of Lent: Exod. 17. 1–7; Ps. 95. 1–2, 6–end; John 4. 5–42.

| Second Service Evening Prayer | | Calendar and Holy Communion | Morning Prayer | Evening Prayer |
|---|---|---|---|---|
| Ps. **4**; 16<br>*alt.* Ps. 81; ***84***<br>Gen. 43. 1–15<br>Gal. ch. 6<br>**ct** | **P** | Ember Day<br>Ember CEG *or*<br>Ezek. 18. 26–end<br>Matt. 17. 1–9<br>*or* Luke 4. 16–21<br>*or* John 10. 1–16 | Jer. 7. 1–20<br>John 6. 27–40 | Gen. 43. 1–15<br>Gal. ch. 6<br>**ct** |
| Ps. 135. 1–14 [15–end]<br>Jer. 22. 1–9, 13–17<br>Luke 14. 27–33 | **P** | **THE SECOND SUNDAY IN LENT**<br>Jer. 17. 5–10<br>Ps. 25. 13–end<br>1 Thess. 4. 1–8<br>Matt. 15. 21–28 | Ps. 119. 161–end<br>Gen. 17. 1–7, 15–16<br>Rom. 11. 13–24 | Ps. 135. 1–14 [15–end]<br>Jer. 22. 1–9, 13–17<br>Luke 14. 27–33 |
| Ps. 70; ***74***<br>*alt.* Ps. ***85***; 86<br>Gen. 43. 16–end<br>Heb. ch. 1 | **P** | Heb. 2. 1–10<br>John 8. 21–30 | Jer. 7. 21–end<br>John 6. 41–51 | Gen. 43. 16–end<br>Heb. ch. 1 |
| Ps. ***52***; 53; 54<br>*alt.* Ps. 89. 19–end<br>Gen. 44. 1–17<br>Heb. 2. 1–9 | **P** | Heb. 2. 11–end<br>Matt. 23. 1–12 | Jer. 8. 1–15<br>John 6. 52–59 | Gen. 44. 1–17<br>Heb. 2. 1–9 |
| Ps. ***3***; 51<br>*alt.* Ps. ***91***; 93<br>Gen. 44. 18–end<br>Heb. 2. 10–end | **Pr** | **Perpetua, Felicity and their Companions, Martyrs at Carthage, 203**<br>Com. Martyr *or*<br>Heb. 3. 1–6<br>Matt. 20. 17–28 | Jer. 8.18 – 9.11<br>John 6. 60–end | Gen. 44. 18–end<br>Heb. 2. 10–end |
| Ps. 71<br>*alt.* Ps. 94<br>Gen. 45. 1–15<br>Heb. 3. 1–6 | **P** | Heb. 3. 7–end<br>John 5. 30–end | Jer. 9. 12–24<br>John 7. 1–13 | Gen. 45. 1–15<br>Heb. 3. 1–6 |
| Ps. ***6***; 38<br>*alt.* Ps. 102<br>Gen. 45. 16–end<br>Heb. 3. 7–end | **P** | Heb. ch. 4<br>Matt. 21. 33–end | Jer. 10. 1–16<br>John 7. 14–24 | Gen. 45. 16–end<br>Heb. 3. 7–end |
| Ps. ***23***; 27<br>*alt.* Ps. 104<br>Gen. 46. 1–7, 28–end<br>Heb. 4. 1–13<br>**ct** | **P** | Heb. ch. 5<br>Luke 15. 11–end | Jer. 10. 17–24<br>John 7. 25–36 | Gen. 46. 1–7, 28–end<br>Heb. 4. 1–13<br>**ct** |
| Ps. 12; 13<br>Gen. 28. 10–19a<br>John 1. 35–end | **P** | **THE THIRD SUNDAY IN LENT**<br>Num. 22. 21–31<br>Ps. 9. 13–end<br>Eph. 5. 1–14<br>Luke 11. 14–28 | Ps. 26; 28<br>Deut. 6. 4–9<br>John 17. 1a, 11b–19 | Ps. 12; 13<br>Gen. 28. 10–19a<br>John 1. 35–end |
| Ps. 11; ***17***<br>*alt.* Ps. ***105***† (*or* 103)<br>Gen. 47. 1–27<br>Heb. 4.14 – 5.10 | **Pw** | **Gregory the Great, Bishop of Rome, 604**<br>Com. Doctor *or*<br>Heb. 6. 1–10<br>Luke 4. 23–30 | Jer. 11. 1–17<br>John 7. 37–52 | Gen. 47. 1–27<br>Heb. 4.14 – 5.10 |
| Ps. 61; 62; ***64***<br>*alt.* Ps. 107†<br>Gen. 47.28 – 48.end<br>Heb. 5.11 – 6.12 | **P** | Heb. 6. 11–end<br>Matt. 18. 15–22 | Jer. 11.18 – 12.6<br>John 7.53 – 8.11 | Gen. 47.28 – 48.end<br>Heb. 5.11 – 6.12 |
| Ps. 36; ***39***<br>*alt.* Ps. 119. 129–152<br>Gen. 49. 1–32<br>Heb. 6. 13–end | **P** | Heb. 7. 1–10<br>Matt. 15. 1–20 | Jer. 13. 1–11<br>John 8. 12–30 | Gen. 49. 1–32<br>Heb. 6. 13–end |

# March 2007

| Date | Day | | Sunday Principal Service<br>Weekday Eucharist | Third Service<br>Morning Prayer |
|---|---|---|---|---|
| **15** | Th<br>**P** | | Jer. 7. 23–28<br>Ps. 95, 1–2, 6–end<br>Luke 11. 14–23 | Ps. **56**; 57<br>*alt.* Ps. 113; ***115***<br>Jer. ch. 14<br>John 8. 31–47 |
| **16** | F<br>**P** | | Hos. 14. 2–10<br>Ps. 81. 6–10, 13, 16<br>Mark 12. 28–34 | Ps. 22<br>*alt.* Ps. 139<br>Jer. 15. 10–end<br>John 8. 48–end |
| **17** | Sa<br>**Pw** | **Patrick, Bishop, Missionary, Patron of Ireland, c. 460**<br>Com. Missionary<br>*also* Ps. 91. 1–4, 13–end<br>Luke 10. 1–12, 17–20 | *or* Hos. 5.15 – 6.6<br>Ps. 51. 1–2, 17–end<br>Luke 18. 9–14 | Ps. 31<br>*alt.* Ps. 120; ***121***; 122<br>Jer. 16.10 – 17.4<br>John 9. 1–17 |
| **18** | **S** | **THE FOURTH SUNDAY OF LENT**<br>(Mothering Sunday) | Josh. 5. 9–12<br>Ps. 32<br>2 Cor. 5. 16–end<br>Luke 15. 1–3, 11b–end | Ps. 84; 85<br>Gen. 37. 3–4, 12–end<br>1 Pet. 2. 16–end |
| | **P** | *or, for Mothering Sunday:* | Exod. 2. 1–10<br>*or* 1 Sam. 1. 20–end<br>Ps. 34. 11–20<br>*or* Ps. 127. 1–4<br>2 Cor. 1. 3–7<br>*or* Col. 3. 12–17<br>Luke 2. 33–35<br>*or* John 19. 25b–27 | |
| **19** | M*<br>**W** | **JOSEPH OF NAZARETH** | 2 Sam. 7. 4–16<br>Ps. 89. 26–36<br>Rom. 4. 13–18<br>Matt. 1. 18–end | *MP:* Ps. 25; 147. 1–12<br>Isa. 11. 1–10<br>Matt. 13. 54–end |
| **20** | Tu<br>**Pw** | **Cuthbert, Bishop of Lindisfarne, Missionary, 687****<br>Com. Missionary<br>*esp.* Ezek. 34. 11–16<br>*also* Matt. 18. 12–14 | *or* Ezek. 47. 1–9, 12<br>Ps. 46. 1–8<br>John 5. 1–3, 5–16 | Ps. 54; **79**<br>*alt.* Ps. **132**; 133<br>Jer. 18. 1–12<br>John 10. 1–10 |
| **21** | W<br>**Pr** | **Thomas Cranmer, Archbishop of Canterbury, Reformation Martyr, 1556**<br>Com. Martyr | *or* Isa. 49. 8–15<br>Ps. 145. 8–18<br>John 5. 17–30 | Ps. 63; **90**<br>*alt.* Ps. 119. 153–end<br>Jer. 18. 13–end<br>John 10. 11–21 |

*The following readings may replace those provided for Holy Communion on any day (except Joseph of Nazareth) during the Fourth Week of Lent: Mic. 7. 7–9; Ps. 27. 1, 9–10, 16–17; John ch. 9.

**Cuthbert may be celebrated on 4 September instead of 20 March.

| Second Service Evening Prayer | | Calendar and Holy Communion | Morning Prayer | Evening Prayer |
|---|---|---|---|---|
| Ps. **59**; 60<br>*alt.* Ps. 114; ***116***; 117<br>Gen. 49.33 – 50.end<br>Heb. 7. 1–10 | **P** | Heb. 7. 11–25<br>John 6. 26–35 | Jer. ch. 14<br>John 8. 31–47 | Gen. 49.33 – 50.end<br>Heb. 7. 1–10 |
| Ps. 69<br>*alt.* Ps. ***130***; 131; 137<br>Exod. 1. 1–14<br>Heb. 7. 11–end | **P** | Heb. 7. 26–end<br>John 4. 5–26 | Jer. 15. 10–end<br>John 8. 48–end | Exod. 1. 1–14<br>Heb. 7. 11–end |
| Ps. ***116***; 130<br>*alt.* Ps. 118<br>Exod. 1.22 – 2.10<br>Heb. ch. 8<br>**ct** | **P** | Heb. 8. 1–6<br>John 8. 1–11 | Jer. 16.10 – 17.4<br>John 9. 1–17 | Exod. 1.22 – 2.10<br>Heb. ch. 8<br>**ct** |
| Ps. 30<br>Prayer of Manasseh<br>*or* Isa. 40.27 – 41.13<br>2 Tim. 4. 1–18<br>*Gospel:* John 11. 17–44<br>*If the Principal Service readings for The Fourth Sunday of Lent are displaced by Mothering Sunday provisions, they may be used at the Second Service.*<br><br>*Or First EP of Joseph*<br>Ps. 132<br>Hos. 11. 1–9<br>Luke 2. 41–end<br>**W ct** | **P** | **THE FOURTH SUNDAY IN LENT**<br>To celebrate Mothering Sunday, see *Common Worship* provision.<br>Exod. 16. 2–7a<br>Ps. 122<br>Gal. 4. 21–end<br>*or* Heb. 12. 22–24<br>John 6. 1–14 | Ps. 84; 85<br>Gen. 37. 3–4, 12–end<br>1 Pet. 2. 16–end | Ps. 30<br>Prayer of Manasseh<br>*or* Isa. 40.27 – 41.13<br>2 Tim. 4. 1–18 |
| *EP*: Ps. 1; 112<br>Gen. 50. 22–end<br>Matt. 2. 13–end | **P** | To celebrate Joseph, see *Common Worship* provision.<br>Heb. 11. 1–6<br>John 2. 13–end | Jer. 17. 5–18<br>John 9. 18–end | Exod. 2. 11–22<br>Heb. 9. 1–14 |
| Ps. **80**; 82<br>*alt.* Ps. (134) ***135***<br>Exod. 2.23 – 3.20<br>Heb. 9. 15–end | **P** | Heb. 11. 13–16a<br>John 7. 14–24 | Jer. 18. 1–12<br>John 10. 1–10 | Exod. 2.23 – 3.20<br>Heb. 9. 15–end |
| Ps. 52; ***91***<br>*alt.* Ps. 136<br>Exod. 4. 1–23<br>Heb. 10. 1–18 | **Pw** | **Benedict, Abbot of Monte Cassino, c. 550**<br>Com. Abbot *or*<br>Heb. 12. 1–11<br>John 9. 1–17 | Jer. 18. 13–end<br>John 10. 11–21 | Exod. 4. 1–23<br>Heb. 10. 1–18 |

# March 2007

| | | | Sunday Principal Service<br>Weekday Eucharist | Third Service<br>Morning Prayer |
|---|---|---|---|---|
| **22** | Th<br>**P** | | Exod. 32. 7–14<br>Ps. 106. 19–23<br>John 5. 31–47 | Ps. 53; ***86***<br>*alt.* Ps. ***143***; 146<br>Jer. 19. 1–13<br>John 10. 22–end |
| **23** | F<br>**P** | | Wisd. 2. 1, 12–22<br>*or* Jer. 26. 8–11<br>Ps. 34. 15–end<br>John 7. 1–2, 10, 25–30 | Ps. 102<br>*alt.* Ps. 142; ***144***<br>Jer. 19.14 – 20.6<br>John 11. 1–16 |
| **24** | Sa<br>**P** | *Walter Hilton of Thurgarton, Augustinian Canon, Mystic, 1396; Oscar Romero, Archbishop of San Salvador, Martyr, 1980* | Jer. 11. 18–20<br>Ps. 7. 1–2, 8–10<br>John 7. 40–52 | Ps. 32<br>*alt.* Ps. 147<br>Jer. 20. 7–end<br>John 11. 17–27 |
| **25** | **S**<br>**P** | **THE FIFTH SUNDAY OF LENT (Passiontide begins)** | Isa. 43. 16–21<br>Ps. 126<br>Phil. 3. 4b–14<br>John 12. 1–8 | Ps. 111; 112<br>Isa. ch. 35<br>Rom. 7.21 – 8.4 |
| **26** | M*<br>**W** | **THE ANNUNCIATION OF OUR LORD TO THE BLESSED VIRGIN MARY**<br>(transferred from 25th) | Isa. 7. 10–14<br>Ps. 40. 5–11<br>Heb. 10. 4–10<br>Luke 1. 26–38 | *MP:* Ps. 111; 113<br>1 Sam. 2. 1–10<br>Rom. 5. 12–end |
| **27** | Tu<br>**P** | | Num. 21. 4–9<br>Ps. 102. 1–3, 16–23<br>John 8. 21–30 | Ps. ***35***; 123<br>*alt.* Ps. ***5***; 6 (8)<br>Jer. 22. 1–5, 13–19<br>John 11. 45–end |
| **28** | W<br>**P** | | Dan. 3. 14–20, 24–25, 28<br>*Canticle:* Bless the Lord<br>John 8. 31–42 | Ps. ***55***; 124<br>*alt.* Ps. 119. 1–32<br>Jer. 22.20 – 23.8<br>John 12. 1–11 |
| **29** | Th<br>**P** | | Gen. 17. 3–9<br>Ps. 105. 4–9<br>John 8. 51–end | Ps. ***40***; 125<br>*alt.* Ps. 14; ***15***; 16<br>Jer. 23. 9–32<br>John 12. 12–19 |
| **30** | F<br>**P** | | Jer. 20. 10–13<br>Ps. 18. 1–6<br>John 10. 31–end | Ps. ***22***; 126<br>*alt.* Ps. 17; ***19***<br>Jer. ch. 24<br>John 12. 20–36a |
| **31** | Sa<br>**P** | *John Donne, Priest, Poet, 1631* | Ezek. 37. 21–28<br>*Canticle:* Jer. 31. 10–13<br>*or* Ps. 121<br>John 11. 45–end | Ps. ***23***; 127<br>*alt.* Ps. 20; 21; ***23***<br>Jer. 25. 1–14<br>John 12. 36b–end |

*The following readings may replace those provided for Holy Communion on any day (except The Annunciation) during the Fifth Week of Lent: 2 Kings 4. 18–21, 32–37; Ps. 17. 1–8, 16; John 11. 1–45.

| Second Service Evening Prayer | | Calendar and Holy Communion | Morning Prayer | Evening Prayer |
|---|---|---|---|---|
| Ps. 94<br>*alt.* Ps. ***138***; 140; 141<br>Exod. 4.27 – 6.1<br>Heb. 10. 19–25 | **P** | Heb. 12. 12–17<br>John 5. 17–27 | Jer. 19. 1–13<br>John 10. 22–end | Exod. 4.27 – 6.1<br>Heb. 10. 19–25 |
| Ps. 13; ***16***<br>*alt.* Ps. 145<br>Exod. 6. 2–13<br>Heb. 10. 26–end | **P** | Heb. 12. 22–end<br>John 11. 33–46 | Jer. 19.14 – 20.6<br>John 11. 1–16 | Exod. 6. 2–13<br>Heb. 10. 26–end |
| Ps. ***140***; 141; 142<br>*alt.* Ps. ***148***; 149; 150<br>Exod. 7. 8–end<br>Heb. 11. 1–16<br>**ct** | **P** | Heb. 13. 7–21<br>John 8. 12–20 | Jer. 20. 7–end<br>John 11. 17–27 | Exod. 7. 8–end<br>Heb. 11. 1–16<br>**ct** |
| Ps. 35. 1–9 [10–end]<br>2 Chron. 35. 1–6, 10–16<br>Luke 22. 1–13<br>*or First EP of The Annunciation*<br>Ps. 85<br>Wisd. 9. 1–12<br>*or* Gen. 3. 8–15<br>Gal. 4. 1–5<br>**𝔚 ct** | **P** | **THE FIFTH SUNDAY IN LENT**<br>Exod. 24. 4–8<br>Ps. 143<br>Heb. 9. 11–15<br>John 8. 46–end | Ps. 111; 112<br>Isa. ch. 35<br>Rom. 7.21 – 8.4 | Ps. 35. 1–9 [10–end]<br>2 Chron. 35. 1–6, 10–16<br>Luke 22. 1–13<br>*or First EP of The Annunciation*<br>Ps. 85<br>Wisd. 9. 1–12<br>*or* Gen. 3. 8–15<br>Gal. 4. 1–5<br>**𝔚 ct** |
| *EP:* Ps. 131; 146<br>Isa. 52. 1–12<br>Heb. 2. 5–end | 𝔚 | **THE ANNUNCIATION OF THE BLESSED VIRGIN MARY**<br>(transferred from 25th)<br>Isa. 7. 10–14 [15]<br>Ps. 113<br>Rom. 5. 12–19<br>Luke 1. 26–38 | Ps. 111<br>1 Sam. 2. 1–10<br>Heb. 10. 4–10 | Ps. 131; 146<br>Isa. 52. 1–12<br>Heb. 2. 5–end |
| Ps. ***61***; 64<br>*alt.* Ps. ***9***; 10†<br>Exod. 8. 20–end<br>Heb. 11.32 – 12.2 | **P** | Col. 2. 8–12<br>John 7. 32–39 | Jer. 22. 1–5, 13–19<br>John 11. 45–end | Exod. 8. 20–end<br>Heb. 11.32 – 12.2 |
| Ps. 56; ***62***<br>*alt.* Ps. ***11***; 12; 13<br>Exod. 9. 1–12<br>Heb. 12. 3–13 | **P** | Col. 2. 13–19<br>John 7. 40–end | Jer. 22.20 – 23.8<br>John 12. 1–11 | Exod. 9. 1–12<br>Heb. 12. 3–13 |
| Ps. 42; ***43***<br>*alt.* Ps. 18†<br>Exod. 9. 13–end<br>Heb. 12. 14–end | **P** | Col. 3. 8–11<br>John 10. 22–38 | Jer. 23. 9–32<br>John 12. 12–19 | Exod. 9. 13–end<br>Heb. 12. 14–end |
| Ps. 31<br>*alt.* Ps. 22<br>Exod. ch. 10<br>Heb. 13. 1–16 | **P** | Col. 3. 12–17<br>John 11. 47–54 | Jer. ch. 24<br>John 12. 20–36a | Exod. ch. 10<br>Heb. 13. 1–16 |
| Ps. 128; 129; ***130***<br>*alt.* Ps. ***24***; 25<br>Exod. ch. 11<br>Heb. 13. 17–end<br>**ct** | **P** | Col. 4. 2–6<br>John 6. 53–end | Jer. 25. 1–14<br>John 12. 36b–end | Exod. ch. 11<br>Heb. 13. 17–end<br>**ct** |

# April 2007

| | | | Sunday Principal Service<br>Weekday Eucharist | Third Service<br>Morning Prayer |
|---|---|---|---|---|
| 1 | S<br>R | **PALM SUNDAY**<br>*Liturgy of the Palms*<br>Luke 19. 28–40<br>Ps. 118. [1–2] 19–24 [25–end] | *Liturgy of the Passion*<br>Isa. 50. 4–9a<br>Ps. 31. 9–16 [17–18]<br>Phil. 2. 5–11<br>Luke 22.14 – 23.end<br>*or* Luke 23. 1–49 | Ps. 61; 62<br>Zech. 9. 9–12<br>1 Cor. 2. 1–12 |
| 2 | M<br>R | **MONDAY OF HOLY WEEK** | Isa. 42. 1–9<br>Ps. 36. 5–11<br>Heb. 9. 11–15<br>John 12. 1–11 | *MP:* Ps. 41<br>Lam. 1. 1–12a<br>Luke 22. 1–23 |
| 3 | Tu<br>R | **TUESDAY OF HOLY WEEK** | Isa. 49. 1–7<br>Ps. 71. 1–8 [9–14]<br>1 Cor. 1. 18–31<br>John 12. 20–36 | *MP:* Ps. 27<br>Lam. 3. 1–18<br>Luke 22. [24–38] 39–53 |
| 4 | W<br>R | **WEDNESDAY OF HOLY WEEK** | Isa. 50. 4–9a<br>Ps. 70<br>Heb. 12. 1–3<br>John 13. 21–32 | *MP:* Ps. 102. 1–17 [18–end]<br>Wisd. 1.16 – 2.1, 12–22<br>*or* Jer. 11. 18–20<br>Luke 22. 54–end |
| 5 | Th<br>W (HC) R | **MAUNDY THURSDAY** | Exod. 12. 1–4 [5–10], 11–14<br>Ps. 116. 1, 10–end (*or* 9–end)<br>1 Cor. 11. 23–26<br>John 13. 1–17, 31b–35 | *MP:* Ps. 42; 43<br>Lev. 16. 2–24<br>Luke 23. 1–25 |
| 6 | F<br>R | **GOOD FRIDAY** | Isa. 52.13 – 53.end<br>Ps. 22 (*or* 22. 1–11 *or* 22. 1–21)<br>Heb. 10. 16–25<br>*or* Heb. 4. 14–16<br>John 18.1 – 19.end | *MP:* Ps. 69<br>Gen. 22. 1–18<br>A part of John 18 – 19 if not read at the Principal Service<br>*or* Heb. 10. 1–10 |
| 7 | Sa | **EASTER EVE**<br>*These readings are for use at services other than the Easter Vigil.* | Job 14. 1–14<br>*or* Lam. 3. 1–9, 19–24<br>Ps. 31. 1–4, 15–16 (*or* 1–5)<br>1 Pet. 4. 1–8<br>Matt. 27. 57–end<br>*or* John 19. 38–end | Ps. 142<br>Hos. 6. 1–6<br>John 2. 18–22 |
| 8 | S | **EASTER DAY**<br>*The following readings and psalms (or canticles) are provided for use at the Easter Vigil. A minimum of three Old Testament readings should be chosen. The reading from* Exodus ch. 14 *should always be used.* | Gen. 1.1 – 2.4a & Ps. 136. 1–9, 23–end<br>Gen. 7. 1–5, 11–18; 8. 6–18; 9. 8–13 & Ps. 46<br>Gen. 22. 1–18 & Ps. 16<br>Exod. 14. 10–end; 15. 20–21 & *Canticle:* Exod. 15. 1b–13, 17–18<br>Isa. 55. 1–11 & *Canticle:* Isa. 12. 2–end<br>Baruch 3.9–15, 32 – 4.4 & Ps. 19 *or*<br>Prov. 8. 1–8, 19–21; 9. 4b–6 & Ps. 19<br>Ezek. 36. 24–28 & Ps. 42; 43<br>Ezek. 37. 1–14 & Ps. 143<br>Zeph. 3. 14–end & Ps. 98<br>Rom. 6. 3–11 & Ps. 114<br>Luke 24. 1–12 | |
| | W | *Easter Day Services*<br>*The reading from Acts must be used as either the first or second reading at the Principal Service.* | Acts 10. 34–43<br>*or* Isa. 65. 17–end<br>Ps. 118. [1–2] 14–24<br>1 Cor. 15. 19–26<br>*or* Acts 10. 34–43<br>John 20. 1–18<br>*or* Luke 24. 1–12 | *MP:* Ps. 114; 117<br>Ezek. 47. 1–12<br>John 2. 13–22 |

| Second Service Evening Prayer | | Calendar and Holy Communion | Morning Prayer | Evening Prayer |
|---|---|---|---|---|
| Ps. 69. 1–20<br>Isa. 5. 1–7<br>Luke 20. 9–19 | R | **PALM SUNDAY**<br>Zech. 9. 9–12<br>Ps. 73. 22–end<br>Phil. 2. 5–11<br>Passion acc. to Matthew<br>Matt. 27. 1–54<br>*or* Matt. 26.1 – 27.61<br>*or* Matt. 21. 1–13 | Ps. 61; 62<br>Isa. 42. 1–9<br>1 Cor. 2. 1–12 | Ps. 69. 1–20<br>Isa. 5. 1–7<br>Luke 20. 9–19 |
| *EP*: Ps. 25<br>Lam. 2. 8–19<br>Col. 1. 18–23 | R | **MONDAY IN HOLY WEEK**<br>Isa. 63. 1–19<br>Ps. 55. 1–8<br>Gal. 6. 1–11<br>Mark ch. 14 | Ps. 41<br>Lam. 1. 1–12a<br>John 12. 1–11 | Ps. 25<br>Lam. 2. 8–19<br>Col. 1. 18–23 |
| *EP*: Ps. 55. 13–24<br>Lam. 3. 40–51<br>Gal. 6. 11–end | R | **TUESDAY IN HOLY WEEK**<br>Isa. 50. 5–11<br>Ps. 13<br>Rom. 5. 6–19<br>Mark 15. 1–39 | Ps. 27<br>Lam. 3. 1–18<br>John 12. 20–36 | Ps. 55. 13–24<br>Lam. 3. 40–51<br>Gal. 6. 11–end |
| *EP*: Ps. 88<br>Isa. 63. 1–9<br>Rev. 14.18 – 15.4 | R | **WEDNESDAY IN HOLY WEEK**<br>Isa. 49. 1–9a<br>Ps. 54<br>Heb. 9. 16–end<br>Luke ch. 22 | Ps. 102. 1–17 [18–end]<br>Wisd. 1.16 – 2.1, 12–22<br>*or* Jer. 11. 18–20<br>John 13. 21–32 | Ps. 88<br>Isa. 63. 1–9<br>Rev. 14.18 – 15.4 |
| *EP*: Ps. 39<br>Exod. ch. 11<br>Eph. 2. 11–18 | W (HC) R | **MAUNDY THURSDAY**<br>Exod. 12. 1–11<br>Ps. 43<br>1 Cor. 11. 17–end<br>Luke 23. 1–49 | Ps. 42; 43<br>Lev. 16. 2–24<br>John 13. 1–17, 31b–35 | Ps. 39<br>Exod. ch. 11<br>Eph. 2. 11–18 |
| *EP*: Ps. 130; 143<br>Lam. 5. 15–end<br>A part of John 18 – 19 if not read at the Principal Service esp. John 19. 38–end<br>*or* Col. 1. 18–23 | R | **GOOD FRIDAY**<br>Alt. Collect Passion acc. to John<br>Alt. Gospel, if Passion is read<br>Num. 21. 4–9<br>Ps. 140. 1–9<br>Heb. 10. 1–25<br>John 19. 1–37<br>*or* John 19. 38–end | Ps. 69<br>Gen. 22. 1–18<br>John ch. 18 | Ps. 130; 143<br>Lam. 5. 15–end<br>John 19. 38–end |
| Ps. 116<br>Job 19. 21–27<br>1 John 5. 5–12 | | **EASTER EVE**<br>Job 14. 1–14<br>1 Pet. 3. 17–22<br>Matt. 27. 57–end | Ps. 142<br>Hos. 6. 1–6<br>John 2. 18–22 | Ps. 116<br>Job 19. 21–27<br>1 John 5. 5–12 |
| *EP*: Ps. 105<br>*or* Ps. 66. 1–11<br>Isa. 43. 1–21<br>1 Cor. 15. 1–11<br>*or* John 20. 19–23 | | **EASTER DAY**<br>Exod. 12. 21–28<br>Ps. 111<br>Col. 3. 1–7<br>John 20. 1–10 | Ps. 114; 117<br>Ezek. 47. 1–12<br>John 2. 13–22 | Ps. 105<br>*or* Ps. 66. 1–11<br>Isa. 43. 1–21<br>1 Cor. 15. 1–11<br>*or* John 20. 19–23 |

# April 2007

| | | | Sunday Principal Service<br>Weekday Eucharist | Third Service<br>Morning Prayer |
|---|---|---|---|---|
| **9** | M<br>**W** | **MONDAY OF EASTER WEEK** | Acts 2. 14, 22–32<br>Ps. 16. 1–2, 6–end<br>Matt. 28. 8–15 | Ps. ***111***; 117; 146<br>Song of Sol. 1.9 – 2.7<br>Mark 16. 1–8 |
| **10** | Tu<br>**W** | **TUESDAY OF EASTER WEEK** | Acts 2. 36–41<br>Ps. 33. 4–5, 18–end<br>John 20. 11–18 | Ps. ***112***; 147. 1–12<br>Song of Sol. 2. 8–end<br>Luke 24. 1–12 |
| **11** | W<br>**W** | **WEDNESDAY OF EASTER WEEK** | Acts 3. 1–10<br>Ps. 105. 1–9<br>Luke 24. 13–35 | Ps. ***113***; 147. 13–end<br>Song of Sol. ch. 3<br>Matt. 28. 16–end |
| **12** | Th<br>**W** | **THURSDAY OF EASTER WEEK** | Acts 3. 11–end<br>Ps. 8<br>Luke 24. 35–48 | Ps. ***114***; 148<br>Song of Sol. 5.2 – 6.3<br>Luke 7. 11–17 |
| **13** | F<br>**W** | **FRIDAY OF EASTER WEEK** | Acts 4. 1–12<br>Ps. 118. 1–4, 22–26<br>John 21. 1–14 | Ps. ***115***; 149<br>Song of Sol. 7.10 – 8.4<br>Luke 8. 41–end |
| **14** | Sa<br>**W** | **SATURDAY OF EASTER WEEK** | Acts 4. 13–21<br>Ps. 118. 1–4, 14–21<br>Mark 16. 9–15 | Ps. ***116***; 150<br>Song of Sol. 8. 5–7<br>John 11. 17–44 |
| **15** | **S**<br>**W** | **THE SECOND SUNDAY OF EASTER**<br>*The reading from Acts must be used as either the first or second reading at the Principal Service.* | Acts 5. 27–32<br>[*or* Exod. 14. 10–end; 15. 20–21]<br>Ps. 118. 14–end<br>*or* Ps. 150<br>Rev. 1. 4–8<br>John 20. 19–31 | Ps. 136. 1–16<br>Exod. 12. 1–13<br>1 Pet. 1. 3–12 |
| **16** | M<br>**W** | *Isabella Gilmore, Deaconess, 1923* | Acts 4. 23–31<br>Ps. 2. 1–9<br>John 3. 1–8 | Ps. 2; ***19***<br>*alt.* Ps. ***1***; 2; 3<br>Deut. 1. 3–18<br>John 20. 1–10 |
| **17** | Tu<br>**W** | | Acts 4. 32–end<br>Ps. 93<br>John 3. 7–15 | Ps. ***8***; 20; 21<br>*alt.* Ps. ***5***; 6 (8)<br>Deut. 1. 19–40<br>John 20. 11–18 |
| **18** | W<br>**W** | | Acts 5. 17–26<br>Ps. 34. 1–8<br>John 3. 16–21 | Ps. 16; ***30***<br>*alt.* Ps. 119. 1–32<br>Deut. 3. 18–end<br>John 20. 19–end |
| **19** | Th<br>**Wr** | **Alphege, Archbishop of Canterbury, Martyr, 1012**<br>Com. Martyr<br>*also* Heb. 5. 1–4 | *or* Acts 5. 27–33<br>Ps. 34. 1, 15–end<br>John 3. 31–end | Ps. ***28***; 29<br>*alt.* Ps. 14; ***15***; 16<br>Deut. 4. 1–14<br>John 21. 1–14 |
| **20** | F<br>**W** | | Acts 5. 34–42<br>Ps. 27. 1–5, 16–17<br>John 6. 1–15 | Ps. 57; ***61***<br>*alt.* Ps. 17; ***19***<br>Deut. 4. 15–31<br>John 21. 15–19 |

| Second Service Evening Prayer | | Calendar and Holy Communion | Morning Prayer | Evening Prayer |
|---|---|---|---|---|
| Ps. 135<br>Exod. 12. 1–14<br>1 Cor. 15. 1–11 | W | **MONDAY IN EASTER WEEK**<br>Hos. 6. 1–6<br>Easter Anthems<br>Acts 10. 34–43<br>Luke 24. 13–35 | Song of Sol. 1.9 – 2.7<br>Mark 16. 1–8 | Exod. 12. 1–14<br>1 Cor. 15. 1–11 |
| Ps. 136<br>Exod. 12. 14–36<br>1 Cor. 15. 12–19 | W | **TUESDAY IN EASTER WEEK**<br>1 Kings 17. 17–end<br>Ps. 16. 9–end<br>Acts 13. 26–41<br>Luke 24. 36b–48 | Song of Sol. 2. 8–end<br>Luke 24. 1–12 | Exod. 12. 14–36<br>1 Cor. 15. 12–19 |
| Ps. 105<br>Exod. 12. 37–end<br>1 Cor. 15. 20–28 | W | **WEDNESDAY IN EASTER WEEK**<br>Isa. 42. 10–16<br>Ps. 111<br>Acts 3. 12–18<br>John 20. 11–18 | Song of Sol. ch. 3<br>Matt. 28. 16–end | Exod. 12. 37–end<br>1 Cor. 15. 20–28 |
| Ps. 106<br>Exod. 13. 1–16<br>1 Cor. 15. 29–34 | W | **THURSDAY IN EASTER WEEK**<br>Isa. 43. 16–21<br>Ps. 113<br>Acts 8. 26–end<br>John 21. 1–14 | Song of Sol. 5.2 – 6.3<br>Luke 7. 11–17 | Exod. 13. 1–16<br>1 Cor. 15. 29–34 |
| Ps. 107<br>Exod. 13.17 – 14.14<br>1 Cor. 15. 35–50 | W | **FRIDAY IN EASTER WEEK**<br>Ezek. 37. 1–14<br>Ps. 116. 1–9<br>1 Pet. 3. 18–end<br>Matt. 28. 16–end | Song of Sol. 7.10 – 8.4<br>Luke 8. 41–end | Exod. 13.17 – 14.14<br>1 Cor. 15. 35–50 |
| Ps. 145<br>Exod. 14. 15–end<br>1 Cor. 15. 51–end<br>**ct** | W | **SATURDAY IN EASTER WEEK**<br>Zech. 8. 1–8<br>Ps. 118. 14–21<br>1 Pet. 2. 1–10<br>John 20. 24–end | Song of Sol. 8. 5–7<br>John 11. 17–44 | Exod. 14. 15–end<br>1 Cor. 15. 51–end<br>**ct** |
| Ps. 16<br>Isa. 52.13 – 53.12<br>(*or* 53. 1–6, 9–12)<br>Luke 24. 13–35 | W | **THE FIRST SUNDAY AFTER EASTER**<br>Ezek. 37. 1–10<br>Ps. 81. 1–4<br>1 John 5. 4–12<br>John 20. 19–23 | Ps. 136. 1–16<br>Exod. 12. 1–13<br>1 Pet. 1. 3–12 | Ps. 16<br>Isa. 52.13 – 53.12<br>(*or* 53. 1–6, 9–12)<br>Luke 24. 13–35 |
| Ps. 139<br>*alt.* Ps. ***4***; 7<br>Exod. 15. 1–21<br>Col. 1. 1–14 | W | | Deut. 1. 3–18<br>John 20. 1–10 | Exod. 15. 1–21<br>Col. 1. 1–14 |
| Ps. 104<br>*alt.* Ps. 9; ***10***†<br>Exod. 15.22 – 16.10<br>Col. 1. 15–end | W | | Deut. 1. 19–40<br>John 20. 11–18 | Exod. 15.22 – 16.10<br>Col. 1. 15–end |
| Ps. 33<br>*alt.* Ps. ***11***; 12; 13<br>Exod. 16. 11–end<br>Col. 2. 1–15 | W | | Deut. 3. 18–end<br>John 20. 19–end | Exod. 16. 11–end<br>Col. 2. 1–15 |
| Ps. 34<br>*alt.* Ps. 18†<br>Exod. ch. 17<br>Col. 2.16 – 3.11 | Wr | **Alphege, Archbishop of Canterbury, Martyr, 1012**<br>Com. Martyr | Deut. 4. 1–14<br>John 21. 1–14 | Exod. ch. 17<br>Col. 2.16 – 3.11 |
| Ps. 118<br>*alt.* Ps. 22<br>Exod. 18. 1–12<br>Col. 3.12 – 4.1 | W | | Deut. 4. 15–31<br>John 21. 15–19 | Exod. 18. 1–12<br>Col. 3.12 – 4.1 |

# April 2007

| Date | Day | | Sunday Principal Service<br>Weekday Eucharist | Third Service<br>Morning Prayer | Colour |
|---|---|---|---|---|---|
| **21** | Sa | **Anselm, Abbot of Le Bec, Archbishop of Canterbury, Teacher, 1109**<br>Com. Teacher<br>*also* Wisd. 9. 13–18<br>Rom. 5. 8–11 | *or* Acts 6. 1–7<br>Ps. 33. 1–5, 18–19<br>John 6. 16–21 | Ps. 63; ***84***<br>*alt.* Ps. 20; 21; ***23***<br>Deut. 4. 32–40<br>John 21. 20–end | **W** |
| **22** | **S** | **THE THIRD SUNDAY OF EASTER**<br>*The reading from Acts must be used as either the first or second reading at the Principal Service.* | Acts 9. 1–6 [7–20]<br>[*or* Zeph. 3. 14–end]<br>Ps. 30<br>Rev. 5. 11–end<br>John 21. 1–19 | Ps. 80. 1–8<br>Exod. 15. 1–2, 9–18<br>John 10. 1–19 | **W** |
| **23** | M | **GEORGE, MARTYR, PATRON OF ENGLAND, c. 304** | 1 Macc. 2. 59–64<br>*or* Rev. 12. 7–12<br>Ps. 126<br>2 Tim. 2. 3–13<br>John 15. 18–21 | *MP:* Ps. 5; 146<br>Josh. 1. 1–9<br>Eph. 6. 10–20 | **R** |
| **24** | Tu | *Mellitus, Bishop of London, first Bishop of St Paul's, 624* | Acts 7.51 – 8.1<br>Ps. 31. 1–5, 16<br>John 6. 30–35 | Ps. ***98***; 99; 100<br>*alt.* Ps. 32; ***36***<br>Deut. 5. 22–end<br>Eph. 1. 15–end | **W** |
| **25** | W | **MARK THE EVANGELIST** | Prov. 15. 28–end<br>*or* Acts 15. 35–end<br>Ps. 119. 9–16<br>Eph. 4. 7–16<br>Mark 13. 5–13 | *MP:* Ps. 37. 23–41; 148<br>Isa. 62. 6–10<br>*or* Ecclus. 51. 13–end<br>Acts 12.25 – 13.13 | **R** |
| **26** | Th | | Acts 8. 26–end<br>Ps. 66. 7–8, 14–end<br>John 6. 44–51 | Ps. 136<br>*alt.* Ps. 37†<br>Deut. 7. 1–11<br>Eph. 2. 11–end | **W** |
| **27** | F | *Christina Rossetti, Poet, 1894* | Acts 9. 1–20<br>Ps. 117<br>John 6. 52–59 | Ps. 107<br>*alt.* Ps. 31<br>Deut. 7. 12–end<br>Eph. 3. 1–13 | **W** |
| **28** | Sa | *Peter Chanel, Missionary in the South Pacific, Martyr, 1841* | Acts 9. 31–42<br>Ps. 116. 10–15<br>John 6. 60–69 | Ps. 108; ***110***; 111<br>*alt.* Ps. 41; **42**; 43<br>Deut. ch. 8<br>Eph. 3. 14–end | **W** |
| **29** | **S** | **THE FOURTH SUNDAY OF EASTER**<br>*The reading from Acts must be used as either the first or second reading at the Principal Service.* | Acts 9. 36–end<br>[*or* Gen. 7. 1–5, 11–18; 8. 6–18; 9. 8–13]<br>Ps. 23<br>Rev. 7. 9–end<br>John 10. 22–30 | Ps. 146<br>1 Kings 17. 17–end<br>Luke 7. 11–23 | **W** |

| Second Service<br>Evening Prayer | | Calendar and Holy Communion | Morning Prayer | Evening Prayer |
|---|---|---|---|---|
| Ps. 66<br>*alt.* Ps. **24**; 25<br>Exod. 18. 13–end<br>Col. 4. 2–end<br>**ct** | **W** | | Deut. 4. 32–40<br>John 21. 20–end | Exod. 18. 13–end<br>Col. 4. 2–end<br>**ct** |
| Ps. 86<br>Isa. 38. 9–20<br>John 11. [17–26] 27–44<br>*or First EP of George*<br>Ps. 111; 116<br>Jer. 15. 15–end<br>Heb. 11.32 – 12.2<br>**R ct** | **W** | **THE SECOND SUNDAY AFTER EASTER**<br>Ezek. 34. 11–16a<br>Ps. 23<br>1 Pet. 2. 19–25<br>John 10. 11–16 | Ps. 80. 1–8<br>Exod. 15. 1–2, 9–18<br>John 21. 1–19 | Ps. 86<br>Isa. 38. 9–20<br>John 11. [17–26]<br>27–44<br>*or First EP of George*<br>Ps. 111; 116<br>Jer. 15. 15–end<br>Heb. 11.32 – 12.2<br>**R ct** |
| *EP*: Ps. 3; 11<br>Isa. 43. 1–7<br>John 15. 1–8 | **Wr** | To celebrate George, see *Common Worship* provision.<br>**George, Martyr, Patron of England, c. 304**<br>*Also* Com. Martyr | Deut. 5. 1–22<br>Eph. 1. 1–14 | Exod. ch. 19<br>Luke 1. 1–25 |
| Ps. 71<br>*alt.* Ps. 33<br>Exod. 20. 1–21<br>Luke 1. 26–38<br>*or First EP of Mark*<br>Ps. 19<br>Isa. 52. 7–10<br>Mark 1. 1–15<br>**R ct** | **W** | | Deut. 5. 22–end<br>Eph. 1. 15–end | Exod. 20. 1–21<br>Luke 1. 26–38<br>*or First EP of Mark*<br>(Ps. 19)<br>Isa. 52. 7–10<br>Mark 1. 1–15<br>**R ct** |
| *EP*: Ps. 45<br>Ezek. 1. 4–14<br>2 Tim. 4. 1–11 | **R** | **MARK THE EVANGELIST**<br>Prov. 15. 28–end<br>Ps. 119. 9–16<br>Eph. 4. 7–16<br>John 15. 1–11 | (Ps. 37. 23–41; 148)<br>Isa. 62. 6–10<br>*or* Ecclus. 51. 13–end<br>Acts 12.25 – 13.13 | (Ps. 45)<br>Ezek. 1. 4–14<br>2 Tim. 4. 1–11 |
| Ps. 73<br>*alt.* Ps. 39; **40**<br>Exod. 25. 1–22<br>Luke 1. 57–end | **W** | | Deut. 7. 1–11<br>Eph. 2. 11–end | Exod. 25. 1–22<br>Luke 1. 57–end |
| Ps. 77<br>*alt.* Ps. 35<br>Exod. 28. 1–4a, 29–38<br>Luke 2. 1–20 | **W** | | Deut. 7. 12–end<br>Eph. 3. 1–13 | Exod. 28. 1–4a, 29–38<br>Luke 2. 1–20 |
| Ps. 23; **27**<br>*alt.* Ps. 45; **46**<br>Exod. 29. 1–9<br>Luke 2. 21–40<br>**ct** | **W** | | Deut. ch. 8<br>Eph. 3. 14–end | Exod. 29. 1–9<br>Luke 2. 21–40<br>**ct** |
| Ps. 113; 114<br>Isa. 63. 7–14<br>Luke 24. 36–49 | **W** | **THE THIRD SUNDAY AFTER EASTER**<br>Gen. 45. 3–10<br>Ps. 57<br>1 Pet. 2. 11–17<br>John 16. 16–22 | Ps. 146<br>1 Kings 17. 17–end<br>Luke 7. 11–23 | Ps. 113; 114<br>Isa. 63. 7–14<br>Luke 24. 36–49 |

# April 2007

| Date | Day | Colour | | Sunday Principal Service<br>Weekday Eucharist | Third Service<br>Morning Prayer |
|---|---|---|---|---|---|
| **30** | M | W | *Pandita Mary Ramabai, Translator of the Scriptures, 1922* | Acts 11. 1–18<br>Ps. 42. 1–2; 43. 1–4<br>John 10. 1–10 (*or* 11–18) | Ps. 103<br>*alt.* Ps. 44<br>Deut. 9. 1–21<br>Eph. 4. 1–16 |

# May 2007

| Date | Day | Colour | | Sunday Principal Service<br>Weekday Eucharist | Third Service<br>Morning Prayer |
|---|---|---|---|---|---|
| **1** | Tu | R | **PHILIP AND JAMES, APOSTLES** | Isa. 30. 15–21<br>Ps. 119. 1–8<br>Eph. 1. 3–10<br>John 14. 1–14 | *MP:* Ps. 139; 146<br>Prov. 4. 10–18<br>James 1. 1–12 |
| **2** | W | W | **Athanasius, Bishop of Alexandria, Teacher, 373**<br>Com. Teacher<br>*also* Ecclus. 4. 20–28<br>Matt. 10. 24–27 | *or* Acts 12.24 –13.5<br>Ps. 67<br>John 12. 44–end | Ps. 135<br>*alt.* Ps. 119. 57–80<br>Deut. 10. 12–end<br>Eph. 5. 1–14 |
| **3** | Th | W | | Acts 13. 13–25<br>Ps. 89. 1–2, 20–26<br>John 13. 16–20 | Ps. 118<br>*alt.* Ps. 56; ***57*** (63†)<br>Deut. 11. 8–end<br>Eph. 5. 15–end |
| **4** | F | W | **The Saints and Martyrs of the Reformation Era**<br>Isa. 43. 1–7<br>*or* Ecclus. 2. 10–17<br>Ps. 87<br>2 Cor. 4. 5–12<br>John 12. 20–26 | *or* Acts 13. 26–33<br>Ps. 2<br>John 14. 1–6 | Ps. 33<br>*alt.* Ps. ***51***; 54<br>Deut. 12. 1–14<br>Eph. 6. 1–9 |
| **5** | Sa | W | | Acts 13. 44–end<br>Ps. 98. 1–5<br>John 14. 7–14 | Ps. 34<br>*alt.* Ps. 68<br>Deut. 15. 1–18<br>Eph. 6. 10–end |
| **6** | **S** | W | **THE FIFTH SUNDAY OF EASTER**<br>*The reading from Acts must be used as either the first or second reading at the Principal Service.* | Acts 11. 1–18<br>[*or* Baruch 3.9–15, 32 – 4.4<br>*or* Gen. 22. 1–18]<br>Ps. 148. 1–6 [7–end]<br>Rev. 21. 1–6<br>John 13. 31–35 | Ps. 16<br>2 Sam. 7. 4–13<br>Acts 2. 14a, 22–32 [33–36] |
| **7** | M | W | | Acts 14. 5–18<br>Ps. 118. 1–3, 14–15<br>John 14. 21–26 | Ps. 145<br>*alt.* Ps. 71<br>Deut. 16. 1–20<br>1 Pet. 1. 1–12 |
| **8** | Tu | W | **Julian of Norwich, Spiritual Writer, c. 1417**<br>Com. Religious<br>*also* 1 Cor. 13. 8–end<br>Matt. 5. 13–16 | *or* Acts 14. 19–end<br>Ps. 145. 10–end<br>John 14. 27–end | Ps. ***19***; 147. 1–12<br>*alt.* Ps. 73<br>Deut. 17. 8–end<br>1 Pet. 1. 13–end |
| **9** | W | W | | Acts 15. 1–6<br>Ps. 122. 1–5<br>John 15. 1–8 | Ps. ***30***; 147. 13–end<br>*alt.* Ps. 77<br>Deut. 18. 9–end<br>1 Pet. 2. 1–10 |

| Second Service<br>Evening Prayer | | Calendar and Holy Communion | Morning Prayer | Evening Prayer |
|---|---|---|---|---|
| Ps. 112; 113; ***114***<br>*alt.* Ps. **47**; 49<br>Exod. 32. 1–14<br>Luke 2. 41–end<br>*or First EP of Philip and James*<br>Ps. 25<br>Isa. 40. 27–end<br>John 12. 20–26<br>**R ct** | **W** | | Deut. 9. 1–21<br>Eph. 4. 1–16 | Exod. 32. 1–14<br>Luke 2. 41–end<br>*or First EP of Philip and James*<br>(Ps. 119. 1–8)<br>Isa. 40. 27–end<br>John 12. 20–26<br>**R ct** |
| | | | | |
| *EP*: Ps. 149<br>Job 23. 1–12<br>John 1. 43–end | **R** | **PHILIP AND JAMES, APOSTLES**<br>Prov. 4. 10–18<br>Ps. 25. 1–9<br>James 1. [1]2–12<br>John 14. 1–14 | (Ps. 139; 146)<br>Isa. 30. 1–5<br>John 12. 20–26 | (Ps. 149)<br>Job 23. 1–12<br>John 1. 43–end |
| Ps. **47**; 48<br>*alt.* Ps. ***59***; 60 (67)<br>Exod. ch. 33<br>Luke 3. 15–22 | **W** | | Deut. 10. 12–end<br>Eph. 5. 1–14 | Exod. ch. 33<br>Luke 3. 15–22 |
| Ps. 81; ***85***<br>*alt.* Ps. 61; **62**; 64<br>Exod. 34. 1–10, 27–end<br>Luke 4. 1–13 | **Wr** | **The Invention of the Cross** | Deut. 11. 8–end<br>Eph. 5. 15–end | Exod. 34. 1–10, 27–end<br>Luke 4. 1–13 |
| Ps. ***36***; 40<br>*alt.* Ps. 38<br>Exod. 35.20 – 36.7<br>Luke 4. 14–30 | **W** | | Deut. 12. 1–14<br>Eph. 6. 1–9 | Exod. 35.20 – 36.7<br>Luke 4. 14–30 |
| Ps. ***84***; 86<br>*alt.* Ps. 65; ***66***<br>Exod. 40. 17–end<br>Luke 4. 31–37<br>**ct** | **W** | | Deut. 15. 1–18<br>Eph. 6. 10–end | Exod. 40. 17–end<br>Luke 4. 31–37<br>**ct** |
| Ps. 98<br>Dan. 6. [1–5] 6–23<br>Mark 15.46 – 16.8 | **W** | **THE FOURTH SUNDAY AFTER EASTER**<br>Job 19. 21–27a<br>Ps. 66. 14–end<br>James 1. 17–21<br>John 16. 5–15 | Ps. 16<br>2 Sam. 7. 4–13<br>Acts 2. 14a, 22–32 [33–36] | Ps. 98<br>Dan. 6. [1–5] 6–23<br>Mark 15.46 – 16.8 |
| Ps. 105<br>*alt.* Ps. ***72***; 75<br>Num. 9. 15–end; 10. 33–end<br>Luke 4. 38–end | **W** | | Deut. 16. 1–20<br>1 Pet. 1. 1–12 | Num. 9. 15–end; 10. 33–end<br>Luke 4. 38–end |
| Ps. 96; ***97***<br>*alt.* Ps. 74<br>Num. 11. 1–33<br>Luke 5. 1–11 | **W** | | Deut. 17. 8–end<br>1 Pet. 1. 13–end | Num. 11. 1–33<br>Luke 5. 1–11 |
| Ps. 98; ***99***; 100<br>*alt.* Ps. 119. 81–104<br>Num. ch. 12<br>Luke 5. 12–26 | **W** | | Deut. 18. 9–end<br>1 Pet. 2. 1–10 | Num. ch. 12<br>Luke 5. 12–26 |

# May 2007

| Date | Day | | Sunday Principal Service<br>Weekday Eucharist | Third Service<br>Morning Prayer |
|---|---|---|---|---|
| **10** | Th<br>**W** | | Acts 15. 7–21<br>Ps. 96. 1–3, 7–10<br>John 15. 9–11 | Ps. **57**; 148<br>*alt.* Ps. 78. 1–39†<br>Deut. ch. 19<br>1 Pet. 2. 11–end |
| **11** | F<br>**W** | | Acts 15. 22–31<br>Ps. 57. 8–end<br>John 15. 12–17 | Ps. ***138***; 149<br>*alt.* Ps. 55<br>Deut. 21.22 – 22.8<br>1 Pet. 3. 1–12 |
| **12** | Sa<br>**W** | | Acts 16. 1–10<br>Ps. 100<br>John 15. 18–21 | Ps. ***146***; 150<br>*alt.* Ps. ***76***; 79<br>Deut. 24. 5–end<br>1 Pet. 3. 13–end |
| **13** | **S**<br>**W** | **THE SIXTH SUNDAY OF EASTER**<br>*The reading from Acts must be used as either the first or second reading at the Principal Service.* | Acts 16. 9–15<br>[*or* Ezek. 37. 1–14]<br>Ps. 67<br>Rev. 21.10, 22 – 22.5<br>John 14. 23–29<br>*or* John 5. 1–9 | Ps. 40. 1–9<br>Gen. 1. 26–28 [29–end]<br>Col. 3. 1–11 |
| **14** | M<br>**R** | **MATTHIAS THE APOSTLE***<br>Rogation Day**<br>*The reading from Acts must be used as either the first or second reading at the Eucharist.* | Isa. 22. 15–end<br>*or* Acts 1. 15–end<br>Ps. 15<br>Acts 1. 15–end<br>*or* 1 Cor. 4. 1–7<br>John 15. 9–17 | *MP:* Ps. 16; 147. 1–12<br>1 Sam. 2. 27–35<br>Acts 2. 37–end |
| | **W** | *or, if Matthias is celebrated on 24 February:* | Acts 16. 11–15<br>Ps. 149. 1–5<br>John 15.26 – 16.4 | Ps. ***65***; 67<br>*alt.* Ps. ***80***; 82<br>Deut. ch. 26<br>1 Pet. 4. 1–11 |
| **15** | Tu<br>**W** | Rogation Day** | Acts 16. 22–34<br>Ps. 138<br>John 16. 5–11 | Ps. 124; 125; ***126***; 127<br>*alt.* Ps. 87; ***89. 1–18***<br>Deut. 28. 1–14<br>1 Pet. 4. 12–end |
| **16** | W<br>**W** | Rogation Day**<br>*Caroline Chisholm, Social Reformer, 1877* | Acts 17.15, 22 – 18.1<br>Ps. 148. 1–2, 11–end<br>John 16. 12–15 | Ps. ***132***; 133<br>*alt.* Ps. 119. 105–128<br>Deut. 28. 58–end<br>1 Peter ch. 5 |
| **17** | Th<br>**W** | **ASCENSION DAY**<br>*The reading from Acts must be used as either the first or second reading at the Eucharist.* | Acts 1. 1–11<br>*or* Dan. 7. 9–14<br>Ps. 47 *or* Ps. 93<br>Eph. 1. 15–end<br>*or* Acts 1. 1–11<br>Luke 24. 44–end | *MP:* Ps. 110; 150<br>Isa. 52. 7–end<br>Heb. 7. [11–25] 26–end |

*Matthias may be celebrated on 24 February instead of 14 May.

**For Rogation Day provision, see p. 12.

| Second Service<br>Evening Prayer | | Calendar and Holy Communion | Morning Prayer | Evening Prayer |
|---|---|---|---|---|
| Ps. 104<br>*alt.* Ps. 78. 40–end†<br>Num. 13. 1–3, 17–end<br>Luke 5. 27–end | **W** | | Deut. ch. 19<br>1 Pet. 2. 11–end | Num. 13. 1–3, 17–end<br>Luke 5. 27–end |
| Ps. 66<br>*alt.* Ps. 69<br>Num. 14. 1–25<br>Luke 6. 1–11 | **W** | | Deut. 21.22 – 22.8<br>1 Pet. 3. 1–12 | Num. 14. 1–25<br>Luke 6. 1–11 |
| Ps. 118<br>*alt.* Ps. 81; ***84***<br>Num. 14. 26–end<br>Luke 6. 12–26<br>**ct** | **W** | | Deut. 24. 5–end<br>1 Pet. 3. 13–end | Num. 14. 26–end<br>Luke 6. 12–26<br>**ct** |
| Ps. 126; 127<br>Zeph. 3. 14–end<br>Matt. 28. 1–10, 16–end<br>*or First EP of Matthias*<br>Ps. 147<br>Isa. 22. 15–22<br>Phil. 3.13b – 4.1<br>**R ct** | **W** | **THE FIFTH SUNDAY AFTER EASTER**<br>Rogation Sunday<br>Joel 2. 21–26<br>Ps. 66. 1–8<br>James 1. 22–end<br>John 16. 23b–end | Ps. 40. 1–9<br>Gen. 1. 26–28<br>[29–end]<br>John 5. 1–9 | Ps. 126; 127<br>Zeph. 3. 14–end<br>Matt. 28. 1–10,<br>16–end |
| *EP:* Ps. 80<br>1 Sam. 16. 1–13a<br>Matt. 7. 15–27<br><br>Ps. ***121***; 122; 123<br>*alt.* Ps. ***85***; 86<br>Num. 16. 1–35<br>Luke 6. 27–38 | **W** | Rogation Day<br>Job 28. 1–11<br>Ps. 107. 1–9<br>James 5. 7–11<br>Luke 6. 36–42 | Deut. ch. 26<br>1 Pet. 4. 1–11 | Num. 16. 1–35<br>Luke 6. 27–38 |
| Ps. ***128***; 129; 130; 131<br>*alt.* Ps. 89. 19–end<br>Num. 16. 36–end<br>Luke 6. 39–end | **W** | Rogation Day<br>Deut. 8. 1–10<br>Ps. 121<br>James 5. 16–end<br>Luke 11. 5–13 | Deut. 28. 1–14<br>1 Pet. 4. 12–end | Num. 16. 36–end<br>Luke 6. 39–end |
| *First EP of Ascension Day*<br>Ps. 15; 24<br>2 Sam. 23. 1–5<br>Col. 2.20 – 3.4<br>**𝔚 ct** | **W** | Rogation Day<br>Deut. 34. 1–7<br>Ps. 108. 1–6<br>Eph. 4. 7–13<br>John 17. 1–11 | Deut. 28. 58–end<br>1 Peter ch. 5 | *First EP of Ascension Day*<br>Ps. 15; 24<br>2 Sam. 23. 1–5<br>Col. 2.20 – 3.4<br>**𝔚 ct** |
| *EP:* Ps. 8<br>Song of the Three 29–37<br>*or* 2 Kings 2. 1–15<br>Rev. ch. 5<br>*Gospel:* Matt. 28. 16–end | **𝔚** | **ASCENSION DAY**<br>Dan. 7. 13–14<br>Ps. 68. 1–6<br>Acts 1. 1–11<br>Mark 16. 14–20<br>*or* Luke 24. 44–end | Ps. 110<br>Isa. 52. 7–end<br>Heb. 7. [11–25]<br>26–end | Ps. 8<br>Song of the Three<br>29–37<br>*or* 2 Kings 2. 1–15<br>Rev. ch. 5 |

# May 2007

| | | | Sunday Principal Service / Weekday Eucharist | Third Service / Morning Prayer |
|---|---|---|---|---|
| **18** | F | | Acts 18. 9–18<br>Ps. 47. 1–6<br>John 16. 20–23 | Ps. 20; ***81***<br>*alt.* Ps. ***88*** (95)<br>Deut. 29. 2–15<br>I John 1.1 – 2.6<br>[Exod. 35.30 – 36.1<br>Gal. 5. 13–end]* |
| | **W** | | | |
| **19** | Sa | **Dunstan, Archbishop of Canterbury, Restorer of Monastic Life, 988**<br>Com. Bishop<br>*esp.* Matt. 24. 42–46<br>*also* Exod. 31. 1–5 | *or* Acts 18. 22–end<br>Ps. 47. 1–2, 7–end<br>John 16. 23–28 | Ps. 21; ***47***<br>*alt.* Ps. 96; **97**; 100<br>Deut. ch. 30<br>I John 2. 7–17<br>[Num. 11. 16–17, 24–29<br>I Cor. ch. 2] |
| | **W** | | | |
| **20** | **S** | **THE SEVENTH SUNDAY OF EASTER (SUNDAY AFTER ASCENSION DAY)**<br>*The reading from Acts must be used as either the first or second reading at the Principal Service.* | Acts 16. 16–34<br>[*or* Ezek. 36. 24–28]<br>Ps. 97<br>Rev. 22. 12–14, 16–17, 20–end<br>John 17. 20–end | Ps. 99<br>Deut. ch. 34<br>Luke 24. 44–end<br>*or* Acts 1. 1–8 |
| | **W** | | | |
| **21** | M | *Helena, Protector of the Holy Places, 330* | Acts 19. 1–8<br>Ps. 68. 1–6<br>John 16. 29–end | Ps. ***93***; 96; 97<br>*alt.* Ps. ***98***; 99; 101<br>Deut. 31. 1–13<br>I John 2. 18–end<br>[Num. 27. 15–end<br>I Cor. ch. 3] |
| | **W** | | | |
| **22** | Tu | | Acts 20. 17–27<br>Ps. 68. 9–10, 18–19<br>John 17. 1–11 | Ps. 98; ***99***; 100<br>*alt.* Ps. ***106***† (*or* 103)<br>Deut. 31. 14–29<br>I John 3. 1–10<br>[I Sam. 10. 1–10<br>I Cor. 12. 1–13] |
| | **W** | | | |
| **23** | W | | Acts 20. 28–end<br>Ps. 68. 27–28, 32–end<br>John 17. 11–19 | Ps. 2; ***29***<br>*alt.* Ps. 110; ***111***; 112<br>Deut. 31.30 – 32.14<br>I John 3. 11–end<br>[I Kings 19. 1–18<br>Matt. 3. 13–end] |
| | **W** | | | |
| **24** | Th | **John and Charles Wesley, Evangelists, Hymn Writers, 1791 and 1788**<br>Com. Pastor<br>*also* Eph. 5. 15–20 | *or* Acts 22. 30; 23. 6–11<br>Ps. 16. 1, 5–end<br>John 17. 20–end | Ps. ***24***; 72<br>*alt.* Ps. 113; ***115***<br>Deut. 32. 15–47<br>I John 4. 1–6<br>[Ezek. 11. 14–20<br>Matt. 9.35 – 10.20] |
| | **W** | | | |
| **25** | F | **The Venerable Bede, Monk at Jarrow, Scholar, Historian, 735**<br>*Aldhelm, Bishop of Sherborne, 709*<br>Com. Religious<br>also Ecclus. 39. 1–10 | *or* Acts 25. 13–21<br>Ps. 103. 1–2, 11–12, 19–20<br>John 21. 15–19 | Ps. ***28***; 30<br>*alt.* Ps. 139<br>Deut. ch. 33<br>I John 4. 7–end<br>[Ezek. 36. 22–28<br>Matt. 12. 22–32] |
| | **W** | | | |
| **26** | Sa | **Augustine, first Archbishop of Canterbury, 605**<br>*John Calvin, Reformer, 1564; Philip Neri, Founder of the Oratorians, Spiritual Guide, 1595*<br>Com. Bishop<br>*also* I Thess. 2. 2b–8<br>Matt. 13. 31–33 | *or* Acts 28. 16–20, 30–end<br>Ps. 11. 4–end<br>John 21. 20–25 | Ps. 42; ***43***<br>*alt.* Ps. 120; ***121***; 122<br>Deut. 32. 48–end; ch. 34<br>I John ch. 5<br>[Mic. 3. 1–8<br>Eph. 6. 10–20] |
| | **W** | | | |

*The alternative readings in square brackets may be used at one of the offices, in preparation for the Day of Pentecost.

| Second Service Evening Prayer | | Calendar and Holy Communion | Morning Prayer | Evening Prayer |
|---|---|---|---|---|
| Ps. 145<br>*alt.* Ps. 102<br>Num. 20. 1–13<br>Luke 7. 11–17 | **W** | Ascension CEG | Deut. 29. 2–15<br>1 John 1.1 – 2.6<br>[Exod. 35.30 – 36.1<br>Gal. 5. 13–end]* | Num. 20. 1–13<br>Luke 7. 11–17 |
| | | **Dunstan, Archbishop of Canterbury, Restorer of Monastic Life, 988** | | |
| Ps. 84; ***85***<br>*alt.* Ps. 104<br>Num. 21. 4–9<br>Luke 7. 18–35<br>**ct** | **W** | Com. Bishop *or*<br>Ascension CEG | Deut. ch. 30<br>1 John 2. 7–17<br>[Num. 11. 16–17, 24–29<br>1 Cor. ch. 2] | Num. 21. 4–9<br>Luke 7. 18–35<br>**ct** |
| | | **THE SUNDAY AFTER ASCENSION DAY** | | |
| Ps. 68. 1–13 [14–17] 18–19 [20–end]<br>Isa. 44. 1–8<br>Eph. 4. 7–16<br>*Gospel:* Luke 24. 44–end | **W** | 2 Kings 2. 9–15<br>Ps. 68. 32–end<br>1 Pet. 4. 7–11<br>John 15.26 – 16.4a | Ps. 99<br>Deut. ch. 34<br>Luke 24. 44–end<br>*or* Acts 1. 1–8 | Ps. 68. 1–13 [14–17] 18–19 [20–end]<br>Isa. 44. 1–8<br>Eph. 4. 7–16 |
| Ps. 18<br>*alt.* Ps. ***105***† (*or* 103)<br>Num. 22. 1–35<br>Luke 7. 36–end | **W** | | Deut. 31. 1–13<br>1 John 2. 18–end<br>[Num. 27. 15–end<br>1 Cor. ch. 3] | Num. 22. 1–35<br>Luke 7. 36–end |
| Ps. 68<br>*alt.* Ps. 107†<br>Num. 22.36 – 23.12<br>Luke 8. 1–15 | **W** | | Deut. 31. 14–29<br>1 John 3. 1–10<br>[1 Sam. 10. 1–10<br>1 Cor. 12. 1–13] | Num. 22.36 – 23.12<br>Luke 8. 1–15 |
| Ps. 36; ***46***<br>*alt.* Ps. 119. 129–152<br>Num. 23. 13–end<br>Luke 8. 16–25 | **W** | | Deut. 31.30 – 32.14<br>1 John 3. 11–end<br>[1 Kings 19. 1–18<br>Matt. 3. 13–end] | Num. 23. 13–end<br>Luke 8. 16–25 |
| Ps. 139<br>*alt.* Ps. 114; ***116***; 117<br>Num. ch. 24<br>Luke 8. 26–39 | **W** | | Deut. 32. 15–47<br>1 John 4. 1–6<br>[Ezek. 11. 14–20<br>Matt. 9.35 – 10.20] | Num. ch. 24<br>Luke 8. 26–39 |
| Ps. 147<br>*alt.* Ps. ***130***; 131; 137<br>Num. 27. 12–end<br>Luke 8. 40–end | **W** | | Deut. ch. 33<br>1 John 4. 7–end<br>[Ezek. 36. 22–28<br>Matt. 12. 22–32] | Num. 27. 12–end<br>Luke 8. 40–end |
| | | **Augustine, first Archbishop of Canterbury, 605** | | |
| *First EP of Pentecost*<br>Ps. 48<br>Deut. 16. 9–15<br>John 7. 37–39<br>**R ct** | **W** | Com. Bishop | Deut. 32. 48–end; ch. 34<br>1 John ch. 5<br>[Mic. 3. 1–8<br>Eph. 6. 10–20] | *First EP of Whit Sunday*<br>Ps. 48<br>Deut. 16. 9–15<br>John 7. 37–39<br>**R ct** |

# May 2007

| Date | Day | | Sunday Principal Service<br>Weekday Eucharist | Third Service<br>Morning Prayer |
|---|---|---|---|---|
| **27** | S<br>**R** | **DAY OF PENTECOST (Whit Sunday)**<br>*The reading from Acts must be used as either the first or second reading at the Principal Service.* | Acts 2. 1–21<br>*or* Gen. 11. 1–9<br>Ps. 104. 26–36, 37b (*or* 26–end)<br>Rom. 8. 14–17<br>*or* Acts 2. 1–21<br>John 14. 8–17 [25–27] | *MP*: Ps. 36. 5–10; 150<br>Isa. 40. 12–23<br>*or* Wisd. 9. 9–17<br>1 Cor. 2. 6–end |
| **28**<br>DEL 8 | M<br>**G** | *Lanfranc, Prior of Le Bec, Archbishop of Canterbury, Scholar, 1089*<br>Ordinary Time resumes today | Ecclus. 17. 24–29<br>*or* James 3. 13–end<br>Ps. 32. 1–8<br>*or* Ps. 19. 7–end<br>Mark 10. 17–27 | Ps. 123; 124; 125; ***126***<br>2 Chron. 17. 1–12<br>Rom. 1. 1–17 |
| **29** | Tu<br>**G** | | Ecclus. 35. 1–12<br>*or* James 4. 1–10<br>Ps. 50. 1–6<br>*or* Ps. 55. 7–9, 24<br>Mark 10. 28–31 | Ps. ***132***; 133<br>2 Chron. 18. 1–27<br>Rom. 1. 18–end |
| **30** | W<br>**Gw** | **Josephine Butler, Social Reformer, 1906**<br>*Joan of Arc, Visionary, 1431; Apolo Kivebulaya, Evangelist in Central Africa, 1933*<br>Com. Saint *or*<br>*esp.* Isa. 58. 6–11<br>*also* 1 John 3. 18–23<br>Matt. 9. 10–13 | Ecclus. 36. 1–2, 4–5, 10–17<br>*or* James 4. 13–end<br>Ps. 79. 8–9, 12, 14<br>*or* Ps. 49. 1–6, 16–18<br>Mark 10. 32–45 | Ps. 119. 153–end<br>2 Chron. 18.28 – 19.end<br>Rom. 2. 1–16 |
| **31** | Th | **THE VISIT OF THE BLESSED VIRGIN MARY TO ELIZABETH***| Zeph. 3. 14–18<br>Ps. 113<br>Rom. 12. 9–16<br>Luke 1. 39–49 [50–56] | *MP*: Ps. 85; 150<br>1 Sam. 2. 1–10<br>Mark 3. 31–end |
| | **W** | *or, if The Visitation is celebrated on 2 July:* | Ecclus. 42. 15–25<br>*or* James 5. 1–6<br>Ps. 33. 1–9<br>*or* Ps. 49. 12–19<br>Mark 10. 46–end | Ps. ***143***; 146<br>2 Chron. 20. 1–23<br>Rom. 2. 17–end |

# June 2007

| Date | Day | | Sunday Principal Service<br>Weekday Eucharist | Third Service<br>Morning Prayer |
|---|---|---|---|---|
| **1** | F<br>**Gr** | **Justin, Martyr at Rome, c. 165**<br>Com. Martyr *or*<br>*esp.* John 15. 18–21<br>*also* 1 Macc. 2. 15–22<br>1 Cor. 1. 18–25 | Ecclus. 44. 1, 9–13<br>*or* James 5. 9–12<br>Ps. 149. 1–5<br>*or* Ps. 103. 1–4, 8–13<br>Mark 11. 11–26 | Ps. ***142***; 144<br>2 Chron. 22.10 – 23.end<br>Rom. 3. 1–20 |
| **2** | Sa<br>**G** | | Ecclus. 51. 12b–20a<br>*or* James 5. 13–end<br>Ps. 19. 7–end<br>*or* Ps. 141. 1–4<br>Mark 11. 27–end | Ps. 147<br>2 Chron. 24. 1–22<br>Rom. 3. 21–end |

*The Visit of the Blessed Virgin Mary to Elizabeth may be celebrated on 2 July instead of 31 May.

| Second Service<br>Evening Prayer | | Calendar and Holy Communion | Morning Prayer | Evening Prayer |
|---|---|---|---|---|
| *EP:* Ps. 33. 1–12<br>Exod. 33. 7–20<br>2 Cor. 3. 4–end<br>*Gospel:* John 16. 4b–15 | **R** | **WHIT SUNDAY**<br>Deut. 16. 9–12<br>Ps. 122<br>Acts 2. 1–11<br>John 14. 15–31a | Ps. 36. 5–10; 150<br>Isa. 40. 12–23<br>*or* Wisd. 9. 9–17<br>1 Cor. 2. 6–end | Ps. 33. 1–12<br>Exod. 33. 7–20<br>2 Cor. 3. 4–end |
| Ps. ***127***; 128; 129<br>Josh. ch. 1<br>Luke 9. 18–27 | **R** | **Monday in Whitsun Week**<br>Acts 10. 34–end<br>John 3. 16–21 | Ezek. 11. 14–20<br>Acts 2. 12–36 | Exod. 35.30 – 36.1<br>Acts 2. 37–end |
| Ps. (134) ***135***<br>Josh. ch. 2<br>Luke 9. 28–36 | **R** | **Tuesday in Whitsun Week**<br>Acts 8. 14–17<br>John 10. 1–10 | Ezek. 37. 1–14<br>1 Cor. 12. 1–13 | 2 Sam. 23. 1–5<br>1 Cor. 12.27 – 13.end |
| Ps. 136<br>Josh. ch. 3<br>Luke 9. 37–50<br>*or First EP of The Visit of Mary to Elizabeth*<br>Ps. 45<br>Song of Sol. 2. 8–14<br>Luke 1. 26–38<br>**W ct** | **R** | Ember Day<br>Ember CEG<br>*or* Acts 2. 14–21<br>John 6. 44–51 | 2 Chron. 18.28 – 19.end<br>Rom. 2. 1–16 | Josh. ch. 3<br>Luke 9. 37–50 |
| *EP:* Ps. 122; 127; 128<br>Zech. 2. 10–end<br>John 3. 25–30<br><br>Ps. ***138***; 140; 141<br>Josh. 4.1 – 5.1<br>Luke 9. 51–end | **R** | Acts 2. 22–28<br>Luke 9. 1–6 | 2 Chron. 20. 1–23<br>Rom. 2. 17–end | Josh. 4.1 – 5.1<br>Luke 9. 51–end |
| | | | | |
| Ps. 145<br>Josh. 5. 2–end<br>Luke 10. 1–16 | **R** | **Nicomede, Priest and Martyr at Rome (date unknown)**<br>Ember Day<br>Com. Martyr *or*<br>Ember CEG *or*<br>Acts 8. 5–8<br>Luke 5. 17–26 | 2 Chron. 22.10 – 23.end<br>Rom. 3. 1–20 | Josh. 5. 2–end<br>Luke 10. 1–16 |
| *First EP of Trinity Sunday*<br>Ps. 97; 98<br>Isa. 40. 12–end<br>Mark 1. 1–13<br>**W ct** | **R** | Ember Day<br>Ember CEG<br>*or* Acts 13. 44–end<br>Matt. 20. 29–end | 2 Chron. 24. 1–22<br>Rom. 3. 21–end | *First EP of Trinity Sunday*<br>Ps. 97; 98<br>Isa. 40. 12–end<br>Mark 1. 1–13<br>**W ct** |

# June 2007

| Date | Day | Observance | Sunday Principal Service<br>Weekday Eucharist | Third Service<br>Morning Prayer |
|---|---|---|---|---|
| **3** | S<br>W | **TRINITY SUNDAY** | Prov. 8. 1–4, 22–31<br>Ps. 8<br>Rom. 5. 1–5<br>John 16. 12–15 | *MP*: Ps. 29<br>Isa. 6. 1–8<br>Rev. ch. 4 |
| **4**<br>DEL 9 | M<br>G | *Petroc, Abbot of Padstow, 6th century* | Tobit 1. 1–2; 2. 1–8<br>*or* 1 Pet. 1. 3–9<br>Ps. 15<br>*or* Ps. 111<br>Mark 12. 1–12 | Ps. ***1***: 2; 3<br>2 Chron. 26. 1–21<br>Rom. 4. 1–12 |
| **5** | Tu<br>**Gr** | **Boniface (Wynfrith) of Crediton, Bishop, Apostle of Germany, Martyr, 754**<br>Com. Martyr<br>*also* Acts 20. 24–28 | *or* Tobit 2. 9–end<br>*or* 1 Pet. 1. 10–16<br>Ps. 112<br>*or* Ps. 98. 1–5<br>Mark 12. 13–17 | Ps. **5**; 6 (8)<br>2 Chron. ch. 28<br>Rom. 4. 13–end |
| **6** | W<br>G | *Ini Kopuria, Founder of the Melanesian Brotherhood, 1945* | Tobit 3. 1–11, 16–end<br>*or* 1 Pet. 1. 18–25<br>Ps. 25. 1–8<br>*or* Ps. 147. 12–end<br>Mark 12. 18–27 | Ps. 119. 1–32<br>2 Chron. 29. 1–19<br>Rom. 5. 1–11 |
| **7** | Th<br>**W** | **DAY OF THANKSGIVING FOR HOLY COMMUNION (CORPUS CHRISTI)** | Gen. 14. 18–20<br>Ps. 116. 10–end<br>1 Cor. 11. 23–26<br>John 6. 51–58 | *MP*: Ps. 147<br>Deut. 8. 2–16<br>1 Cor. 10. 1–17 |
| | **G** | *or the ferial readings for the day*: | Tobit 6. 9–11; 7. 1–15; 8. 4–8<br>*or* 1 Pet. 2. 2–5, 9–12<br>Ps. 128<br>*or* Ps. 100<br>Mark 12. 28–34 | Ps. 14; ***15***; 16<br>2 Chron. 29. 20–end<br>Rom. 5. 12–end |
| **8** | F<br>**Gw** | **Thomas Ken, Bishop of Bath and Wells, Nonjuror, Hymn Writer, 1711**<br>Com. Bishop<br>*esp.* 2 Cor. 4. 1–10<br>Matt. 24. 42–46 | *or* Tobit 11. 5–15<br>*or* 1 Pet. 4. 7–13<br>Ps. 146<br>*or* Ps. 96. 10–end<br>Mark 12. 35–37 | Ps. 17; ***19***<br>2 Chron. ch. 30<br>Rom. 6. 1–14 |
| **9** | Sa<br>**Gw** | **Columba, Abbot of Iona, Missionary, 597**<br>*Ephrem of Syria, Deacon, Hymn Writer, Teacher, 373*<br>Com. Missionary<br>*also* Titus 2. 11–15 | *or* Tobit 12. 1, 5–15, 20a<br>*or* Jude 17, 20–25<br>Ps. 103. 1, 8–13<br>*or* Ps. 63. 1–6<br>Mark 12. 38–end | Ps. 20; 21; **23**<br>2 Chron. 32. 1–22<br>Rom. 6. 15–end |
| **10** | **S**<br>**G** | **THE FIRST SUNDAY AFTER TRINITY (Proper 5)**<br>*Track 1*<br>1 Kings 17. 8–16 [17–end]<br>Ps. 146<br>Gal. 1. 11–end<br>Luke 7. 11–17 | *Track 2*<br>1 Kings 17. 17–end<br>Ps. 30<br>Gal. 1. 11–end<br>Luke 7. 11–17 | Ps. 45<br>Deut. 6. 10–end<br>Acts 22.22 – 23.11 |

| Second Service Evening Prayer | | Calendar and Holy Communion | Morning Prayer | Evening Prayer |
|---|---|---|---|---|
| *EP*: Ps. 73. 1–3, 16–end<br>Exod. 3. 1–15<br>John 3. 1–17 | W | **TRINITY SUNDAY**<br>Isa. 6. 1–8<br>Ps. 8<br>Rev. 4. 1–11<br>John 3. 1–15 | Ps. 29<br>Prov. 8. 1–4, 22–31<br>Rom. 5. 1–5 | Ps. 73. 1–3, 16–end<br>Exod. 3. 1–15<br>Matt. 28. 16–20 |
| Ps. **4**; 7<br>Josh. 7. 1–15<br>Luke 10. 25–37 | **G** | | 2 Chron. 26. 1–21<br>Rom. 4. 1–12 | Josh. 7. 1–15<br>Luke 10. 25–37 |
| Ps. **9**; 10†<br>Josh. 7. 16–end<br>Luke 10. 38–end | **Gr** | **Boniface (Wynfrith) of Crediton, Bishop, Apostle of Germany, Martyr, 754**<br>Com. Martyr | 2 Chron. ch. 28<br>Rom. 4. 13–end | Josh. 7. 16–end<br>Luke 10. 38–end |
| Ps. ***11***; 12; 13<br>Josh. 8. 1–29<br>Luke 11. 1–13<br>*or First EP of Corpus Christi*<br>Ps. 110; 111<br>Exod. 16. 2–15<br>John 6. 22–35<br>**W ct** | **G** | | 2 Chron. 29. 1–19<br>Rom. 5. 1–11 | Josh. 8. 1–29<br>Luke 11. 1–13 |
| *EP*: Ps. 23; 42; 43<br>Prov. 9. 1–5<br>Luke 9. 11–17<br><br>Ps. 18†<br>Josh. 8. 30–end<br>Luke 11. 14–28 | **G** | To celebrate Corpus Christi, see *Common Worship* provision. | 2 Chron. 29. 20–end<br>Rom. 5. 12–end | Josh. 8. 30–end<br>Luke 11. 14–28 |
| Ps. 22<br>Josh. 9. 3–26<br>Luke 11. 29–36 | **G** | | 2 Chron. ch. 30<br>Rom. 6. 1–14 | Josh. 9. 3–26<br>Luke 11. 29–36 |
| Ps. **24**; 25<br>Josh. 10. 1–15<br>Luke 11. 37–end<br>**ct** | **G** | | 2 Chron. 32. 1–22<br>Rom. 6. 15–end | Josh. 10. 1–15<br>Luke 11. 37–end<br>**ct** |
| Ps. 44. 1–9 [10–end]<br>Gen. 8.15 – 9.17<br>Mark 4. 1–20<br>*or First EP of Barnabas*<br>Ps. 1; 15<br>Isa. 42. 5–12<br>Acts 14. 8–end<br>**R ct** | **G** | **THE FIRST SUNDAY AFTER TRINITY**<br>2 Sam. 9. 6–end<br>Ps. 41. 1–4<br>1 John 4. 7–end<br>Luke 16. 19–31 | Ps. 45<br>Deut. 6. 10–end<br>Acts 22.2 – 23.11 | Ps. 44. 1–9 [10–end]<br>Gen. 8.15 – 9.17<br>Mark 4. 1–20<br>*or First EP of Barnabas*<br>Ps. 1; 15<br>Isa. 42. 5–12<br>Acts 14. 8–end<br>**R ct** |

# June 2007

| Date | Day / Colour | | Sunday Principal Service<br>Weekday Eucharist | Third Service<br>Morning Prayer |
|---|---|---|---|---|
| **11**<br>DEL 10 | M<br>**R** | **BARNABAS THE APOSTLE**<br>*The reading from Acts must be used as either the first or second reading at the Eucharist.* | Job 29. 11–16<br>*or* Acts 11. 19–end<br>Ps. 112<br>Acts 11. 19–end<br>*or* Gal. 2. 1–10<br>John 15. 12–17 | *MP:* Ps. 100; 101; 117<br>Jer. 9. 23–24<br>Acts 4. 32–end |
| **12** | Tu<br>**G** | | 2 Cor. 1. 18–22<br>Ps. 119. 129–136<br>Matt. 5. 13–16 | Ps. 32; ***36***<br>2 Chron. 34. 1–18<br>Rom. 7. 7–end |
| **13** | W<br>**G** | | 2 Cor. 3. 4–11<br>Ps. 78. 1–4<br>Matt. 5. 17–19 | Ps. 34<br>2 Chron. 34. 19–end<br>Rom. 8. 1–11 |
| **14** | Th<br>**G** | *Richard Baxter, Puritan Divine, 1691* | 2 Cor. 3.15 – 4.1, 3–6<br>Ps. 78. 36–40<br>Matt. 5. 20–26 | Ps. 37†<br>2 Chron. 35. 1–19<br>Rom. 8. 12–17 |
| **15** | F<br>**G** | *Evelyn Underhill, Spiritual Writer, 1941* | 2 Cor. 4. 7–15<br>Ps. 99<br>Matt. 5. 27–32 | Ps. 31<br>2 Chron. 35.20 – 36.10<br>Rom. 8. 18–30 |
| **16** | Sa<br>**Gw** | **Richard, Bishop of Chichester, 1253**<br>*Joseph Butler, Bishop of Durham, Philosopher, 1752*<br>Com. Bishop<br>*also* John 21. 15–19 | *or* 2 Cor. 5. 14–end<br>Ps. 103. 1–12<br>Matt. 5. 33–37 | Ps. 41; **42**; 43<br>2 Chron. 36. 11–end<br>Rom. 8. 31–end |
| **17** | **S**<br>**G** | **THE SECOND SUNDAY AFTER TRINITY (Proper 6)**<br>*Track 1*<br>1 Kings 21. 1–10 [11–14] 15–21a<br>Ps. 5. 1–8<br>Gal. 2. 15–end<br>Luke 7.36 – 8.3 | *Track 2*<br>2 Sam. 11.26 – 12.10, 13–15<br>Ps. 32<br>Gal. 2. 15–end<br>Luke 7.36 – 8.3 | Ps. 49<br>Deut. 10.12 – 11.1<br>Acts 23. 12–end |
| **18**<br>DEL 11 | M<br>**G** | *Bernard Mizeki, Apostle of the MaShona, Martyr, 1896* | 2 Cor. 6. 1–10<br>Ps. 98<br>Matt. 5. 38–42 | Ps. 44<br>Ezra ch. 1<br>Rom. 9. 1–18 |
| **19** | Tu<br>**G** | *Sundar Singh of India, Sadhu (holy man), Evangelist, Teacher, 1929* | 2 Cor. 8. 1–9<br>Ps. 146<br>Matt. 5. 43–end | Ps. ***48***; 52<br>Ezra ch. 3<br>Rom. 9. 19–end |
| **20** | W<br>**G** | | 2 Cor. 9. 6–11<br>Ps. 112<br>Matt. 6. 1–6, 16–18 | Ps. 119. 57–80<br>Ezra 4. 1–5<br>Rom. 10. 1–10 |
| **21** | Th<br>**G** | | 2 Cor. 11. 1–11<br>Ps. 111<br>Matt. 6. 7–15 | Ps. 56; **57** (63†)<br>Ezra 4. 7–end<br>Rom. 10. 11–end |
| **22** | F<br>**Gr** | **Alban, first Martyr of Britain, c. 250**<br>Com. Martyr<br>*esp.* 2 Tim. 2. 3–13<br>John 12. 24–26 | *or* 2 Cor. 11. 18, 21a–30<br>Ps. 34. 1–6<br>Matt. 6. 19–23 | Ps. ***51***; 54<br>Ezra ch. 5<br>Rom. 11. 1–12 |
| **23** | Sa<br>**Gw** | **Etheldreda, Abbess of Ely, c. 678**<br>Com. Religious<br>*also* Matt. 25. 1–13 | *or* 2 Cor. 12. 1–10<br>Ps. 89. 20–33<br>Matt. 6. 24–end | Ps. 68<br>Ezra ch. 6<br>Rom. 11. 13–24 |

| Second Service Evening Prayer | | Calendar and Holy Communion | Morning Prayer | Evening Prayer |
|---|---|---|---|---|
| *EP*: Ps. 147<br>Eccles. 12. 9–end<br>*or* Tobit 4. 5–11<br>Acts 9. 26–31 | R | **BARNABAS THE APOSTLE**<br>Job 29. 11–16<br>Ps. 112<br>Acts 11. 22–end<br>John 15. 12–16 | (Ps. 100; 101; 117)<br>Jer. 9. 23–24<br>Acts 4. 32–end | (Ps. 147)<br>Eccles. 12. 9–end<br>*or* Tobit 4. 5–11<br>Acts 9. 26–31 |
| Ps. 33<br>Josh. 21.43 – 22.8<br>Luke 12. 13–21 | G | | 2 Chron. 34. 1–18<br>Rom. 7. 7–end | Josh. 21.43 – 22.8<br>Luke 12. 13–21 |
| Ps. 119. 33–56<br>Josh. 22. 9–end<br>Luke 12. 22–31 | G | | 2 Chron. 34. 19–end<br>Rom. 8. 1–11 | Josh. 22. 9–end<br>Luke 12. 22–31 |
| Ps. 39; ***40***<br>Josh. ch. 23<br>Luke 12. 32–40 | G | | 2 Chron. 35. 1–19<br>Rom. 8. 12–17 | Josh. ch. 23<br>Luke 12. 32–40 |
| Ps. 35<br>Josh. 24. 1–28<br>Luke 12. 41–48 | G | | 2 Chron. 35.20 – 36.10<br>Rom. 8. 18–30 | Josh. 24. 1–28<br>Luke 12. 41–48 |
| Ps. 45; ***46***<br>Josh. 24. 29–end<br>Luke 12. 49–end<br>**ct** | G | | 2 Chron. 36. 11–end<br>Rom. 8. 31–end | Josh. 24. 29–end<br>Luke 12. 49–end<br>**ct** |
| Ps. 52 [53]<br>Gen. ch. 13<br>Mark 4. 21–end | G | **THE SECOND SUNDAY AFTER TRINITY**<br>Gen. 12. 1–4<br>Ps. 120<br>1 John 3. 13–end<br>Luke 14. 16–24 | Ps. 49<br>Deut. 10.12 – 11.1<br>Acts 23. 12–end | Ps. 52 [53]<br>Gen. ch. 13<br>Mark 4. 21–end |
| Ps. ***47***; 49<br>Judg. ch. 2<br>Luke 13. 1–9 | G | | Ezra ch. 1<br>Rom. 9. 1–18 | Judg. ch. 2<br>Luke 13. 1–9 |
| Ps. 50<br>Judg. 4. 1–23<br>Luke 13. 10–21 | G | | Ezra ch. 3<br>Rom. 9. 19–end | Judg. 4. 1–23<br>Luke 13. 10–21 |
| Ps. ***59***; 60 (67)<br>Judg. ch. 5<br>Luke 13. 22–end | Gr | **Translation of Edward, King of the West Saxons, 979**<br>Com. Martyr | Ezra 4. 1–5<br>Rom. 10. 1–10 | Judg. ch. 5<br>Luke 13. 22–end |
| Ps. 61; ***62***; 64<br>Judg. 6. 1–24<br>Luke 14. 1–11 | G | | Ezra 4. 7–end<br>Rom. 10. 11–end | Judg. 6. 1–24<br>Luke 14. 1–11 |
| Ps. 38<br>Judg. 6. 25–end<br>Luke 14. 12–24 | G | | Ezra ch. 5<br>Rom. 11. 1–12 | Judg. 6. 25–end<br>Luke 14. 12–24 |
| Ps. 65; ***66***<br>Judg. ch. 7<br>Luke 14. 25–end<br>**ct**<br>*or First EP of The Birth of John the Baptist*<br>Ps. 71<br>Judg. 13. 2–7, 24–end<br>Luke 1. 5–25<br>**W ct** | G | | Ezra ch. 6<br>Rom. 11. 13–24 | Judg. ch. 7<br>Luke 14. 25–end<br>**ct**<br>*or First EP of The Nativity of John the Baptist*<br>(Ps. 71)<br>Judg. 13. 2–7, 24–end<br>Luke 1. 5–25<br>**W ct** |

# June 2007

| | | | Sunday Principal Service<br>Weekday Eucharist | Third Service<br>Morning Prayer |
|---|---|---|---|---|
| **24** | **S** | **THE BIRTH OF JOHN THE BAPTIST** (or transferred to 25th) | Isa. 40. 1–11<br>Ps. 85. 7–end<br>Acts 13. 14b–26<br>*or* Gal. 3. 23–end<br>Luke 1. 57–66, 80 | *MP*: Ps. 50; 149<br>Ecclus. 48. 1–10<br>*or* Mal. 3. 1–6<br>Luke 3. 1–17 |
| | **W** | | | |
| | | *or, for The Third Sunday after Trinity (Proper 7):*<br>*Track 1*<br>1Kings 19. 1–4 [5–7] 8–15a<br>Ps. 42; 43 (*or* Ps. 42 *or* 43)<br>Gal. 3. 23–end<br>Luke 8. 26–39 | *Track 2*<br>Isa. 65. 1–9<br>Ps. 22. 19–28<br>Gal. 3. 23–end<br>Luke 8. 26–39 | Ps. 55. 1–16, 18–21<br>Deut. 11. 1–15<br>Acts 27. 1–12 |
| | **G** | | | |
| **25**<br>DEL 12 | M | For The Birth of John the Baptist, see 24th | Gen. 12. 1–9<br>Ps. 33. 12–end<br>Matt. 7. 1–5 | Ps. 71<br>Ezra ch. 7<br>Rom. 11. 25–end |
| | **G** | | | |
| **26** | Tu | | Gen. 13. 2, 5–end<br>Ps. 15<br>Matt. 7. 6, 12–14 | Ps. 73<br>Ezra 8. 15–end<br>Rom. 12. 1–8 |
| | **G** | | | |
| **27** | W | Ember Day*<br>*Cyril, Bishop of Alexandria, Teacher, 444* | Gen. 15. 1–12, 17–18<br>Ps. 105. 1–9<br>Matt. 7. 15–20 | Ps. 77<br>Ezra ch. 9<br>Rom. 12. 9–end |
| | **G** *or* **R** | | | |
| **28** | Th | **Irenaeus, Bishop of Lyons, Teacher, c. 200**<br>Com. Teacher<br>*also* 2 Pet. 1. 16–21 | *or* Gen. 16. 1–12, 15–16<br>Ps. 106. 1–5<br>Matt. 7. 21–end | Ps. 78. 1–39†<br>Ezra 10. 1–17<br>Rom. 13. 1–7 |
| | **Gw** | | | |
| **29** | F | **PETER AND PAUL, APOSTLES**<br>Ember Day*<br>*The reading from Acts must be used as either the first or second reading at the Eucharist.* | Zech. 4. 1–6a, 10b–end<br>*or* Acts 12. 1–11<br>Ps. 125<br>Acts 12. 1–11<br>*or* 2 Tim. 4. 6–8, 17–18<br>Matt. 16. 13–19 | *MP*: Ps. 71; 113<br>Isa. 49. 1–6<br>Acts 11. 1–18 |
| | **R** | | | |
| | | *or, if Peter is commemorated alone:*<br>*The reading from Acts must be used as either the first or second reading at the Eucharist.* | Ezek. 3. 22–end<br>*or* Acts 12. 1–11<br>Ps. 125<br>Acts 12. 1–11<br>*or* 1 Pet. 2. 19–end<br>Matt. 16. 13–19 | *MP*: Ps. 71; 113<br>Isa. 49. 1–6<br>Acts 11. 1–18 |
| | **R** | | | |
| **30** | Sa | Ember Day* | Gen. 18. 1–15<br>*Canticle*: Luke 1. 46b–55<br>Matt. 8. 5–17 | Ps. **76**; 79<br>Neh. ch. 2<br>Rom. 14. 1–12 |
| | **G** *or* **R** | | | |

*For Ember Day provision, see p. 13.

| Second Service Evening Prayer | | Calendar and Holy Communion | Morning Prayer | Evening Prayer |
|---|---|---|---|---|
| | | **THE NATIVITY OF JOHN THE BAPTIST** (or transferred to 25th) | | |
| *EP*: Ps. 80; 82<br>Mal. ch. 4<br>Matt. 11. 2–19 | **W** | Isa. 40. 1–11<br>Ps. 80. 1–7<br>Acts 13. 22–26<br>Luke 1. 57–80 | (Ps. 50; 149)<br>Ecclus. 48. 1–10<br>*or* Mal. 3. 1–6<br>Luke 3. 1–17 | (Ps. 82)<br>Mal. ch. 4<br>Matt. 11. 2–19 |
| | | *or, for The Third Sunday after Trinity:* | | |
| Ps. [50] 57<br>Gen. 24. 1–27<br>Mark 5. 21–end | **G** | 2 Chron. 33. 9–13<br>Ps. 55. 17–23<br>1 Pet. 5. 5b–11<br>Luke 15. 1–10 | Ps. 52; 53<br>Deut. 11. 1–15<br>Acts 27. 1–12 | Ps. [50] 57<br>Gen. 24. 1–27<br>Mark 5. 21–end |
| Ps. **72**; 75<br>Judg. 8. 22–end<br>Luke 15. 1–10 | **G** | For The Nativity of John the Baptist, see 24th | Ezra ch. 7<br>Rom. 11. 25–end | Judg. 8. 22–end<br>Luke 15. 1–10 |
| Ps. 74<br>Judg. 9. 1–21<br>Luke 15. 11–end | **G** | | Ezra 8. 15–end<br>Rom. 12. 1–8 | Judg. 9. 1–21<br>Luke 15. 11–end |
| Ps. 119. 81–104<br>Judg. 9. 22–end<br>Luke 16. 1–18 | **G** | | Ezra ch. 9<br>Rom. 12. 9–end | Judg. 9. 22–end<br>Luke 16. 1–18 |
| Ps. 78. 40–end†<br>Judg. 11. 1–11<br>Luke 16. 19–end<br>*or First EP of Peter and Paul*<br>Ps. 66; 67<br>Ezek. 3. 4–11<br>Gal. 1.13 – 2.8<br>*or, for Peter alone:*<br>Acts 9. 32–end<br>**R ct** | **G** | | Ezra 10. 1–17<br>Rom. 13. 1–7 | Judg. 11. 1–11<br>Luke 16. 19–end<br>*or First EP of Peter*<br>(Ps. 66; 67)<br>Ezek. 3. 4–11<br>Acts 9. 32–end<br>**R ct** |
| | | **PETER THE APOSTLE** | | |
| *EP*: Ps. 124; 138<br>Ezek. 34. 11–16<br>John 21. 15–22<br><br>*EP*: Ps. 124; 138<br>Ezek. 34. 11–16<br>John 21. 15–22 | **R** | Ezek. 3. 4–11<br>Ps. 125<br>Acts 12. 1–11<br>Matt. 16. 13–19 | (Ps. 71; 113)<br>Isa. 49. 1–6<br>Acts 11. 1–18 | (Ps. 124; 138)<br>Ezek. 34. 11–16<br>John 21. 15–22 |
| Ps. 81; ***84***<br>Judg. 12. 1–7<br>Luke 17. 11–19<br>**ct** | **G** | | Neh. ch. 2<br>Rom. 14. 1–12 | Judg. 12. 1–7<br>Luke 17. 11–19<br>**ct** |

# July 2007

| Date | Day | | Sunday Principal Service<br>Weekday Eucharist | Third Service<br>Morning Prayer |
|---|---|---|---|---|
| **1** | S<br>**G** | THE FOURTH SUNDAY AFTER TRINITY **(Proper 8)**<br>*Track 1*<br>2 Kings 2. 1–2, 6–14<br>Ps. 77. [1–2] 11–end<br>Gal. 5. 1, 13–25<br>Luke 9. 51–end | *Track 2*<br>1 Kings 19. 15–16, 19–end<br>Ps. 16<br>Gal. 5. 1, 13–25<br>Luke 9. 51–end | Ps. 64<br>Deut. 15. 1–11<br>Acts 27. [13–32] 33–end |
| **2**<br>DEL 13 | M<br>**G** | | Gen. 18. 16–end<br>Ps. 103. 6–17<br>Matt. 8. 18–22 | Ps. ***80***; 82<br>Neh. ch. 4<br>Rom. 14. 13–end |
| **3** | Tu<br>**R**<br>**G** | THOMAS THE APOSTLE**<br><br>*or, if Thomas is not celebrated:* | Hab. 2. 1–4<br>Ps. 31. 1–6<br>Eph. 2. 19–end<br>John 20. 24–29<br>Gen. 19. 15–29<br>Ps. 26<br>Matt. 8. 23–27 | *MP:* Ps. 92; 146<br>2 Sam. 15. 17–21<br>*or* Ecclus. ch. 2<br>John 11. 1–16<br>Ps. 87; ***89. 1–18***<br>Neh. ch. 5<br>Rom. 15. 1–13 |
| **4** | W<br>**G** | | Gen. 21. 5, 8–20<br>Ps. 34. 1–12<br>Matt. 8. 28–end | Ps. 119. 105–128<br>Neh. 6.1 – 7.4<br>Rom. 15. 14–21 |
| **5** | Th<br>**G** | | Gen. 22. 1–19<br>Ps. 116. 1–7<br>Matt. 9. 1–8 | Ps. 90; **92**<br>Neh. 7.73b – 8.end<br>Rom. 15. 22–end |
| **6** | F<br>**G** | *Thomas More, Scholar, and John Fisher, Bishop of Rochester, Reformation Martyrs, 1535* | Gen. 23. 1–4, 19; 24. 1–8, 62–end<br>Ps. 106. 1–5<br>Matt. 9. 9–13 | Ps. ***88***; (95)<br>Neh. 9. 1–23<br>Rom. 16. 1–16 |
| **7** | Sa<br>**G** | *** | Gen. 27. 1–5a, 15–29<br>Ps. 135. 1–6<br>Matt. 9. 14–17 | Ps. 96; **97**; 100<br>Neh. 9. 24–end<br>Rom. 16. 17–end |
| **8** | S<br>**G** | THE FIFTH SUNDAY AFTER TRINITY **(Proper 9)**<br>*Track 1*<br>2 Kings 5. 1–14<br>Ps. 30<br>Gal. 6. [1–6] 7–16<br>Luke 10. 1–11, 16–20 | *Track 2*<br>Isa. 66. 10–14<br>Ps. 66. 1–8<br>Gal. 6. [1–6] 7–16<br>Luke 10. 1–11, 16–20 | Ps. 74<br>Deut. 24. 10–end<br>Acts 28. 1–16 |
| **9**<br>DEL 14 | M<br>**G** | | Gen. 28. 10–end<br>Ps. 91. 1–10<br>Matt. 9. 18–26 | Ps. ***98***; 99; 101<br>Neh. 12. 27–47<br>2 Cor. 1. 1–14 |
| **10** | Tu<br>**G** | | Gen. 32. 22–end<br>Ps. 17. 1–8<br>Matt. 9. 32–end | Ps. ***106***† (*or* 103)<br>Neh. 13. 1–14<br>2 Cor. 1.15 – 2.4 |
| **11** | W<br>**Gw** | **Benedict of Nursia, Abbot of Monte Cassino, Father of Western Monasticism, c. 550**<br>Com. Religious<br>*also* 1 Cor. 3. 10–11<br>Luke 18. 18–22 | *or* Gen. 41. 55–end; 42. 5–7, 17–end<br>Ps. 33. 1–4, 18–end<br>Matt. 10. 1–7 | Ps. 110; ***111***; 112<br>Neh. 13. 15–end<br>2 Cor. 2. 5–end |
| **12** | Th<br>**G** | | Gen. 44. 18–21, 23–29; 45. 1–5<br>Ps. 105. 11–17<br>Matt. 10. 7–15 | Ps. 113; ***115***<br>Esther ch. 1<br>2 Cor. ch. 3 |
| **13** | F<br>**G** | | Gen. 46. 1–7, 28–30<br>Ps. 37. 3–6, 27–28<br>Matt. 10. 16–23 | Ps. 139<br>Esther ch. 2<br>2 Cor. ch. 4 |

**Common Worship* Morning and Evening Prayer provision for 31 May may be used.

**Thomas the Apostle may be celebrated on 21 December instead of 3 July.

***Thomas Becket may be celebrated on 7 July instead of 29 December.

| Second Service Evening Prayer | | Calendar and Holy Communion | Morning Prayer | Evening Prayer |
|---|---|---|---|---|
| | | **THE FOURTH SUNDAY AFTER TRINITY** | | |
| Ps. [59. 1–6, 18–end] 60<br>Gen. 27. 1–40<br>Mark 6. 1–6 | **G** | Gen. 3. 17–19<br>Ps. 79. 8–10<br>Rom. 8. 18–23<br>Luke 6. 36–42 | Ps. 64<br>Deut. 15. 1–11<br>Acts 27. [13–32] 33–end | Ps. [59. 1–6, 18–end] 60<br>Gen. 27. 1–40<br>Mark 6. 1–6 |
| Ps. ***85***; 86<br>Judg. 13. 1–24<br>Luke 17. 20–end<br>*or First EP of Thomas*<br>Ps. 27<br>Isa. ch. 35<br>Heb. 10.35 – 11.1<br>**R ct** | **Gw** | **The Visitation of the Blessed Virgin Mary***<br>1 Sam. 2. 1–3<br>Ps. 113<br>Gal. 4. 1–5<br>Luke 1. 39–45 | Neh. ch. 4<br>Rom. 14. 13–end | Judg. 13. 1–24<br>Luke 17. 20–end |
| *EP*: Ps. 139<br>Job 42. 1–6<br>1 Pet. 1. 3–12<br><br>Ps. 89. 19–end<br>Judg. ch. 14<br>Luke 18. 1–14 | **G** | | Neh. ch. 5<br>Rom. 15. 1–13 | Judg. ch. 14<br>Luke 18. 1–14 |
| Ps. ***91***; 93<br>Judg. 15.1 – 16.3<br>Luke 18. 15–30 | **Gw** | **Translation of Martin, Bishop of Tours, c. 397**<br>Com. Bishop | Neh. 6.1 – 7.4<br>Rom. 15. 14–21 | Judg. 15.1 – 16.3<br>Luke 18. 15–30 |
| Ps. 94<br>Judg. 16. 4–end<br>Luke 18. 31–end | **G** | | Neh. 7.73b – 8.end<br>Rom. 15. 22–end | Judg. 16. 4–end<br>Luke 18. 31–end |
| Ps. 102<br>Judg. ch. 17<br>Luke 19. 1–10 | **G** | | Neh. 9. 1–23<br>Rom. 16. 1–16 | Judg. ch. 17<br>Luke 19. 1–10 |
| Ps. 104<br>Judg. 18. 1–20, 27–end<br>Luke 19. 11–27<br>**ct** | **G** | | Neh. 9. 24–end<br>Rom. 16. 17–end | Judg. 18. 1–20, 27–end<br>Luke 19. 11–27<br>**ct** |
| | | **THE FIFTH SUNDAY AFTER TRINITY** | | |
| Ps. 65 [70]<br>Gen. 29. 1–20<br>Mark 6. 7–29 | **G** | 1 Kings 19. 19–21<br>Ps. 84. 8–end<br>1 Pet. 3. 8–15a<br>Luke 5. 1–11 | Ps. 73<br>Deut. 24. 10–end<br>Acts 28. 1–16 | Ps. 65 [70]<br>Gen. 29. 1–20<br>Mark 6. 7–29 |
| Ps. ***105***† (*or* 103)<br>1 Sam. 1. 1–20<br>Luke 19. 28–40 | **G** | | Neh. 12. 27–47<br>2 Cor. 1. 1–14 | 1 Sam. 1. 1–20<br>Luke 19. 28–40 |
| Ps. 107†<br>1 Sam. 1.21 – 2.11<br>Luke 19. 41–end | **G** | | Neh. 13. 1–14<br>2 Cor. 1.15 – 2.4 | 1 Sam. 1.21 – 2.11<br>Luke 19. 41–end |
| Ps. 119. 129–152<br>1 Sam. 2. 12–26<br>Luke 20. 1–8 | **G** | | Neh. 13. 15–end<br>2 Cor. 2. 5–end | 1 Sam. 2. 12–26<br>Luke 20. 1–8 |
| Ps. 114; ***116***; 117<br>1 Sam. 2. 27–end<br>Luke 20. 9–19 | **G** | | Esther ch. 1<br>2 Cor. ch. 3 | 1 Sam. 2. 27–end<br>Luke 20. 9–19 |
| Ps. ***130***; 131; 137<br>1 Sam. 3.1 – 4.1a<br>Luke 20. 20–26 | **G** | | Esther ch. 2<br>2 Cor. ch. 4 | 1 Sam. 3.1 – 4.1a<br>Luke 20. 20–26 |

# July 2007

| Date | Day | | Sunday Principal Service<br>Weekday Eucharist | Third Service<br>Morning Prayer |
|---|---|---|---|---|
| **14** | Sa | **John Keble, Priest, Tractarian, Poet, 1866** | | |
| | | Com. Pastor | *or* Gen. 49. 29–end; 50. 15–25 | Ps. 120; ***121***; 122 |
| | | *also* Lam. 3. 19–26 | Ps. 105. 1–7 | Esther ch. 3 |
| | | Matt. 5. 1–8 | Matt. 10. 24–33 | 2 Cor. ch. 5 |
| | **Gw** | | | |
| **15** | **S** | THE SIXTH SUNDAY AFTER TRINITY **(Proper 10)** | | |
| | | *Track 1* | *Track 2* | |
| | | Amos 7. 7–end | Deut. 30. 9–14 | Ps. 76 |
| | | Ps. 82 | Ps. 25. 1–10 | Deut. 28. 1–14 |
| | | Col. 1. 1–14 | Col. 1. 1–14 | Acts 28. 17–end |
| | **G** | Luke 10. 25–37 | Luke 10. 25–37 | |
| **16** | M | *Osmund, Bishop of Salisbury, 1099* | | |
| | | | Exod. 1. 8–14, 22 | Ps. 123; 124; 125; ***126*** |
| DEL 15 | | | Ps. 124 | Esther ch. 4 |
| | **G** | | Matt. 10.34 – 11.1 | 2 Cor. 6.1 – 7.1 |
| **17** | Tu | | Exod. 2. 1–15 | Ps. ***132***; 133 |
| | | | Ps. 69. 1–2, 31–end | Esther ch. 5 |
| | **G** | | Matt. 11. 20–24 | 2 Cor. 7. 2–end |
| **18** | W | *Elizabeth Ferard, first Deaconess of the Church of England, Founder of the Community of St Andrew, 1883* | | |
| | | | Exod. 3. 1–6, 9–12 | Ps. 119. 153–end |
| | | | Ps. 103. 1–7 | Esther 6. 1–13 |
| | **G** | | Matt. 11. 25–27 | 2 Cor. 8. 1–15 |
| **19** | Th | **Gregory, Bishop of Nyssa, and his sister Macrina, Deaconess, Teachers, c. 394 and c. 379** | | |
| | | Com. Teacher | *or* Exod. 3. 13–20 | Ps. ***143***; 146 |
| | | *esp.* 1 Cor. 2. 9–13 | Ps. 105. 1–2, 23 | Esther 6.14 – 7.end |
| | **Gw** | *also* Wisd. 9. 13–17 | Matt. 11. 28–end | 2 Cor. 8.16 – 9.5 |
| **20** | F | *Margaret of Antioch, Martyr, 4th century; Bartolomé de las Casas, Apostle to the Indies, 1566* | | |
| | | | Exod. 11.10 – 12.14 | Ps. 142; ***144*** |
| | | | Ps. 116. 10–end | Esther ch. 8 |
| | **G** | | Matt. 12. 1–8 | 2 Cor. 9. 6–end |
| **21** | Sa | | Exod. 12. 37–42 | Ps. 147 |
| | | | Ps. 136. 1–4, 10–15 | Esther 9. 20–28 |
| | | | Matt. 12. 14–21 | 2 Cor. ch. 10 |
| | **G** | | | |
| **22** | **S** | MARY MAGDALENE (or transferred to 23rd) | | |
| | | | Song of Sol. 3. 1–4 | *MP:* Ps. 30; 32; 150 |
| | | | Ps. 42. 1–10 | 1 Sam. 16. 14–end |
| | | | 2 Cor. 5. 14–17 | Luke 8. 1–3 |
| | **W** | | John 20. 1–2, 11–18 | |
| | | *or, for The Seventh Sunday after Trinity (Proper 11):* | | |
| | | *Track 1* | *Track 2* | |
| | | Amos 8. 1–12 | Gen. 18. 1–10a | Ps. 82; 100 |
| | | Ps. 52 | Ps. 15 | Deut. 30. 1–10 |
| | | Col. 1. 15–28 | Col. 1. 15–28 | 1 Pet. 3. 8–18 |
| | **G** | Luke 10. 38–end | Luke 10. 38–end | |
| **23** | M | For Mary Magdalene, see 22nd | | |
| | | *Bridget of Sweden, Abbess of Vadstena, 1373* | | |
| DEL 16 | | | Exod. 14. 5–18 | Ps. ***1***; 2; 3 |
| | | | Ps. 136. 1–4, 10–15 | Jer. ch. 26 |
| | | | *or Canticle:* Exod. 15. 1–6 | 2 Cor. 11. 1–15 |
| | **G** | | Matt. 12. 38–42 | |

| Second Service Evening Prayer | | Calendar and Holy Communion | Morning Prayer | Evening Prayer |
|---|---|---|---|---|
| Ps. 118<br>I Sam. 4. 1b–end<br>Luke 20. 27–40<br>**ct** | **G** | | Esther ch. 3<br>2 Cor. ch. 5 | I Sam. 4. 1b–end<br>Luke 20. 27–40<br>**ct** |
| Ps. 77. 1–12 [13–end]<br>Gen. 32. 9–30<br>Mark 7. 1–23 | **G** | **THE SIXTH SUNDAY AFTER TRINITY**<br>Gen. 4. 2b–15<br>Ps. 90. 12–end<br>Rom. 6. 3–11<br>Matt. 5. 20–26 | Ps. 76<br>Deut. 28. 1–14<br>Acts 28. 17–end | Ps. 77. 1–12 [13–end]<br>Gen. 32. 9–30<br>Mark 7. 1–23 |
| Ps. ***127***; 128; 129<br>I Sam. ch. 5<br>Luke 20.41 – 21.4 | **G** | | Esther ch. 4<br>2 Cor. 6.1 – 7.1 | I Sam. ch. 5<br>Luke 20.41 – 21.4 |
| Ps. (134) ***135***<br>I Sam. 6. 1–16<br>Luke 21. 5–19 | **G** | | Esther ch. 5<br>2 Cor. 7. 2–end | I Sam. 6. 1–16<br>Luke 21. 5–19 |
| Ps. 136<br>I Sam. ch. 7<br>Luke 21. 20–28 | **G** | | Esther 6. 1–13<br>2 Cor. 8. 1–15 | I Sam. ch. 7<br>Luke 21. 20–28 |
| Ps. ***138***; 140; 141<br>I Sam. ch. 8<br>Luke 21. 29–end | **G** | | Esther 6.14 – 7.end<br>2 Cor. 8.16 – 9.5 | I Sam. ch. 8<br>Luke 21. 29–end |
| Ps. 145<br>I Sam. 9. 1–14<br>Luke 22. 1–13 | **Gr** | **Margaret of Antioch, Martyr, 4th century**<br>Com. Virgin Martyr | Esther ch. 8<br>2 Cor. 9. 6–end | I Sam. 9. 1–14<br>Luke 22. 1–13 |
| Ps. ***148***; 149; 150<br>I Sam. 9.15 – 10.1<br>Luke 22. 14–23<br>**ct**<br>*or First EP of Mary Magdalene*<br>Ps. 139<br>Isa. 25. 1–9<br>2 Cor. 1. 3–7<br>**W ct** | **G** | | Esther 9. 20–28<br>2 Cor. ch. 10 | I Sam. 9.15 – 10.1<br>Luke 22. 14–23<br>**ct**<br>*or First EP of Mary Magdalene*<br>(Ps. 139)<br>Isa. 25. 1–9<br>2 Cor. 1. 3–7<br>**W ct** |
| *EP:* Ps. 63<br>Zeph. 3. 14–end<br>Mark 15.40 – 16.7 | **W** | **MARY MAGDALENE** (or transferred to 23rd)<br>Zeph. 3. 14–end<br>Ps. 30. 1–5<br>2 Cor. 5. 14–17<br>John 20. 11–18 | (Ps. 30; 32; 150)<br>I Sam. 16. 14–end<br>Luke 8. 1–3 | (Ps. 63)<br>Song of Sol. 3. 1–4<br>Mark 15.40 – 16.7 |
| Ps. 81<br>Gen. 41. 1–16, 25–37<br>I Cor. 4. 8–13<br>*Gospel:* John 4. 31–35 | **G** | *or, for The Seventh Sunday after Trinity:*<br>I Kings 17. 8–16<br>Ps. 34. 11–end<br>Rom. 6. 19–end<br>Mark 8. 1–10a | Ps. 82; 100<br>Deut. 30. 1–10<br>I Pet. 3. 8–18 | Ps. 81<br>Gen. 41. 1–16, 25–37<br>I Cor. 4. 8–13 |
| Ps. **4**; 7<br>I Sam. 10. 1–16<br>Luke 22. 24–30 | **G** | For Mary Magdalene, see 22nd | Jer. ch. 26<br>2 Cor. 11. 1–15 | I Sam. 10. 1–16<br>Luke 22. 24–30 |

## July 2007

| Date | Day / Colour | | Sunday Principal Service<br>Weekday Eucharist | Third Service<br>Morning Prayer |
|---|---|---|---|---|
| **24** | Tu<br>**G** | | Exod. 14.21 – 15.1<br>Ps. 105. 37–44<br>*or Canticle*: Exod. 15. 8–10, 12, 17<br>Matt. 12. 46–end | Ps. **5**; 6 (8)<br>Jer. ch. 28<br>2 Cor. 11. 16–end |
| **25** | W<br>**R** | JAMES THE APOSTLE<br>*The reading from Acts must be used as either the first or second reading at the Principal Service.* | Jer. 45. 1–5<br>*or* Acts 11.27 – 12.2<br>Ps. 126<br>Acts 11.27 – 12.2<br>*or* 2 Cor. 4. 7–15<br>Matt. 20. 20–28 | *MP*: Ps. 7; 29; 117<br>2 Kings 1. 9–15<br>Luke 9. 46–56 |
| **26** | Th<br>**Gw** | **Anne and Joachim, Parents of the Blessed Virgin Mary**<br>Zeph. 3. 14–18a<br>Ps. 127<br>Rom. 8. 28–30<br>Matt. 13. 16–17 | *or* Exod. 19. 1–2, 9–11, 16–20<br>*Canticle:* Bless the Lord<br>Matt. 13. 10–17 | Ps. 14; ***15***; 16<br>Jer. 30. 1–11<br>2 Cor. ch. 13 |
| **27** | F<br>**G** | *Brooke Foss Westcott, Bishop of Durham, Teacher, 1901* | Exod. 20. 1–17<br>Ps. 19. 7–11<br>Matt. 13. 18–23 | Ps. 17; ***19***<br>Jer. 30. 12–22<br>James 1. 1–11 |
| **28** | Sa<br>**G** | | Exod. 24. 3–8<br>Ps. 50. 1–6, 14–15<br>Matt. 13. 24–30 | Ps. 20; 21; ***23***<br>Jer. 31. 1–22<br>James 1. 12–end |
| **29** | **S**<br>**G** | THE EIGHTH SUNDAY AFTER TRINITY **(Proper 12)**<br>*Track 1*<br>Hos. 1. 2–10<br>Ps. 85. 1–7 [8–end]<br>Col. 2. 6–15 [16–19]<br>Luke 11. 1–13 | *Track 2*<br>Gen. 18. 20–32<br>Ps. 138<br>Col. 2. 6–15 [16–19]<br>Luke 11. 1–13 | Ps. 95<br>Song of Sol. ch. 2<br>*or* 1 Macc. 2. [1–14] 15–22<br>1 Pet. 4. 7–14 |
| **30**<br>DEL 17 | M<br>**Gw** | **William Wilberforce, Social Reformer, 1833**<br>Com. Saint<br>*also* Job 31. 16–23<br>Gal. 3. 26–end; 4. 6–7<br>Luke 4. 16–21 | *or* Exod. 32. 15–24, 30–34<br>Ps. 106. 18–22<br>Matt. 13. 31–35 | Ps. 27; ***30***<br>Jer. 31. 23–25, 27–37<br>James 2. 1–13 |
| **31** | Tu<br>**G** | *Ignatius of Loyola, Founder of the Society of Jesus, 1556* | Exod. 33. 7–11; 34. 5–9, 28<br>Ps. 103. 8–12<br>Matt. 13. 36–43 | Ps. 32; ***36***<br>Jer. 32. 1–15<br>James 2. 14–end |

## August 2007

| Date | Day / Colour | | Sunday Principal Service<br>Weekday Eucharist | Third Service<br>Morning Prayer |
|---|---|---|---|---|
| **1** | W<br>**G** | | Exod. 34. 29–end<br>Ps. 99<br>Matt. 13. 44–46 | Ps. 34<br>Jer. 33. 1–13<br>James ch. 3 |
| **2** | Th<br>**G** | | Exod. 40. 16–21, 34–end<br>Ps. 84. 1–6<br>Matt. 13. 47–53 | Ps. 37†<br>Jer. 33. 14–end<br>James 4. 1–12 |
| **3** | F<br>**G** | | Lev. 23. 1, 4–11, 15–16, 27, 34–37<br>Ps. 81. 1–8<br>Matt. 13. 54–end | Ps. 31<br>Jer. ch. 35<br>James 4.13 – 5.6 |
| **4** | Sa<br>**G** | *Jean-Baptiste Vianney, Curé d'Ars, Spiritual Guide, 1859* | Lev. 25. 1, 8–17<br>Ps. 67<br>Matt. 14. 1–12 | Ps. 41; **42**; 43<br>Jer. 36. 1–18<br>James 5. 7–end |

| Second Service Evening Prayer | | Calendar and Holy Communion | Morning Prayer | Evening Prayer |
|---|---|---|---|---|
| Ps. **9**; 10† I Sam. 10. 17–end Luke 22. 31–38 *or First EP of James* Ps. 144 Deut. 30. 11–end Mark 5. 21–end **R ct** | **G** | | Jer. ch. 28 2 Cor. 11. 16–end | I Sam. 10. 17–end Luke 22. 31–38 *or First EP of James* (Ps. 144) Deut. 30. 11–end Mark 5. 21–end **R ct** |
| *EP:* Ps. 94 Jer. 26. 1–15 Mark 1. 14–20 | **R** | **JAMES THE APOSTLE** 2 Kings 1. 9–15 Ps. 15 Acts 11.27 – 12.3a Matt. 20. 20–28 | (Ps. 7; 29; 117) Jer. 45. 1–5 Luke 9. 46–56 | (Ps. 94) Jer. 26. 1–15 Mark 1. 14–20 |
| Ps. 18† I Sam. ch. 12 Luke 22. 47–62 | **Gw** | **Anne, Mother of the Blessed Virgin Mary** Com. Saint | Jer. 30. 1–11 2 Cor. ch. 13 | I Sam. ch. 12 Luke 22. 47–62 |
| Ps. 22 I Sam. 13. 5–18 Luke 22. 63–end | **G** | | Jer. 30. 12–22 James 1. 1–11 | I Sam. 13. 5–18 Luke 22. 63–end |
| Ps. ***24***; 25 I Sam. 13.19 – 14.15 Luke 23. 1–12 **ct** | **G** | | Jer. 31. 1–22 James 1. 12–end | I Sam. 13.19 – 14.15 Luke 23. 1–12 **ct** |
| Ps. 88. 1–10 [11–end] Gen. 42. 1– 25 I Cor. 10. 1–24 *Gospel:* Matt. 13. 24–30 [31–43] | **G** | **THE EIGHTH SUNDAY AFTER TRINITY** Jer. 23. 16–24 Ps. 31. 1–6 Rom. 8. 12–17 Matt. 7. 15–21 | Ps. 96 Song of Sol. ch. 2 *or* I Macc. 2. [1–14] 15–22 I Pet. 4. 7–14 | Ps. 88. 1–10 [11–end] Gen. 42. 1– 25 I Cor. 9. 16–end |
| Ps. 26; ***28***; 29 I Sam. 14. 24–46 Luke 23. 13–25 | **G** | | Jer. 31. 23–25, 27–37 James 2. 1–13 | I Sam. 14. 24–46 Luke 23. 13–25 |
| Ps. 33 I Sam. 15. 1–23 Luke 23. 26–43 | **G** | | Jer. 32. 1–15 James 2. 14–end | I Sam. 15. 1–23 Luke 23. 26–43 |
| | | | | |
| Ps. 119. 33–56 I Sam. ch. 16 Luke 23. 44–56a | **G** | Lammas Day | Jer. 33. 1–13 James ch. 3 | I Sam. ch. 16 Luke 23. 44–56a |
| Ps. 39; ***40*** I Sam. 17. 1–30 Luke 23.56b – 24.12 | **G** | | Jer. 33. 14–end James 4. 1–12 | I Sam. 17. 1–30 Luke 23.56b – 24.12 |
| Ps. 35 I Sam. 17. 31–54 Luke 24. 13–35 | **G** | | Jer. ch. 35 James 4.13 – 5.6 | I Sam. 17. 31–54 Luke 24. 13–35 |
| Ps. 45; ***46*** I Sam. 17.55 – 18.16 Luke 24. 36–end **ct** | **G** | | Jer. 36. 1–18 James 5. 7–end | I Sam. 17.55 – 18.16 Luke 24. 36–end **ct** |

# August 2007

| Date | Day | | Sunday Principal Service<br>Weekday Eucharist | Third Service<br>Morning Prayer |
|---|---|---|---|---|
| **5** | S<br>G | THE NINTH SUNDAY AFTER TRINITY **(Proper 13)**<br>*Track 1*<br>Hos. 11. 1–11<br>Ps. 107. 1–9 [43]<br>Col. 3. 1–11<br>Luke 12. 13–21 | *Track 2*<br>Eccles. 1. 2, 12–14; 2. 18–23<br>Ps. 49. 1–9 [10–12]<br>Col. 3. 1–11<br>Luke 12. 13–21 | Ps. 106. 1–10<br>Song of Sol. 5. 2–end<br>*or* 1 Macc. 3. 1–12<br>2 Pet. 1. 1–15 |
| **6**<br>DEL 18 | M<br>W | THE TRANSFIGURATION OF OUR LORD | Dan. 7. 9–10, 13–14<br>Ps. 97<br>2 Pet. 1. 16–19<br>Luke 9. 28–36 | *MP:* Ps. 27; 150<br>Ecclus. 48. 1–10<br>*or* 1 Kings 19. 1–16<br>1 John 3. 1–3 |
| **7** | Tu<br>G | *John Mason Neale, Priest, Hymn Writer, 1866* | Num. 12. 1–13<br>Ps. 51. 1–8<br>Matt. 14. 22–end *or* 15. 1–2, 10–14 | Ps. ***48***; 52<br>Jer. ch. 37<br>Mark 1. 14–20 |
| **8** | W<br>Gw | **Dominic, Priest, Founder of the Order of Preachers, 1221**<br>Com. Religious<br>*also* Ecclus. 39. 1–10 | *or* Num. 13.1–2, 10–14, 25 – 14.1, 26–35<br>Ps. 106. 14–24<br>Matt. 15. 21–28 | Ps. 119. 57–80<br>Jer. 38. 1–13<br>Mark 1. 21–28 |
| **9** | Th<br>Gw | **Mary Sumner, Founder of the Mothers' Union, 1921**<br>Com. Saint<br>*also* Heb. 13. 1–5 | *or* Num. 20. 1–13<br>Ps. 95. 1, 8–end<br>Matt. 16. 13–23 | Ps. 56; **57** (63†)<br>Jer. 38. 14–end<br>Mark 1. 29–end |
| **10** | F<br>Gr | **Laurence, Deacon at Rome, Martyr, 258**<br>Com. Martyr<br>*also* 2 Cor. 9. 6–10 | *or* Deut. 4. 32–40<br>Ps. 77. 11–end<br>Matt. 16. 24–end | Ps. ***51***; 54<br>Jer. ch. 39<br>Mark 2. 1–12 |
| **11** | Sa<br>Gw | **Clare of Assisi, Founder of the Minoresses (Poor Clares), 1253**<br>*John Henry Newman, Priest, Tractarian, 1890*<br>Com. Religious<br>*esp.* Song of Sol. 8. 6–7 | *or* Deut. 6. 4–13<br>Ps. 18. 1–2, 48–end<br>Matt. 17. 14–20 | Ps. 68<br>Jer. ch. 40<br>Mark 2. 13–22 |
| **12** | S<br>G | THE TENTH SUNDAY AFTER TRINITY **(Proper 14)**<br>*Track 1*<br>Isa. 1. 1, 10–20<br>Ps. 50. 1–7 [8, 23–24]<br>Heb. 11. 1–3, 8–16<br>Luke 12. 32–40 | *Track 2*<br>Gen. 15. 1–6<br>Ps. 33. 12–21 [22]<br>Heb. 11. 1–3, 8–16<br>Luke 12. 32–40 | Ps. 115<br>Song of Sol. 8. 5–7<br>*or* 1 Macc. 14. 4–15<br>2 Pet. 3. 8–13 |
| **13**<br>DEL 19 | M<br>Gw | **Jeremy Taylor, Bishop of Down and Connor, Teacher, 1667**<br>*Florence Nightingale, Nurse, Social Reformer, 1910; Octavia Hill, Social Reformer, 1912*<br>Com. Teacher<br>*also* Titus 2. 7–8, 11–14 | *or* Deut. 10. 12–end<br>Ps. 147. 13–end<br>Matt. 17. 22–end | Ps. 71<br>Jer. ch. 41<br>Mark 2.23 – 3.6 |
| **14** | Tu<br>G | *Maximilian Kolbe, Friar, Martyr, 1941* | Deut. 31. 1–8<br>Ps. 107. 1–3, 42–end<br>Matt. 18. 1–5, 10, 12–14 | Ps. 73<br>Jer. ch. 42<br>Mark 3. 7–19a |

| Second Service Evening Prayer | | Calendar and Holy Communion | Morning Prayer | Evening Prayer |
|---|---|---|---|---|
| | | **THE NINTH SUNDAY AFTER TRINITY** | | |
| Ps. 107. 1–12 [13–32]<br>Gen. 50. 4–end<br>1 Cor. 14. 1–19<br>*Gospel:* Mark 6. 45–52<br>*or First EP of The Transfiguration*<br>Ps. 99; 110<br>Exod. 24. 12–end<br>John 12. 27–36a<br>**W ct** | **G** | Num. 10.35 – 11.3<br>Ps. 95<br>1 Cor. 10. 1–13<br>Luke 16. 1–9<br>*or* Luke 15. 11–end | Ps. 106. 1–10<br>Song of Sol. 5. 2–end<br>*or* 1 Macc. 3. 1–12<br>2 Pet. 1. 1–15 | Ps. 107. 1–12 [13–32]<br>Gen. 50. 4–end<br>1 Cor. 14. 1–19<br>*or First EP of The Transfiguration*<br>(Ps. 99; 110)<br>Exod. 24. 12–end<br>John 12. 27–36a<br>**W ct** |
| | | **THE TRANSFIGURATION OF OUR LORD** | | |
| *EP:* Ps. 72<br>Exod. 34. 29–end<br>2 Cor. ch. 3 | **W** | Exod. 24. 12–end<br>Ps. 84. 1–7<br>1 John 3. 1–3<br>Mark 9. 2–7 | Ps. 27; 150<br>Ecclus. 48. 1–10<br>*or* 1 Kings 19. 1–16<br>2 Pet. 1. 16–19 | Ps. 72<br>Exod. 34. 29–end<br>2 Cor. ch. 3 |
| | | **The Name of Jesus** | | |
| Ps. 50<br>1 Sam. 20. 1–17<br>Acts 1. 15–end | **Gw** | Jer. 14. 7–9<br>Ps. 8<br>Acts 4. 8–12<br>Matt. 1. 20–23 | Jer. ch. 37<br>Mark 1. 14–20 | 1 Sam. 20. 1–17<br>Acts 1. 15–end |
| Ps. **59**; 60 (67)<br>1 Sam. 20. 18–end<br>Acts 2. 1–21 | **G** | | Jer. 38. 1–13<br>Mark 1. 21–28 | 1 Sam. 20. 18–end<br>Acts 2. 1–21 |
| Ps. 61; **62**; 64<br>1 Sam. 21.1 – 22.5<br>Acts 2. 22–36 | **G** | | Jer. 38. 14–end<br>Mark 1. 29–end | 1 Sam. 21.1 – 22.5<br>Acts 2. 22–36 |
| | | **Laurence, Deacon at Rome, Martyr, 258** | | |
| Ps. 38<br>1 Sam. 22. 6–end<br>Acts 2. 37–end | **Gr** | Com. Martyr | Jer. ch. 39<br>Mark 2. 1–12 | 1 Sam. 22. 6–end<br>Acts 2. 37–end |
| Ps. 65; **66**<br>1 Sam. ch. 23<br>Acts 3. 1–10<br>**ct** | **G** | | Jer. ch. 40<br>Mark 2. 13–22 | 1 Sam. ch. 23<br>Acts 3. 1–10<br>**ct** |
| | | **THE TENTH SUNDAY AFTER TRINITY** | | |
| Ps. 108 [116]<br>Isa. 11.10 – 12.end<br>2 Cor. 1. 1–22<br>*Gospel:* Mark 7. 24–30 | **G** | Jer. 7. 9–15<br>Ps. 17. 1–8<br>1 Cor. 12. 1–11<br>Luke 19. 41–47a | Ps. 115<br>Song of Sol. 8. 5–7<br>*or* 1 Macc. 14. 4–15<br>2 Pet. 3. 8–13 | Ps. 108 [116]<br>Isa. 11.10 – 12.end<br>2 Cor. 1. 1–22 |
| Ps. **72**; 75<br>1 Sam. ch. 24<br>Acts 3. 11–end | **G** | | Jer. ch. 41<br>Mark 2.23 – 3.6 | 1 Sam. ch. 24<br>Acts 3. 11–end |
| Ps. 74<br>1 Sam. ch. 26<br>Acts 4. 1–12<br>*or First EP of The Blessed Virgin Mary*<br>Ps. 72<br>Prov. 8. 22–31<br>John 19. 23–27<br>**W ct** | **G** | | Jer. ch. 42<br>Mark 3. 7–19a | 1 Sam. ch. 26<br>Acts 4. 1–12 |

# August 2007

| Date | | | Sunday Principal Service<br>Weekday Eucharist | Third Service<br>Morning Prayer |
|---|---|---|---|---|
| **15** | W<br>W | THE BLESSED VIRGIN MARY* | Isa. 61. 10–end<br>*or* Rev. 11.19 – 12.6, 10<br>Ps. 45. 10–end<br>Gal. 4. 4–7<br>Luke 1. 46–55 | *MP*: Ps. 98; 138; 147. 1–12<br>Isa. 7. 10–15<br>Luke 11. 27–28 |
| | G | *or, if The Blessed Virgin Mary is celebrated on 8 September:* | Deut. ch. 34<br>Ps. 66. 14–end<br>Matt. 18. 15–20 | Ps. 77<br>Jer. ch. 43<br>Mark 3. 19b–end |
| **16** | Th<br>G | | Josh. 3. 7–11, 13–17<br>Ps. 114<br>Matt. 18.21 – 19.1 | Ps. 78. 1–39†<br>Jer. 44. 1–14<br>Mark 4. 1–20 |
| **17** | F<br>G | | Josh. 24. 1–13<br>Ps. 136. 1–3, 16–22<br>Matt. 19. 3–12 | Ps. 55<br>Jer. 44. 15–end<br>Mark 4. 21–34 |
| **18** | Sa<br>G | | Josh. 24. 14–29<br>Ps. 16. 1, 5–end<br>Matt. 19. 13–15 | Ps. ***76***; 79<br>Jer. ch. 45<br>Mark 4. 35–end |
| **19** | S<br>G | THE ELEVENTH SUNDAY AFTER TRINITY **(Proper 15)**<br>*Track 1*<br>Isa. 5. 1–7<br>Ps. 80. [1–2] 9–end<br>Heb. 11.29 – 12.2<br>Luke 12. 49–56 | *Track 2*<br>Jer. 23. 23–29<br>Ps. 82<br>Heb. 11.29 – 12.2<br>Luke 12. 49–56 | Ps. 119. 33–48<br>Jonah ch. 1<br>*or* Ecclus. 3. 1–15<br>2 Pet. 3. 14–end |
| **20**<br>DEL 20 | M<br>Gw | **Bernard, Abbot of Clairvaux, Teacher, 1153**<br>*William and Catherine Booth, Founders of the Salvation Army, 1912 and 1890*<br>Com. Teacher<br>*esp.* Rev. 19. 5–9 | *or* Judg. 2. 11–19<br>Ps. 106. 34–42<br>Matt. 19. 16–22 | Ps. ***80***; 82<br>Mic. 1. 1–9<br>Mark 5. 1–20 |
| **21** | Tu<br>G | | Judg. 6. 11–24<br>Ps. 85. 8–end<br>Matt. 19. 23–end | Ps. 87; ***89. 1–18***<br>Mic. ch. 2<br>Mark 5. 21–34 |
| **22** | W<br>G | | Judg. 9. 6–15<br>Ps. 21. 1–6<br>Matt. 20. 1–16 | Ps. 119. 105–128<br>Mic. ch. 3<br>Mark 5. 35–end |
| **23** | Th<br>G | | Judg. 11. 29–end<br>Ps. 40. 4–11<br>Matt. 22. 1–14 | Ps. 90; **92**<br>Mic. 4.1 – 5.1<br>Mark 6. 1–13 |
| **24** | F<br>R | BARTHOLOMEW THE APOSTLE<br>*The reading from Acts must be used as either the first or second reading at the Eucharist.* | Isa. 43. 8–13<br>*or* Acts 5. 12–16<br>Ps. 145. 1–7<br>Acts 5. 12–16<br>*or* 1 Cor. 4. 9–15<br>Luke 22. 24–30 | *MP*: Ps. 86; 117<br>Gen. 28. 10–17<br>John 1. 43–end |
| **25** | Sa<br>G | | Ruth 2. 1–3, 8–11; 4. 13–17<br>Ps. 128<br>Matt. 23. 1–12 | Ps. 96; **97**; 100<br>Mic. ch. 6<br>Mark 6. 30–44 |
| **26** | S<br>G | THE TWELFTH SUNDAY AFTER TRINITY **(Proper 16)**<br>*Track 1*<br>Jer. 1. 4–10<br>Ps. 71. 1–6<br>Heb. 12. 18–end<br>Luke 13. 10–17 | *Track 2*<br>Isa. 58. 9b–end<br>Ps. 103. 1–8<br>Heb. 12. 18–end<br>Luke 13. 10–17 | Ps. 119. 73–88<br>Jonah ch. 2<br>*or* Ecclus. 3. 17–29<br>Rev. ch. 1 |

*The Blessed Virgin Mary may be celebrated on 8 September instead of 15 August.

| Second Service Evening Prayer | | Calendar and Holy Communion | Morning Prayer | Evening Prayer |
|---|---|---|---|---|
| | | To celebrate The Blessed Virgin Mary, see *Common Worship* provision. | | |
| *EP*: Ps. 132<br>Song of Sol. 2. 1–7<br>Acts 1. 6–14<br><br>Ps. 119. 81–104<br>1 Sam. 28. 3–end<br>Acts 4. 13–31 | G | | Jer. ch. 43<br>Mark 3. 19b–end | 1 Sam. 28. 3–end<br>Acts 4. 13–31 |
| Ps. 78. 40–end†<br>1 Sam. ch. 31<br>Acts 4.32 – 5.11 | G | | Jer. 44. 1–14<br>Mark 4. 1–20 | 1 Sam. ch. 31<br>Acts 4.32 – 5.11 |
| Ps. 69<br>2 Sam. ch. 1<br>Acts 5. 12–26 | G | | Jer. 44. 15–end<br>Mark 4. 21–34 | 2 Sam. ch. 1<br>Acts 5. 12–26 |
| Ps. 81; ***84***<br>2 Sam. 2. 1–11<br>Acts 5. 27–end<br>**ct** | G | | Jer. ch. 45<br>Mark 4. 35–end | 2 Sam. 2. 1–11<br>Acts 5. 27–end<br>**ct** |
| | | **THE ELEVENTH SUNDAY AFTER TRINITY** | | |
| Ps. 119. 17–24 [25–32]<br>Isa. 28. 9–22<br>2 Cor. 8. 1–9<br>*Gospel:* Matt. 20. 1–16 | G | 1 Kings 3. 5–15<br>Ps. 28<br>1 Cor. 15. 1–11<br>Luke 18. 9–14 | Ps. 119. 33–48<br>Jonah ch. 1<br>*or* Ecclus. 3. 1–15<br>2 Pet. 3. 14–end | Ps. 119. 17–24 [25–32]<br>Isa. 28. 9–22<br>2 Cor. 8. 1–9 |
| Ps. ***85***; 86<br>2 Sam. 3. 12–end<br>Acts ch. 6 | G | | Mic. 1. 1–9<br>Mark 5. 1–20 | 2 Sam. 3. 12–end<br>Acts ch. 6 |
| Ps. 89. 19–end<br>2 Sam. 5. 1–12<br>Acts 7. 1–16 | G | | Mic. ch. 2<br>Mark 5. 21–34 | 2 Sam. 5. 1–12<br>Acts 7. 1–16 |
| Ps. ***91***; 93<br>2 Sam. 6. 1–19<br>Acts 7. 17–43 | G | | Mic. ch. 3<br>Mark 5. 35–end | 2 Sam. 6. 1–19<br>Acts 7. 17–43 |
| Ps. 94<br>2 Sam. 7. 1–17<br>Acts 7. 44–53<br>*or First EP of Bartholomew*<br>Ps. 97<br>Isa. 61. 1–9<br>2 Cor. 6. 1–10<br>**R ct** | G | | Mic. 4.1 – 5.1<br>Mark 6. 1–13 | 2 Sam. 7. 1–17<br>Acts 7. 44–53<br>*or First EP of Bartholomew*<br>(Ps. 97)<br>Isa. 61. 1–9<br>2 Cor. 6. 1–10<br>**R ct** |
| *EP*: Ps. 91; 116<br>Ecclus. 39. 1–10<br>*or* Deut. 18. 15–19<br>Matt. 10. 1–22 | R | **BARTHOLOMEW THE APOSTLE**<br>Gen. 28. 10–17<br>Ps. 15<br>Acts 5. 12–16<br>Luke 22. 24–30 | (Ps. 86; 117)<br>Isa. 43. 8–13<br>John 1. 43–end | (Ps. 91; 116)<br>Ecclus. 39. 1–10<br>*or* Deut. 18. 15–19<br>Matt. 10. 1–22 |
| Ps. 104<br>2 Sam. ch. 9<br>Acts 8. 4–25<br>**ct** | G | | Mic. ch. 6<br>Mark 6. 30–44 | 2 Sam. ch. 9<br>Acts 8. 4–25<br>**ct** |
| | | **THE TWELFTH SUNDAY AFTER TRINITY** | | |
| Ps. 119. 49–56 [57–72]<br>Isa. 30. 8–21<br>2 Cor. ch. 9<br>*Gospel:* Matt. 21. 28–32 | G | Exod. 34. 29–end<br>Ps. 34. 1–10<br>2 Cor. 3. 4–9<br>Mark 7. 31–37 | Ps. 119. 73–88<br>Jonah ch. 2<br>*or* Ecclus. 3. 17–29<br>Rev. ch. 1 | Ps. 119. 49–56 [57–72]<br>Isa. 30. 8–21<br>2 Cor. ch. 9 |

## August 2007

| Date | Day | Sunday Principal Service<br>Weekday Eucharist | | Third Service<br>Morning Prayer |
|---|---|---|---|---|
| **27**<br>DEL 21 | M<br>**Gw** | **Monica, Mother of Augustine of Hippo, 387**<br>Com. Saint<br>*also* Ecclus. 26. 1–3, 13–16 | <br>*or* 1 Thess. 1. 2–5, 8–10<br>Ps. 149. 1–5<br>Matt. 23. 13–22 | <br>Ps. ***98***; 99; 101<br>Mic. 7. 1–7<br>Mark 6. 45–end |
| **28** | Tu<br>**Gw** | **Augustine, Bishop of Hippo, Teacher, 430**<br>Com. Teacher<br>*esp.* Ecclus. 39. 1–10<br>*also* Rom. 13. 11–13 | <br>*or* 1 Thess. 2. 1–8<br>Ps. 139. 1–9<br>Matt. 23. 23–26 | <br>Ps. ***106***† (*or* 103)<br>Mic. 7. 8–end<br>Mark 7. 1–13 |
| **29** | W<br>**Gr** | **The Beheading of John the Baptist**<br>Jer. 1. 4–10<br>Ps. 11<br>Heb. 11.32 – 12.2<br>Matt. 14. 1–12 | <br>*or* 1 Thess. 2. 9–13<br>Ps. 126<br>Matt. 23. 27–32 | <br>Ps. 110; ***111***; 112<br>Hab. 1. 1–11<br>Mark 7. 14–23 |
| **30** | Th<br>**Gw** | **John Bunyan, Spiritual Writer, 1688**<br>Com. Teacher<br>*also* Heb. 12. 1–2<br>Luke 21. 21, 34–36 | <br>*or* 1 Thess. 3. 7–end<br>Ps. 90. 13–end<br>Matt. 24. 42–end | <br>Ps. 113; ***115***<br>Hab. 1.12 – 2.5<br>Mark 7. 24–30 |
| **31** | F<br>**Gw** | **Aidan, Bishop of Lindisfarne, Missionary, 651**<br>Com. Missionary<br>*also* 1 Cor. 9. 16–19 | <br>*or* 1 Thess. 4. 1–8<br>Ps. 97<br>Matt. 25. 1–13 | <br>Ps. 139<br>Hab. 2. 6–end<br>Mark 7. 31–end |

## September 2007

| Date | Day | Sunday Principal Service<br>Weekday Eucharist | | Third Service<br>Morning Prayer |
|---|---|---|---|---|
| **1** | Sa<br>**G** | *Giles of Provence, Hermit, c. 710* | <br>1 Thess. 4. 9–12<br>Ps. 98. 1–2, 8–end<br>Matt. 25. 14–30 | <br>Ps. 120; ***121***; 122<br>Hab. 3. 2–19a<br>Mark 8. 1–10 |
| **2** | S<br>**G** | **THE THIRTEENTH SUNDAY AFTER TRINITY** (Proper 17)<br>*Track 1*<br>Jer. 2. 4–13<br>Ps. 81. 1, 10–end (or 1–11)<br>Heb. 13. 1–8, 15–16<br>Luke 14. 1, 7–14 | <br>*Track 2*<br>Ecclus. 10. 12–18<br>*or* Prov. 25. 6–7<br>Ps. 112<br>Heb. 13. 1–8, 15–16<br>Luke 14. 1, 7–14 | <br><br>Ps. 119. 161–end<br>Jonah 3. 1–9<br>*or* Ecclus. 11. [7–17] 18–28<br>Rev. 3. 14–22 |
| **3**<br>DEL 22 | M<br>**Gw** | **Gregory the Great, Bishop of Rome, Teacher, 604**<br>Com. Teacher<br>*also* 1 Thess. 2. 3–8 | <br>*or* 1 Thess. 4. 13–end<br>Ps. 96<br>Luke 4. 16–30 | <br>Ps. 123; 124; 125; ***126***<br>Hag. 1. 1–11<br>Mark 8. 11–21 |
| **4** | Tu<br>**G** | *Birinus, Bishop of Dorchester (Oxon), Apostle of Wessex, 650** | <br>1 Thess. 5. 1–6, 9–11<br>Ps. 27. 1–8<br>Luke 4. 31–37 | <br>Ps. ***132***; 133<br>Hag. 1.12 – 2.9<br>Mark 8. 22–26 |
| **5** | W<br>**G** | | Col. 1. 1–8<br>Ps. 34. 11–18<br>Luke 4. 38–end | Ps. 119. 153–end<br>Hag. 2. 10–end<br>Mark 8.27 – 9.1 |
| **6** | Th<br>**G** | *Allen Gardiner, Missionary, Founder of the South American Missionary Society, 1851* | <br>Col. 1. 9–14<br>Ps. 98. 1–5<br>Luke 5. 1–11 | <br>Ps. ***143***; 146<br>Zech. 1. 1–17<br>Mark 9. 2–13 |
| **7** | F<br>**G** | | Col. 1. 15–20<br>Ps. 89. 19b–28<br>Luke 5. 33–end | Ps. 142; ***144***<br>Zech. 1.18 – 2.end<br>Mark 9. 14–29 |
| **8** | Sa<br>**Gw** | **The Birth of the Blessed Virgin Mary****<br>Com. BVM | <br>*or* Col. 1. 21–23<br>Ps. 117<br>Luke 6. 1–5 | <br>Ps. 147<br>Zech. ch. 3<br>Mark 9. 30–37 |

*Cuthbert may be celebrated on 4 September instead of 20 March.

**The Blessed Virgin Mary may be celebrated on 8 September instead of 15 August.

| Second Service Evening Prayer | | Calendar and Holy Communion | Morning Prayer | Evening Prayer |
|---|---|---|---|---|
| Ps. ***105***† (*or* 103)<br>2 Sam. ch. 11<br>Acts 8. 26–end | **G** | | Mic. 7. 1–7<br>Mark 6. 45–end | 2 Sam. ch. 11<br>Acts 8. 26–end |
| Ps. 107†<br>2 Sam. 12. 1–25<br>Acts 9. 1–19a | **Gw** | **Augustine, Bishop of Hippo, 430**<br>Com. Doctor | Mic. 7. 8–end<br>Mark 7. 1–13 | 2 Sam. 12. 1–25<br>Acts 9. 1–19a |
| Ps. 119. 129–152<br>2 Sam. 15. 1–12<br>Acts 9. 19b–31 | **Gr** | **The Beheading of John the Baptist**<br>2 Chron. 24. 17–21<br>Ps. 92. 11–end<br>Heb. 11.32 – 12.2<br>Matt. 14. 1–12 | Hab. 1. 1–11<br>Mark 7. 14–23 | 2 Sam. 15. 1–12<br>Acts 9. 19b–31 |
| Ps. 114; ***116***; 117<br>2 Sam. 15. 13–end<br>Acts 9. 32–end | **G** | | Hab. 1.12 – 2.5<br>Mark 7. 24–30 | 2 Sam. 15. 13–end<br>Acts 9. 32–end |
| Ps. ***130***; 131; 137<br>2 Sam. 16. 1–14<br>Acts 10. 1–16 | **G** | | Hab. 2. 6–end<br>Mark 7. 31–end | 2 Sam. 16. 1–14<br>Acts 10. 1–16 |
| | | | | |
| Ps. 118<br>2 Sam. 17. 1–23<br>Acts 10. 17–33<br>**ct** | **Gw** | **Giles of Provence, Hermit, *c.* 710**<br>Com. Abbot | Hab. 3. 2–19a<br>Mark 8. 1–10 | 2 Sam. 17. 1–23<br>Acts 10. 17–33<br>**ct** |
| Ps. 119. 81–88 [89–96]<br>Isa. 33. 13–22<br>John 3. 22–36 | **G** | **THE THIRTEENTH SUNDAY AFTER TRINITY**<br>Lev. 19. 13–18<br>Ps. 74. 20–end<br>Gal. 3. 16–22<br>*or* Heb. 13. 1–6<br>Luke 10. 23b–37 | Ps. 119. 161–end<br>Jonah 3. 1–9<br>*or* Ecclus. 11. [7–17] 18–28<br>Rev. 3. 14–22 | Ps. 119. 81–88 [89–96]<br>Isa. 33. 13–22<br>John 3. 22–36 |
| Ps. ***127***; 128; 129<br>2 Sam. 18. 1–18<br>Acts 10. 34–end | **G** | | Hag. 1. 1–11<br>Mark 8. 11–21 | 2 Sam. 18. 1–18<br>Acts 10. 34–end |
| Ps. (134); ***135***<br>2 Sam 18.19 – 19.8a<br>Acts 11. 1–18 | **G** | | Hag. 1.12 – 2.9<br>Mark 8. 22–26 | 2 Sam 18.19 – 19.8a<br>Acts 11. 1–18 |
| Ps. 136<br>2 Sam 19. 8b–23<br>Acts 11. 19–end | **G** | | Hag. 2. 10–end<br>Mark 8.27 – 9.1 | 2 Sam 19. 8b–23<br>Acts 11. 19–end |
| Ps. ***138***; 140; 141<br>2 Sam. 19. 24–end<br>Acts 12. 1–17 | **G** | | Zech. 1. 1–17<br>Mark 9. 2–13 | 2 Sam. 19. 24–end<br>Acts 12. 1–17 |
| Ps. 145<br>2 Sam. 23. 1–7<br>Acts 12. 18–end | **Gw** | **Evurtius, Bishop of Orleans, 4th century**<br>Com. Bishop | Zech. 1.18 – 2.end<br>Mark 9. 14–29 | 2 Sam. 23. 1–7<br>Acts 12. 18–end |
| Ps. ***148***; 149; 150<br>2 Sam. ch. 24<br>Acts 13. 1–12<br>**ct** | **Gw** | **The Nativity of the Blessed Virgin Mary**<br>Gen. 3. 9–15<br>Ps. 45. 11–18<br>Rom. 5. 12–17<br>Luke 11. 27–28 | Zech. ch. 3<br>Mark 9. 30–37 | 2 Sam. ch. 24<br>Acts 13. 1–12<br>**ct** |

# September 2007

| Date | Day / Colour | Sunday Principal Service<br>Weekday Eucharist | | Third Service<br>Morning Prayer |
|---|---|---|---|---|
| **9** | **S**<br>**G** | THE FOURTEENTH SUNDAY AFTER TRINITY **(Proper 18)**<br>*Track 1*<br>Jer. 18. 1–11<br>Ps. 139. 1–5, 12–18 (*or* 1–7)<br>Philemon 1–21<br>Luke 14. 25–33 | <br>*Track 2*<br>Deut. 30. 15–end<br>Ps. 1<br>Philemon 1–21<br>Luke 14. 25–33 | <br><br>Ps. 122; 123<br>Jonah 3.10 – 4.end<br>*or* Ecclus. 27.30 – 28.9<br>Rev. 8. 1–5 |
| **10**<br>DEL 23 | M<br>**G** | | Col. 1.24 – 2.3<br>Ps. 62. 1–7<br>Luke 6. 6–11 | Ps. ***1***; 2; 3<br>Zech. ch. 4<br>Mark 9. 38–end |
| **11** | Tu<br>**G** | | Col. 2. 6–15<br>Ps. 8<br>Luke 6. 12–19 | Ps. ***5***; 6 (8)<br>Zech. 6. 9–end<br>Mark 10. 1–16 |
| **12** | W<br>**G** | | Col. 3. 1–11<br>Ps. 15<br>Luke 6. 20–26 | Ps. 119. 1–32<br>Zech. ch. 7<br>Mark 10. 17–31 |
| **13** | Th<br>**Gw** | **John Chrysostom, Bishop of Constantinople, Teacher, 407**<br>Com. Teacher<br>*esp.* Matt. 5. 13–19<br>*also* Jer. 1. 4–10 | <br>*or* Col. 3. 12–17<br>Ps. 149. 1–5<br>Luke 6. 27–38 | <br>Ps. 14; ***15***; 16<br>Zech. 8. 1–8<br>Mark 10. 32–34 |
| **14** | F<br>**R** | HOLY CROSS DAY | Num. 21. 4–9<br>Ps. 22. 23–28<br>Phil. 2. 6–11<br>John 3. 13–17 | *MP*: Ps. 2; 8; 146<br>Gen. 3. 1–15<br>John 12. 27–36a |
| **15** | Sa<br>**Gr** | **Cyprian, Bishop of Carthage, Martyr, 258**<br>Com. Martyr<br>*esp.* 1 Pet. 4. 12–end<br>*also* Matt. 18. 18–22 | <br>*or* 1 Tim. 1. 15–17<br>Ps. 113<br>Luke 6. 43–end | <br>Ps. 20; 21; ***23***<br>Zech. 9. 1–12<br>Mark 10. 46–end |
| **16** | **S**<br>**G** | THE FIFTEENTH SUNDAY AFTER TRINITY **(Proper 19)**<br>*Track 1*<br>Jer. 4. 11–12, 22–28<br>Ps. 14<br>1 Tim. 1. 12–17<br>Luke 15. 1–10 | <br>*Track 2*<br>Exod. 32. 7–14<br>Ps. 51. 1–11<br>1 Tim. 1. 12–17<br>Luke 15. 1–10 | <br><br>Ps. 126; 127<br>Isa. 44.24 – 45.8<br>Rev. 12. 1–12 |
| **17**<br>DEL 24 | M<br>**Gw** | **Hildegard, Abbess of Bingen, Visionary, 1179**<br>Com. Religious<br>*also* 1 Cor. 2. 9–13<br>Luke 10. 21–24 | <br>*or* 1 Tim. 2. 1–8<br>Ps. 28<br>Luke 7. 1–10 | <br>Ps. 27; ***30***<br>Zech. ch. 10<br>Mark 11. 1–11 |
| **18** | Tu<br>**G** | | 1 Tim. 3. 1–13<br>Ps. 101<br>Luke 7. 11–17 | Ps. 32; ***36***<br>Zech. 11. 4–end<br>Mark 11. 12–26 |
| **19** | W<br>**G** | *Theodore of Tarsus, Archbishop of Canterbury, 690* | 1 Tim. 3. 14–end<br>Ps. 111. 1–5<br>Luke 7. 31–35 | Ps. 34<br>Zech. 12. 1–10<br>Mark 11. 27–end |
| **20** | Th<br>**Gr** | **John Coleridge Patteson, first Bishop of Melanesia and his Companions, Martyrs, 1871**<br>Com. Martyr<br>*esp.* 2 Chron. 24. 17–21<br>*also* Acts 7. 55–60 | <br>*or* 1 Tim. 4. 12–end<br>Ps. 111. 6–end<br>Luke 7. 36–end | <br>Ps. 37†<br>Zech. ch. 13<br>Mark 12. 1–12 |

| Second Service Evening Prayer | | Calendar and Holy Communion | Morning Prayer | Evening Prayer |
|---|---|---|---|---|
| | | **THE FOURTEENTH SUNDAY AFTER TRINITY** | | |
| Ps. [120] 121<br>Isa. 43.14 – 44.5<br>John 5. 30–end | **G** | 2 Kings 5. 9–16<br>Ps. 118. 1–9<br>Gal. 5. 16–24<br>Luke 17. 11–19 | Ps. 123; 133<br>Jonah 3.10 – 4.end<br>*or* Ecclus. 27.30 – 28.9<br>Rev. 8. 1–5 | Ps. [120] 121<br>Isa. 43.14 – 44.5<br>John 5. 30–end |
| Ps. **4**; 7<br>1 Kings 1. 5–31<br>Acts 13. 13–43 | **G** | | Zech. ch. 4<br>Mark 9. 38–end | 1 Kings 1. 5–31<br>Acts 13. 13–43 |
| Ps. **9**; 10†<br>1 Kings 1.32 – 2.4, 10–12<br>Acts 13.44 – 14.7 | **G** | | Zech. 6. 9–end<br>Mark 10. 1–16 | 1 Kings 1.32 – 2.4, 10–12<br>Acts 13.44 – 14.7 |
| Ps. ***11***; 12; 13<br>1 Kings ch. 3<br>Acts 14. 8–end | **G** | | Zech. ch. 7<br>Mark 10. 17–31 | 1 Kings ch. 3<br>Acts 14. 8–end |
| Ps. 18†<br>1 Kings 4.29 – 5.12<br>Acts 15. 1–21<br>*or First EP of Holy Cross Day*<br>Ps. 66<br>Isa. 52.13 – 53.end<br>Eph. 2. 11–end<br>**R ct** | **G** | | Zech. 8. 1–8<br>Mark 10. 32–34 | 1 Kings 4.29 – 5.12<br>Acts 15. 1–21 |
| *EP*: Ps. 110; 150<br>Isa. 63. 1–16<br>1 Cor. 1. 18–25 | **Gr** | **Holy Cross Day**<br>To celebrate Holy Cross as a festival, see *Common Worship* provision.<br>Num. 21. 4–9<br>Ps. 67<br>1 Cor. 1. 17–25<br>John 12. 27–33 | Zech. 8. 9–end<br>Mark 10. 35–45 | 1 Kings 6. 1, 11–28<br>Acts 15. 22–35 |
| Ps. ***24***; 25<br>1 Kings 8. 1–30<br>Acts 15.36 – 16.5<br>**ct** | **G** | | Zech. 9. 1–12<br>Mark 10. 46–end | 1 Kings 8. 1–30<br>Acts 15.36 – 16.5<br>**ct** |
| | | **THE FIFTEENTH SUNDAY AFTER TRINITY** | | |
| Ps. 124; 125<br>Isa. ch. 60<br>John 6. 51–69 | **G** | Josh. 24. 14–25<br>Ps. 92. 1–6<br>Gal. 6. 11–end<br>Matt. 6. 24–end | Ps. 126; 127<br>Isa. 44.24 – 45.8<br>Rev. 12. 1–12 | Ps. 124; 125<br>Isa. ch. 60<br>John 6. 51–69 |
| Ps. 26; ***28***; 29<br>1 Kings 8. 31–62<br>Acts 16. 6–24 | **Gr** | **Lambert, Bishop of Maastricht, Martyr, 709**<br>Com. Martyr | Zech. ch. 10<br>Mark 11. 1–11 | 1 Kings 8. 31–62<br>Acts 16. 6–24 |
| Ps. 33<br>1 Kings 8.63 – 9. 9<br>Acts 16. 25–end | **G** | | Zech. 11. 4–end<br>Mark 11. 12–26 | 1 Kings 8.63 – 9.9<br>Acts 16. 25–end |
| Ps. 119. 33–56<br>1 Kings 10. 1–25<br>Acts 17. 1–15 | **G** | | Zech. 12. 1–10<br>Mark 11. 27–end | 1 Kings 10. 1–25<br>Acts 17. 1–15 |
| Ps. 39; ***40***<br>1 Kings 11. 1–13<br>Acts 17. 16–end<br>*or First EP of Matthew*<br>Ps. 34<br>Isa. 33. 13–17<br>Matt. 6. 19–end<br>**R ct** | **G** | | Zech. ch. 13<br>Mark 12. 1–12 | 1 Kings 11. 1–13<br>Acts 17. 16–end<br>*or First EP of Matthew*<br>(Ps. 34)<br>Prov. 3. 3–18<br>Matt. 6. 19–end<br>**R ct** |

# September 2007

| Date | Day / Colour | | Sunday Principal Service<br>Weekday Eucharist | Third Service<br>Morning Prayer |
|---|---|---|---|---|
| **21** | F<br>**R** | MATTHEW, APOSTLE AND EVANGELIST | Prov. 3. 13–18<br>Ps. 119. 65–72<br>2 Cor. 4. 1–6<br>Matt. 9. 9–13 | *MP:* Ps. 49; 117<br>1 Kings 19. 15–end<br>2 Tim. 3. 14–end |
| **22** | Sa<br>**G** | | 1 Tim. 6. 3–16<br>Ps. 100<br>Luke 8. 4–15 | Ps. 41; ***42***; 43<br>Zech. 14. 12–end<br>Mark 12. 18–27 |
| **23** | **S**<br>**G** | **THE SIXTEENTH SUNDAY AFTER TRINITY (Proper 20)**<br>*Track 1*<br>Jer. 8.18 – 9.1<br>Ps. 79. 1–9<br>1 Tim. 2. 1–7<br>Luke 16. 1–13 | *Track 2*<br>Amos 8. 4–7<br>Ps. 113<br>1 Tim. 2. 1–7<br>Luke 16. 1–13 | Ps. 130; 131<br>Isa. 45. 9–22<br>Rev. 14. 1–5 |
| **24**<br>DEL 25 | M<br>**G** | | Ezra 1. 1–6<br>Ps. 126<br>Luke 8. 16–18 | Ps. 44<br>Ecclus. 1. 1–10<br>*or* Ezek. 1. 1–14<br>Mark 12. 28–34 |
| **25** | Tu<br>**Gw** | **Lancelot Andrewes, Bishop of Winchester, Spiritual Writer, 1626**<br>*Sergei of Radonezh, Russian Monastic Reformer, Teacher, 1392*<br>Com. Bishop<br>*esp.* Isa. 6. 1–8 | *or* Ezra 6. 7–8, 12, 14–20<br>Ps. 124<br>Luke 8. 19–21 | Ps. ***48***; 52<br>Ecclus. 1. 11–end<br>*or* Ezek. 1.15 – 2.2<br>Mark 12. 35–end |
| **26** | W<br>**G** *or* **R** | Ember Day*<br>*Wilson Carlile, Founder of the Church Army, 1942* | Ezra 9. 5–9<br>*Canticle:* Song of Tobit<br>*or* Ps. 103. 1–6<br>Luke 9. 1–6 | Ps. 119. 57–80<br>Ecclus. ch. 2<br>*or* Ezek. 2.3 – 3.11<br>Mark 13. 1–13 |
| **27** | Th<br>**Gw** | **Vincent de Paul, Founder of the Congregation of the Mission (Lazarists), 1660**<br>Com. Religious<br>*also* 1 Cor. 1. 25–end<br>Matt. 25. 34–40 | *or* Hag. 1. 1–8<br>Ps. 149. 1–5<br>Luke 9. 7–9 | Ps. 56; **57** (63†)<br>Ecclus. 3. 17–29<br>*or* Ezek. 3. 12–end<br>Mark 13. 14–23 |
| **28** | F<br>**G** *or* **R** | Ember Day* | Hag. 1.15b – 2.9<br>Ps. 43<br>Luke 9. 18–22 | Ps. ***51***; 54<br>Ecclus. 4. 11–28<br>*or* Ezek. ch. 8<br>Mark 13. 24–31 |
| **29** | Sa<br>**W** | MICHAEL AND ALL ANGELS<br>Ember Day*<br>*The reading from Revelation must be used as either the first or second reading at the Eucharist.* | Gen. 28. 10–17<br>*or* Rev. 12. 7–12<br>Ps. 103. 19–end<br>Rev. 12. 7–12<br>*or* Heb. 1. 5–end<br>John 1. 47–end | *MP:* Ps. 34; 150<br>Tobit 12. 6–end<br>*or* Dan. 12. 1–4<br>Acts 12. 1–11 |

*For Ember Day provision, see p. 13.

| Second Service Evening Prayer | | Calendar and Holy Communion | Morning Prayer | Evening Prayer |
|---|---|---|---|---|
| *EP*: Ps. 119. 33–40, 89–96<br>Eccles. 5. 4–12<br>Matt. 19. 16–end | R | **MATTHEW, APOSTLE AND EVANGELIST**<br>Isa. 33. 13–17<br>Ps. 119. 65–72<br>2 Cor. 4. 1–6<br>Matt. 9. 9–13 | (Ps. 49; 117)<br>1 Kings 19. 15–end<br>2 Tim. 3. 14–end | (Ps. 119. 33–40, 89–96)<br>Eccles. 5. 4–12<br>Matt. 19. 16–end |
| Ps. 45; **46**<br>1 Kings 12. 1–24<br>Acts 18.22 – 19.7<br>**ct** | G | | Zech. 14. 12–end<br>Mark 12. 18–27 | 1 Kings 12. 1–24<br>Acts 18.22 – 19.7<br>**ct** |
| Ps. [128] 129<br>Ezra ch. 1<br>John 7. 14–36 | G | **THE SIXTEENTH SUNDAY AFTER TRINITY**<br>1 Kings 17. 17–end<br>Ps. 102. 12–17<br>Eph. 3. 13–end<br>Luke 7. 11–17 | Ps. 130; 131<br>Isa. 45. 9–22<br>Rev. 14. 1–5 | Ps. [128] 129<br>Ezra ch. 1<br>John 7. 14–36 |
| Ps. ***47***; 49<br>1 Kings 12.25 – 13.10<br>Acts 19. 8–20 | G | | Ecclus. 1. 1–10<br>*or* Ezek. 1. 1–14<br>Mark 12. 28–34 | 1 Kings 12.25 – 13.10<br>Acts 19. 8–20 |
| Ps. 50<br>1 Kings 13. 11–end<br>Acts 19. 21–end | G | | Ecclus. 1. 11–end<br>*or* Ezek. 1.15 – 2.2<br>Mark 12. 35–end | 1 Kings 13. 11–end<br>Acts 19. 21–end |
| Ps. ***59***; 60 (67)<br>1 Kings ch. 17<br>Acts 20. 1–16 | **Gr** *or* **R** | **Cyprian, Bishop of Carthage, Martyr, 258**<br>Ember Day<br>Ember CEG *or*<br>Com. Martyr | Ecclus. ch. 2<br>*or* Ezek. 2.3 – 3.11<br>Mark 13. 1–13 | 1 Kings ch. 17<br>Acts 20. 1–16 |
| Ps. 61; ***62***; 64<br>1 Kings 18. 1–20<br>Acts 20. 17–end | G | | Ecclus. 3. 17–29<br>*or* Ezek. 3. 12–end<br>Mark 13. 14–23 | 1 Kings 18. 1–20<br>Acts 20. 17–end |
| Ps. 38<br>1 Kings 18. 21–end<br>Acts 21. 1–16<br>*or First EP of Michael and All Angels*<br>Ps. 91<br>2 Kings 6. 8–17<br>Matt. 18. 1–6, 10<br>**W ct** | **G** *or* **R** | Ember Day<br>Ember CEG | Ecclus. 4. 11–28<br>*or* Ezek. ch. 8<br>Mark 13. 24–31 | 1 Kings 18. 21–end<br>Acts 21. 1–16<br>*or First EP of Michael and All Angels*<br>(Ps. 91)<br>2 Kings 6. 8–17<br>John 1. 47–51<br>**W ct** |
| *EP*: Ps. 138; 148<br>Dan. 10. 4–end<br>Rev. ch. 5 | W | **MICHAEL AND ALL ANGELS**<br>Ember Day<br>Dan. 10. 10–19a<br>Ps. 103. 17–22<br>Rev. 12. 7–12<br>Matt. 18. 1–10 | (Ps. 34; 150)<br>Tobit 12. 6–end<br>*or* Dan. 12. 1–4<br>Acts 12. 1–11 | (Ps. 138; 148)<br>Gen. 28. 10–17<br>Rev. ch. 5 |

## September 2007

| Date | Day | | Sunday Principal Service<br>Weekday Eucharist | Third Service<br>Morning Prayer |
|---|---|---|---|---|
| **30** | **S**<br>G | THE SEVENTEENTH SUNDAY AFTER TRINITY **(Proper 21)**<br>*Track 1*<br>Jer. 32. 1–3a, 6–15<br>Ps. 91. 1–6, 14–end (*or* 11–end)<br>1 Tim. 6. 6–19<br>Luke 16. 19–end | *Track 2*<br>Amos. 6. 1a, 4–7<br>Ps. 146<br>1 Tim. 6. 6–19<br>Luke 16. 19–end | Ps. 132<br>Isa. 48. 12–end<br>Luke 11. 37–end |

## October 2007

| Date | Day | | Sunday Principal Service<br>Weekday Eucharist | Third Service<br>Morning Prayer |
|---|---|---|---|---|
| **1**<br>DEL 26 | M<br>G | *Remigius, Bishop of Rheims, Apostle of the Franks, 533; Anthony Ashley Cooper, Earl of Shaftesbury, Social Reformer, 1885* | Zech. 8. 1–18<br>Ps. 102. 12–22<br>Luke 9. 46–50 | Ps. 71<br>Ecclus. 6. 14–end<br>*or* Ezek. 10. 1–19<br>Mark 14. 1–11 |
| **2** | Tu<br>G | | Zech. 8. 20–end<br>Ps. 87<br>Luke 9. 51–56 | Ps. 73<br>Ecclus. 7. 27–end<br>*or* Ezek. 11. 14–end<br>Mark 14. 12–25 |
| **3** | W<br>G | | Neh. 2. 1–8<br>Ps. 137. 1–6<br>Luke 9. 57–end | Ps. 77<br>Ecclus. 10. 6–8, 12–24<br>*or* Ezek. 12. 1–16<br>Mark 14. 26–42 |
| **4** | Th<br>Gw | **Francis of Assisi, Friar, Deacon, Founder of the Friars Minor, 1226**<br>Com. Religious<br>*also* Gal. 6. 14–end<br>Luke 12. 22–34 | *or* Neh. 8. 1–12<br>Ps. 19. 7–11<br>Luke 10. 1–12 | Ps. 78. 1–39†<br>Ecclus. 11. 7–28<br>*or* Ezek. 12. 17–end<br>Mark 14. 43–52 |
| **5** | F<br>G | | Baruch 1. 15–end<br>*or* Deut. 31. 7–13<br>Ps. 79. 1–9<br>Luke 10. 13–16 | Ps. 55<br>Ecclus. 14.20 – 15.10<br>*or* Ezek. 13. 1–16<br>Mark 14. 53–65 |
| **6** | Sa<br>Gr | **William Tyndale, Translator of the Scriptures, Reformation Martyr, 1536**<br>Com. Martyr<br>*also* Prov. 8. 4–11<br>2 Tim. 3. 12–end | *or* Baruch 4. 5–12, 27–29<br>*or* Josh. 22. 1–6<br>Ps. 69. 33–37<br>Luke 10. 17–24 | Ps. **76**; 79<br>Ecclus. 15. 11–end<br>*or* Ezek. 14. 1–11<br>Mark 14. 66–end |
| **7** | **S**<br>G | THE EIGHTEENTH SUNDAY AFTER TRINITY **(Proper 22)**<br>*Track 1*<br>Lam. 1. 1–6<br>*Canticle:* Lam. 3. 19–26<br>*or* Ps. 137. 1–6 [7–end]<br>2 Tim. 1. 1–14<br>Luke 17. 5–10 | *Track 2*<br>Hab. 1. 1–4; 2. 1–4<br>Ps. 37. 1–9<br>2 Tim. 1. 1–14<br>Luke 17. 5–10 | Ps. 141<br>Isa. 49. 13–23<br>Luke 12. 1–12 |
| | 𝔚 | *or, if observed as Dedication Festival:* | 1 Chron. 29. 6–19<br>Ps. 122<br>Eph. 2. 19–end<br>John 2. 13–22 | *MP:* Ps. 48; 150<br>Hag. 2. 6–9<br>Heb. 10. 19–25 |

| Second Service Evening Prayer | | Calendar and Holy Communion | Morning Prayer | Evening Prayer |
|---|---|---|---|---|
| | | THE SEVENTEENTH SUNDAY AFTER TRINITY | | |
| Ps. [134] 135. 1–14 [15–end]<br>Neh. ch. 2<br>John 8. 31–38, 48–end | G | Prov. 25. 6–14<br>Ps. 33. 6–12<br>Eph. 4. 1–6<br>Luke 14. 1–11 | Ps. 132<br>Isa. 48. 12–end<br>Luke 11. 37–end | Ps. [134] 135. 1–14 [15–end]<br>Neh. ch. 2<br>John 8. 31–38, 48–end |
| | | | | |
| | | **Remigius, Bishop of Rheims, Apostle of the Franks, 533** | | |
| Ps. **72**; 75<br>1 Kings ch. 21<br>Acts 21.37 – 22.21 | Gw | Com. Bishop | Ecclus. 6. 14–end<br>*or* Ezek. 10. 1–19<br>Mark 14. 1–11 | 1 Kings ch. 21<br>Acts 21.37 – 22.21 |
| Ps. 74<br>1 Kings 22. 1–28<br>Acts 22.22 – 23.11 | G | | Ecclus. 7. 27–end<br>*or* Ezek. 11. 14–end<br>Mark 14. 12–25 | 1 Kings 22. 1–28<br>Acts 22.22 – 23.11 |
| Ps. 119. 81–104<br>1 Kings 22. 29–45<br>Acts 23. 12–end | G | | Ecclus. 10. 6–8, 12–24<br>*or* Ezek. 12. 1–16<br>Mark 14. 26–42 | 1 Kings 22. 29–45<br>Acts 23. 12–end |
| Ps. 78. 40–end†<br>2 Kings 1. 2–17<br>Acts 24. 1–23 | G | | Ecclus. 11. 7–28<br>*or* Ezek. 12. 17–end<br>Mark 14. 43–52 | 2 Kings 1. 2–17<br>Acts 24. 1–23 |
| Ps. 69<br>2 Kings 2. 1–18<br>Acts 24.24 – 25.12 | G | | Ecclus. 14.20 – 15.10<br>*or* Ezek. 13. 1–16<br>Mark 14. 53–65 | 2 Kings 2. 1–18<br>Acts 24.24 – 25.12 |
| Ps. 81; ***84***<br>2 Kings 4. 1–37<br>Acts 25. 13–end<br>**ct**<br>*or First EP of Dedication Festival*<br>Ps. 24<br>2 Chron. 7. 11–16<br>John 4. 19–29<br>**𝔚 ct** | Gr | **Faith of Aquitaine, Martyr, *c.* 304**<br>Com. Virgin Martyr | Ecclus. 15. 11–end<br>*or* Ezek. 14. 1–11<br>Mark 14. 66–end | 2 Kings 4. 1–37<br>Acts 25. 13–end<br>**ct**<br>*or First EP of Dedication Festival*<br>Ps. 24<br>2 Chron. 7. 11–16<br>John 4. 19–29<br>**𝔚 ct** |
| | | THE EIGHTEENTH SUNDAY AFTER TRINITY | | |
| Ps. 142<br>Neh. 5. 1–13<br>John ch. 9 | G | Deut. 6. 4–9<br>Ps. 122<br>1 Cor. 1. 4–8<br>Matt. 22. 34–end | Ps. 141<br>Isa. 49. 13–23<br>Luke 12. 1–12 | Ps. 142<br>Neh. 5. 1–13<br>John ch. 9 |
| *EP*: Ps. 132<br>Jer. 7. 1–11<br>Luke 19. 1–10 | 𝔚 | *or, if observed as Dedication Festival:*<br>2 Chron. 7. 11–16<br>Ps. 122<br>1 Cor. 3. 9–17<br>*or* 1 Pet. 2. 1–5<br>Matt. 21. 12–16<br>*or* John 10. 22–29 | Ps. 48; 150<br>Hag. 2. 6–9<br>Heb. 10. 19–25 | Ps. 132<br>Jer. 7. 1–11<br>Luke 19. 1–10 |

# October 2007

| Date | Day | | Sunday Principal Service<br>Weekday Eucharist | Third Service<br>Morning Prayer | Colour |
|---|---|---|---|---|---|
| **8**<br>DEL 27 | M | | Jonah 1.1 – 2.2, 10<br>*Canticle:* Jonah 2. 2–4, 7<br>*or* Ps. 69. 1–6<br>Luke 10. 25–37 | Ps. ***80***; 82<br>Ecclus. 16. 17–end<br>*or* Ezek. 14. 12–end<br>Mark 15. 1–15 | **G** |
| **9** | Tu | *Denys, Bishop of Paris, and his Companions, Martyrs, c. 250; Robert Grosseteste, Bishop of Lincoln, Philosopher, Scientist, 1253* | Jonah ch. 3<br>Ps. 130<br>Luke 10. 38–end | Ps. 87; ***89. 1–18***<br>Ecclus. 17. 1–24<br>*or* Ezek. 18. 1–20<br>Mark 15. 16–32 | **G** |
| **10** | W | **Paulinus, Bishop of York, Missionary, 644**<br>*Thomas Traherne, Poet, Spiritual Writer, 1674*<br>Com. Missionary<br>*esp.* Matt. 28. 16–end | *or* Jonah ch. 4<br>Ps. 86. 1–9<br>Luke 11. 1–4 | Ps. 119. 105–128<br>Ecclus. 18. 1–14<br>*or* Ezek. 18. 21–32<br>Mark 15. 33–41 | **Gw** |
| **11** | Th | *Ethelburga, Abbess of Barking, 675; James the Deacon, Companion of Paulinus, 7th century* | Mal. 3.13 – 4.2a<br>Ps. 1<br>Luke 11. 5–13 | Ps. 90; **92**<br>Ecclus. 19. 4–17<br>*or* Ezek. 20. 1–20<br>Mark 15. 42–end | **G** |
| **12** | F | **Wilfrid of Ripon, Bishop, Missionary, 709**<br>*Elizabeth Fry, Prison Reformer, 1845; Edith Cavell, Nurse, 1915*<br>Com. Missionary<br>*esp.* Luke 5. 1–11<br>*also* 1 Cor. 1. 18–25 | *or* Joel 1. 13–15; 2. 1–2<br>Ps. 9. 1–7<br>Luke 11. 15–26 | Ps. ***88*** (95)<br>Ecclus. 19. 20–end<br>*or* Ezek. 20. 21–38<br>Mark 16. 1–8 | **Gw** |
| **13** | Sa | **Edward the Confessor, King of England, 1066**<br>Com. Saint<br>*also* 2 Sam. 23. 1–5<br>1 John 4. 13–16 | *or* Joel 3. 12–21<br>Ps. 97. 1, 8–end<br>Luke 11. 27–28 | Ps. 96; **97**; 100<br>Ecclus. 21. 1–17<br>*or* Ezek. 24. 15–end<br>Mark 16. 9–end | **Gw** |
| **14** | **S** | **THE NINETEENTH SUNDAY AFTER TRINITY (Proper 23)**<br>*Track 1*<br>Jer. 29. 1, 4–7<br>Ps. 66. 1–11<br>2 Tim. 2. 8–15<br>Luke 17. 11–19 | *Track 2*<br>2 Kings 5. 1–3, 7–15c<br>Ps. 111<br>2 Tim. 2. 8–15<br>Luke 17. 11–19 | Ps. 143<br>Isa. 50. 4–10<br>Luke 13. 22–30 | **G** |
| **15**<br>DEL 28 | M | **Teresa of Avila, Teacher, 1582**<br>Com. Teacher<br>*also* Rom. 8. 22–27 | *or* Rom. 1. 1–7<br>Ps. 98<br>Luke 11. 29–32 | Ps. ***98***; 99; 101<br>Ecclus. 22. 6–22<br>*or* Ezek. 28. 1–19<br>John 13. 1–11 | **Gw** |
| **16** | Tu | *Nicholas Ridley, Bishop of London, and Hugh Latimer, Bishop of Worcester, Reformation Martyrs, 1555* | Rom. 1. 16–25<br>Ps. 19. 1–4<br>Luke 11. 37–41 | Ps. ***106***† (*or* 103)<br>Ecclus. 22.27 – 23.15<br>*or* Ezek. 33. 1–20<br>John 13. 12–20 | **G** |
| **17** | W | **Ignatius, Bishop of Antioch, Martyr, c. 107**<br>Com. Martyr<br>*also* Phil. 3. 7–12<br>John 6. 52–58 | *or* Rom. 2. 1–11<br>Ps. 62. 1–8<br>Luke 11. 42–46 | Ps. 110; ***111***; 112<br>Ecclus. 24. 1–22<br>*or* Ezek. 33. 21–end<br>John 13. 21–30 | **Gr** |

| Second Service Evening Prayer | | Calendar and Holy Communion | Morning Prayer | Evening Prayer |
|---|---|---|---|---|
| Ps. ***85***; 86<br>2 Kings ch. 5<br>Acts 26. 1–23 | **G** | | Ecclus. 16. 17–end<br>*or* Ezek. 14. 12–end<br>Mark 15. 1–15 | 2 Kings ch. 5<br>Acts 26. 1–23 |
| Ps. 89. 19–end<br>2 Kings 6. 1–23<br>Acts 26. 24–end | **Gr** | **Denys, Bishop of Paris, Martyr, *c.* 250**<br>Com. Martyr | Ecclus. 17. 1–24<br>*or* Ezek. 18. 1–20<br>Mark 15. 16–32 | 2 Kings 6. 1–23<br>Acts 26. 24–end |
| Ps. ***91***; 93<br>2 Kings 9. 1–16<br>Acts 27. 1–26 | **G** | | Ecclus. 18. 1–14<br>*or* Ezek. 18. 21–32<br>Mark 15. 33–41 | 2 Kings 9. 1–16<br>Acts 27. 1–26 |
| Ps. 94<br>2 Kings 9. 17–end<br>Acts 27. 27–end | **G** | | Ecclus. 19. 4–17<br>*or* Ezek. 20. 1–20<br>Mark 15. 42–end | 2 Kings 9. 17–end<br>Acts 27. 27–end |
| Ps. 102<br>2 Kings 12. 1–19<br>Acts 28. 1–16 | **G** | | Ecclus. 19. 20–end<br>*or* Ezek. 20. 21–38<br>Mark 16. 1–8 | 2 Kings 12. 1–19<br>Acts 28. 1–16 |
| Ps. 104<br>2 Kings 17. 1–23<br>Acts 28. 17–end<br>**ct** | **Gw** | **Edward the Confessor, King of England, 1066, translated 1163**<br>Com. Saint | Ecclus. 21. 1–17<br>*or* Ezek. 24. 15–end<br>Mark 16. 9–end | 2 Kings 17. 1–23<br>Acts 28. 17–end<br>**ct** |
| Ps. 144<br>Neh. 6. 1–16<br>John 15. 12–end | **G** | **THE NINETEENTH SUNDAY AFTER TRINITY**<br>Gen. 18. 23–32<br>Ps. 141. 1–9<br>Eph. 4. 17–end<br>Matt. 9. 1–8 | Ps. 143<br>Isa. 50. 4–10<br>Luke 13. 22–30 | Ps. 144<br>Neh. 6. 1–16<br>John 15. 12–end |
| Ps. ***105***† (*or* 103)<br>2 Kings 17. 24–end<br>Phil. 1. 1–11 | **G** | | Ecclus. 22. 6–22<br>*or* Ezek. 28. 1–19<br>John 13. 1–11 | 2 Kings 17. 24–end<br>Phil. 1. 1–11 |
| Ps. 107†<br>2 Kings 18. 1–12<br>Phil. 1. 12–end | **G** | | Ecclus. 22.27 – 23.15<br>*or* Ezek. 33. 1–20<br>John 13. 12–20 | 2 Kings 18. 1–12<br>Phil. 1. 12–end |
| Ps. 119. 129–152<br>2 Kings 18. 13–end<br>Phil. 2. 1–13<br>*or First EP of Luke*<br>Ps. 33<br>Hos. 6. 1–3<br>2 Tim. 3. 10–end<br>**R ct** | **Gw** | **Etheldreda, Abbess of Ely, 679**<br>Com. Abbess | Ecclus. 24. 1–22<br>*or* Ezek. 33. 21–end<br>John 13. 21–30 | 2 Kings 18. 13–end<br>Phil. 2. 1–13<br>*or First EP of Luke*<br>(Ps. 33)<br>Hos. 6. 1–3<br>2 Tim. 3. 10–end<br>**R ct** |

# October 2007

| Date | Day | | Sunday Principal Service<br>Weekday Eucharist | Third Service<br>Morning Prayer |
|---|---|---|---|---|
| **18** | Th<br>**R** | LUKE THE EVANGELIST | Isa. 35. 3–6<br>*or* Acts 16. 6–12a<br>Ps. 147. 1–7<br>2 Tim. 4. 5–17<br>Luke 10. 1–9 | *MP:* Ps. 145; 146<br>Isa. ch. 55<br>Luke 1. 1–4 |
| **19** | F<br>**Gw** | **Henry Martyn, Translator of the Scriptures, Missionary in India and Persia, 1812**<br>Com. Missionary *or*<br>*esp.* Mark 16. 15–end<br>*also* Isa. 55. 6–11 | Rom. 4. 1–8<br>Ps. 32<br>Luke 12. 1–7 | Ps. 139<br>Ecclus. 27.30 – 28.9<br>*or* Ezek. 34. 17–end<br>John 14. 1–14 |
| **20** | Sa<br>**G** | | Rom. 4. 13, 16–18<br>Ps. 105. 6–10, 41–44<br>Luke 12. 8–12 | Ps. 120; ***121***; 122<br>Ecclus. 28. 14–end<br>*or* Ezek. 36. 16–36<br>John 14. 15–end |
| **21** | **S**<br>**G** | THE TWENTIETH SUNDAY AFTER TRINITY **(Proper 24)**<br>*Track 1*<br>Jer. 31. 27–34<br>Ps. 119. 97–104<br>2 Tim. 3.14 – 4.5<br>Luke 18. 1–8 | *Track 2*<br>Gen. 32. 22–31<br>Ps. 121<br>2 Tim. 3.14 – 4.5<br>Luke 18. 1–8 | Ps. 147<br>Isa. 54. 1–14<br>Luke 13. 31–end |
| **22**<br>DEL 29 | M<br>**G** | | Rom. 4. 20–end<br>*Canticle:* Benedictus 1–6<br>Luke 12. 13–21 | Ps. 123; 124; 125; ***126***<br>Ecclus. 31. 1–11<br>*or* Ezek. 37. 1–14<br>John 15. 1–11 |
| **23** | Tu<br>**G** | | Rom. 5. 12, 15, 17–end<br>Ps. 40. 7–12<br>Luke 12. 35–38 | Ps. ***132***; 133<br>Ecclus. 34. 9–end<br>*or* Ezek. 37. 15–end<br>John 15. 12–17 |
| **24** | W<br>**G** | | Rom. 6. 12–18<br>Ps. 124<br>Luke 12. 39–48 | Ps. 119. 153–end<br>Ecclus. ch. 35<br>*or* Ezek. 39. 21–end<br>John 15. 18–end |
| **25** | Th<br>**G** | *Crispin and Crispinian, Martyrs at Rome, c. 287* | Rom. 6. 19–end<br>Ps. 1<br>Luke 12. 49–53 | Ps. ***143***; 146<br>Ecclus. 37. 7–24<br>*or* Ezek. 43. 1–12<br>John 16. 1–15 |
| **26** | F<br>**Gw** | **Alfred the Great, King of the West Saxons, Scholar, 899**<br>*Cedd, Abbot of Lastingham, Bishop of the East Saxons, 664**<br>Com. Saint *or*<br>*also* 2 Sam. 23. 1–5<br>John 18. 33–37 | Rom. 7. 18–end<br>Ps. 119. 33–40<br>Luke 12. 54–end | Ps. 142; ***144***<br>Ecclus. 38. 1–14<br>*or* Ezek. 44. 4–16<br>John 16. 16–22 |
| **27** | Sa<br>**G** | | Rom. 8. 1–11<br>Ps. 24. 1–6<br>Luke 13. 1–9 | Ps. 147<br>Ecclus. 38. 24–end<br>*or* Ezek. 47. 1–12<br>John 16. 23–end |

*Chad may be celebrated with Cedd on 26 October instead of 2 March.

| Second Service<br>Evening Prayer | | Calendar and Holy Communion | Morning Prayer | Evening Prayer |
|---|---|---|---|---|
| *EP*: Ps. 103<br>Ecclus. 38. 1–14<br>*or* Isa. 61. 1–6<br>Col. 4. 7–end | **R** | **LUKE THE EVANGELIST**<br>Isa. 35. 3–6<br>Ps. 147. 1–6<br>2 Tim. 4. 5–15<br>Luke 10. 1–9<br>*or* Luke 7. 36–50 | (Ps. 145; 146)<br>Isa. ch. 55<br>Luke 1. 1–4 | (Ps. 103)<br>Ecclus. 38. 1–14<br>*or* Isa. 61. 1–6<br>Col. 4. 7–end |
| Ps. ***130***; 131; 137<br>2 Kings 19. 20–36<br>Phil. 3.1 – 4.1 | **G** | | Ecclus. 27.30 – 28.9<br>*or* Ezek. 34. 17–end<br>John 14. 1–14 | 2 Kings 19. 20–36<br>Phil. 3.1 – 4.1 |
| Ps. 118<br>2 Kings ch. 20<br>Phil. 4. 2–end<br>**ct** | **G** | | Ecclus. 28. 14–end<br>*or* Ezek. 36. 16–36<br>John 14. 15–end | 2 Kings ch. 20<br>Phil. 4. 2–end<br>**ct** |
| Ps. [146] 149<br>Neh. 8. 9–end<br>John 16. 1–11 | **G** | **THE TWENTIETH SUNDAY AFTER TRINITY**<br>Prov. 9. 1–6<br>Ps. 145. 15–end<br>Eph. 5. 15–21<br>Matt. 22. 1–14 | Ps. 147<br>Isa. 54. 1–14<br>Luke 13. 31–end | Ps. [146] 149<br>Neh. 8. 9–end<br>John 16. 1–11 |
| Ps. ***127***; 128; 129<br>2 Kings 21. 1–18<br>1 Tim. 1. 1–17 | **G** | | Ecclus. 31. 1–11<br>*or* Ezek. 37. 1–14<br>John 15. 1–11 | 2 Kings 21. 1–18<br>1 Tim. 1. 1–17 |
| Ps. (134) ***135***<br>2 Kings 22.1 – 23.3<br>1 Tim. 1.18 – 2.end | **G** | | Ecclus. 34. 9–end<br>*or* Ezek. 37. 15–end<br>John 15. 12–17 | 2 Kings 22.1 – 23.3<br>1 Tim. 1.18 – 2.end |
| Ps. 136<br>2 Kings 23. 4–25<br>1 Tim. ch. 3 | **G** | | Ecclus. ch. 35<br>*or* Ezek. 39. 21–end<br>John 15. 18–end | 2 Kings 23. 4–25<br>1 Tim. ch. 3 |
| Ps. ***138***; 140; 141<br>2 Kings. 23.36 – 24.17<br>1 Tim. ch. 4 | **Gr** | **Crispin, Martyr at Rome, c. 287**<br>Com. Martyr | Ecclus. 37. 7–24<br>*or* Ezek. 43. 1–12<br>John 16. 1–15 | 2 Kings. 23.36 – 24.17<br>1 Tim. ch. 4 |
| Ps. 145<br>2 Kings 24.18 – 25.12<br>1 Tim. 5. 1–16 | **G** | | Ecclus. 38. 1–14<br>*or* Ezek. 44. 4–16<br>John 16. 16–22 | 2 Kings 24.18 – 25.12<br>1 Tim. 5. 1–16 |
| Ps. ***148***; 149; 150<br>2 Kings 25. 22–end<br>1 Tim. 5. 17–end<br>**ct**<br>*or First EP of Simon and Jude*<br>Ps. 124; 125; 126<br>Deut. 32. 1–4<br>John 14. 15–26<br>**R ct** | **G** | | Ecclus. 38. 24–end<br>*or* Ezek. 47. 1–12<br>John 16. 23–end | 2 Kings 25. 22–end<br>1 Tim. 5. 17–end<br>**ct**<br>*or First EP of Simon and Jude*<br>(Ps. 124; 125; 126)<br>Deut. 32. 1–4<br>John 14. 15–26<br>**R ct** |

## October 2007

| Date | Day | | Sunday Principal Service / Weekday Eucharist | Third Service / Morning Prayer |
|---|---|---|---|---|
| **28** | S | **SIMON AND JUDE, APOSTLES** (or transferred to 29th)* | | |
| | | | Isa. 28. 14–16 | *MP*: Ps. 116; 117 |
| | | | Ps. 119. 89–96 | Wisd. 5. 1–16 |
| | | | Eph. 2. 19–end | *or* Isa. 45. 18–end |
| | | | John 15. 17–end | Luke 6. 12–16 |
| | R | | | |
| | | *or, for The Last Sunday after Trinity:* | | |
| | | *Track 1* | *Track 2* | |
| | | Joel 2. 23–end | Ecclus. 35. 12–17 | Ps. 119. 105–128 |
| | | Ps. 65. 1–7 [8–end] | *or* Jer. 14. 7–10, 19–end | Isa. 59. 9–20 |
| | | 2 Tim. 4. 6–8, 16–18 | Ps. 84. 1–7 | Luke 14. 1–14 |
| | | Luke 18. 9–14 | 2 Tim. 4. 6–8, 16–18 | |
| | G | | Luke 18. 9–14 | |
| | | *or, if being observed as Bible Sunday:* | | |
| | | | Isa. 45. 22–end | Ps. 119. 105–128 |
| | | | Ps. 119. 129–136 | 1 Kings 22. 1–17 |
| | | | Rom. 15. 1–6 | Rom. 15. 4–13 |
| | G | | Luke 4. 16–24 | *or* Luke 14. 1–14 |
| **29** | M | For Simon and Jude, Apostles, see 28th | | |
| | | **James Hannington, Bishop of Eastern Equatorial Africa, Martyr in Uganda, 1885** | | |
| DEL 30 | | Com. Martyr *or* | Rom. 8. 12–17 | Ps. ***1***; 2; 3 |
| | | *esp.* Matt. 10. 28–39 | Ps. 68. 1–6, 19 | Ecclus. 39. 1–11 |
| | | | Luke 13. 10–17 | *or* Eccles. ch. 1 |
| | Gr | | | John 17. 1–5 |
| **30** | Tu | | Rom. 8. 18–25 | Ps. **5**; 6 (8) |
| | | | Ps. 126 | Ecclus. 39. 13–end |
| | | | Luke 13. 18–21 | *or* Eccles. ch. 2 |
| | G | | | John 17. 6–19 |
| **31** | W | *Martin Luther, Reformer, 1546* | | |
| | | | Rom. 8. 26–30 | Ps. 119. 1–32 |
| | | | Ps. 13 | Ecclus. 42. 15–end |
| | | | Luke 13. 22–30 | *or* Eccles. 3. 1–15 |
| | | | | John 17. 20–end |
| | G | | | |

## November 2007

| Date | Day | | Sunday Principal Service / Weekday Eucharist | Third Service / Morning Prayer |
|---|---|---|---|---|
| **1** | Th | **ALL SAINTS' DAY** | | |
| | | | Dan. 7. 1–3, 15–18 | *MP*: Ps. 15; 84; 149 |
| | | | Ps. 149 | Isa. ch. 35 |
| | | | Eph. 1. 11–end | Luke 9. 18–27 |
| | W | | Luke 6. 20–31 | |
| | | *or, if the readings above are used* | Isa. 56. 3–8 | *MP*: Ps. 111; 112; 117 |
| | | *on Sunday 4 November:* | *or* 2 Esdras 2. 42–end | Wisd. 5. 1–16 |
| | | | Ps. 33. 1–5 | *or* Jer. 31. 31–34 |
| | | | Heb. 12. 18–24 | 2 Cor. 4. 5–12 |
| | W | | Matt. 5. 1–12 | |
| | | *or, if kept as a feria:* | Rom. 8. 31–end | Ps. 14; ***15***; 16 |
| | | | Ps. 109. 20–21 | Ecclus. 43. 1–12 |
| | | | Luke 13. 31–end | *or* Eccles. 3.16 – 4.end |
| | G | | | John 18. 1–11 |

*If the Dedication Festival is kept on this Sunday, use the provision given on 6 and 7 October.

| Second Service Evening Prayer | | Calendar and Holy Communion | Morning Prayer | Evening Prayer |
|---|---|---|---|---|
| | | **SIMON AND JUDE, APOSTLES** | | |
| *EP:* Ps. 119. 1–16<br>1 Macc. 2. 42–66<br>*or* Jer. 3. 11–18<br>Jude 1–4, 17–end | R | Isa. 28. 9–16<br>Ps. 116. 11–end<br>Jude 1–8<br>*or* Rev. 21. 9–14<br>John 15. 17–end | Ps. 119. 89–96<br>Wisd. 5. 1–16<br>*or* Isa. 45. 18–end<br>Luke 6. 12–16 | Ps. 119. 1–16<br>1 Macc. 2. 42–66<br>*or* Jer. 3. 11–18<br>Eph. 2. 19–end |
| | | *or, for The Twenty-First Sunday after Trinity:* | | |
| Ps. 119. 1–16<br>Eccles. chs. 11 & 12<br>2 Tim. 2. 1–7<br>*Gospel:* Matt. 22. 34–end | G | Gen. 32. 24–29<br>Ps. 90. 1–12<br>Eph. 6. 10–20<br>John 4. 46b–end | Ps. 119. 105–128<br>Isa. 59. 9–20<br>Luke 14. 12–24 | Ps. 119. 1–16<br>Eccles. chs. 11 & 12<br>2 Tim. 2. 1–7 |
| Ps. 119. 1–16<br>Jer. 36. 9–end<br>Rom. 10. 5–17<br>*Gospel:* Matt. 22. 34–40 | | | | |
| Ps. **4**; 7<br>Judith ch. 4<br>*or* Exod. 22. 21–27<br>1 Tim. 6. 1–10 | G | | Ecclus. 39. 1–11<br>*or* Eccles. ch. 1<br>John 17. 1–5 | Judith ch. 4<br>*or* Exod. 22. 21–27<br>1 Tim. 6. 1–10 |
| Ps. **9**; 10†<br>Judith 5.1 – 6.4<br>*or* Exod. 29.38 – 30.16<br>1 Tim. 6. 11–end | G | | Ecclus. 39. 13–end<br>*or* Eccles. ch. 2<br>John 17. 6–19 | Judith 5.1 – 6.4<br>*or* Exod. 29.38 – 30.16<br>1 Tim. 6. 11–end |
| *First EP of All Saints*<br>Ps. 1; 5<br>Ecclus. 44. 1–15<br>*or* Isa. 40. 27–end<br>Rev. 19. 6–10<br>**W ct**<br>*or, if All Saints is observed on 4th:*<br>Ps. ***11***; 12; 13<br>Judith 6.10 – 7.7<br>*or* Lev. ch. 8<br>2 Tim. 1. 1–14 | G | | Ecclus. 42. 15–end<br>*or* Eccles. 3. 1–15<br>John 17. 20–end | *First EP of All Saints*<br>Ps. 1; 5<br>Ecclus. 44. 1–15<br>*or* Isa. 40. 27–end<br>Rev. 19. 6–10<br>**W ct** |
| | | | | |
| *EP:* Ps. 148; 150<br>Isa. 65. 17–end<br>Heb. 11.32 – 12.2 | | **ALL SAINTS' DAY**<br>Isa. 66. 20–23<br>Ps. 33. 1–5<br>Rev. 7. 2–4 [5–8] 9–12<br>Matt. 5. 1–12 | Ps. 15; 84; 149<br>Isa. ch. 35<br>Luke 9. 18–27 | Ps. 148; 150<br>Isa. 65. 17–end<br>Heb. 11.32 – 12.2 |
| *EP:* Ps. 145<br>Isa. 66. 20–23<br>Col. 1. 9–14 | | | | |
| Ps. 18†<br>Judith 7. 19–end<br>*or* Lev. ch. 9<br>2 Tim. 1.15 – 2.13 | W | | | |

# November 2007

| | | | Sunday Principal Service<br>Weekday Eucharist | Third Service<br>Morning Prayer |
|---|---|---|---|---|
| **2** | F<br>**Rp** *or*<br>**Gp** | **Commemoration of the Faithful Departed (All Souls' Day)**<br>Lam. 3. 17–26, 31–33<br>*or* Wisd. 3. 1–9<br>Ps. 23<br>*or* Ps. 27. 1–6, 16–end<br>Rom. 5. 5–11<br>*or* 1 Pet. 1. 3–9<br>John 5. 19–25<br>*or* John 6. 37–40 | *or* Rom. 9. 1–5<br>Ps. 147. 13–end<br>Luke 14. 1–6 | Ps. 17; ***19***<br>Ecclus. 43. 13–end<br>*or* Eccles. ch. 5<br>John 18. 12–27 |
| **3** | Sa<br>**Rw** *or* **Gw** | **Richard Hooker, Priest, Anglican Apologist, Teacher, 1600**<br>*Martin of Porres, Friar, 1639*<br>Com. Teacher<br>*esp.* John 16. 12–15<br>*also* Ecclus. 44. 10–15 | *or* Rom. 11. 1–2, 11–12, 25–29<br>Ps. 94. 14–19<br>Luke 14. 1, 7–11 | Ps. 20; 21; ***23***<br>Ecclus. 44. 1–15<br>*or* Eccles. ch. 6<br>John 18. 28–end |
| **4** | **S**<br>**R** *or* **G**<br>W | **THE FOURTH SUNDAY BEFORE ADVENT**<br><br><br><br><br>*Or ALL SAINTS' SUNDAY (see readings for 1 November throughout the day)* | Isa. 1. 10–18<br>Ps. 32. 1–8<br>2 Thess. ch. 1<br>Luke 19. 1–10 | Ps. 87<br>Job ch. 26<br>Col. 1. 9–14 |
| **5**<br>DEL 31 | M<br>**R** *or* **G** | | Rom. 11. 29–end<br>Ps. 69. 31–37<br>Luke 14. 12–14 | Ps. **2**; 146<br>*alt.* Ps. 27; ***30***<br>Isa. 1. 1–20<br>Matt. 1. 18–end |
| **6** | Tu<br>**R** *or* **G** | *Leonard, Hermit, 6th century; William Temple, Archbishop of Canterbury, Teacher, 1944* | Rom. 12. 5–16<br>Ps. 131<br>Luke 14. 15–24 | Ps. ***5***; 147. 1–12<br>*alt.* Ps. 32; ***36***<br>Isa. 1. 21–end<br>Matt. 2. 1–15 |
| **7** | W<br>**Rw** *or* **Gw** | **Willibrord of York, Bishop, Apostle of Fresia, 739**<br>Com. Missionary<br>*esp.* Isa. 52. 7–10<br>Matt. 28. 16–end | *or* Rom. 13. 8–10<br>Ps. 112<br>Luke 14. 25–33 | Ps. ***9***; 147. 13–end<br>*alt.* Ps. 34<br>Isa. 2. 1–11<br>Matt. 2. 16–end |
| **8** | Th<br>**Rw** *or*<br>**Gw** | **The Saints and Martyrs of England**<br>Isa. 61. 4–9<br>*or* Ecclus. 44. 1–15<br>Ps. 15<br>Rev. 19. 5–10<br>John 17. 18–23 | *or* Rom. 14. 7–12<br>Ps. 27. 14–end<br>Luke 15. 1–10 | Ps. 11; ***15***; 148<br>*alt.* Ps. 37†<br>Isa. 2. 12–end<br>Matt. ch. 3 |
| **9** | F<br>**R** *or* **G** | *Margery Kempe, Mystic, c. 1440* | Rom. 15. 14–21<br>Ps. 98<br>Luke 16. 1–8 | Ps. ***16***; 149<br>*alt.* Ps. 31<br>Isa. 3. 1–15<br>Matt. 4. 1–11 |
| **10** | Sa<br>**Rw** *or* **Gw** | **Leo the Great, Bishop of Rome, Teacher, 461**<br>Com. Teacher<br>*also* 1 Pet. 5. 1–11 | *or* Rom. 6. 3–9, 16, 22–end<br>Ps. 145. 1–7<br>Luke 16. 9–15 | Ps. ***18. 31–end***; 150<br>*alt.* Ps. 41; ***42***; 43<br>Isa. 4.2 – 5.7<br>Matt. 4. 12–22 |
| **11** | **S**<br>**R** *or* **G** | **THE THIRD SUNDAY BEFORE ADVENT**<br>(Remembrance Sunday) | Job 19. 23–27a<br>Ps. 17. 1–8 [9]<br>2 Thess. 2. 1–5, 13–end<br>Luke 20. 27–38 | Ps. 20; 90<br>Isa. 2. 1–5<br>James 3. 13–end |

| Second Service Evening Prayer | | Calendar and Holy Communion | Morning Prayer | Evening Prayer |
|---|---|---|---|---|
| Ps. 22<br>Judith 8. 9–end<br>*or* Lev. 16. 2–24<br>2 Tim. 2. 14–end | **G** | To celebrate All Souls' Day, see *Common Worship* provision. | Ecclus. 43. 13–end<br>*or* Eccles. ch. 5<br>John 18. 12–27 | Judith 8. 9–end<br>*or* Lev. 16. 2–24<br>2 Tim. 2. 14–end |
| Ps. 24; ***25***<br>Judith ch. 9<br>*or* Lev. ch. 17<br>2 Tim. ch. 3<br>**ct** | **G** | | Ecclus. 44. 1–15<br>*or* Eccles. ch. 6<br>John 18. 28–end | Judith ch. 9<br>*or* Lev. ch. 17<br>2 Tim. ch. 3<br>**ct** |
| Ps. 145. 1–9 [10–end]<br>Lam. 3. 22–33<br>John 11. [1–31] 32–44 | **G** | **THE TWENTY-SECOND SUNDAY AFTER TRINITY**<br>Gen. 45. 1–7, 15<br>Ps. 133<br>Phil. 1. 3–11<br>Matt. 18. 21–end | Ps. 87<br>Job ch. 26<br>Luke 19. 1–10 | Ps. 145. 1–9 [10–end]<br>Lam. 3. 22–33<br>John 11. [1–31] 32–44 |
| Ps. ***92***; 96; 97<br>*alt.* Ps. 26; ***28***; 29<br>Dan. ch. 1<br>Rev. ch. 1 | **G** | | Isa. 1. 1–20<br>Matt. 1. 18–end | Dan. ch. 1<br>Rev. ch. 1 |
| Ps. 98; 99; ***100***<br>*alt.* Ps. 33<br>Dan. 2. !–24<br>Rev. 2. 1–11 | **Gw** | **Leonard, Hermit, 6th century**<br>Com. Abbot | Isa. 1. 21–end<br>Matt. 2. 1–15 | Dan. 2. 1–24<br>Rev. 2. 1–11 |
| Ps. 111; ***112***; 116<br>*alt.* Ps. 119. 33–56<br>Dan. 2. 25–end<br>Rev. 2. 12–end | **G** | | Isa. 2. 1–11<br>Matt. 2. 16–end | Dan. 2. 25–end<br>Rev. 2. 12–end |
| Ps. 118<br>*alt.* Ps. 39; ***40***<br>Dan. 3. 1–18<br>Rev. 3. 1–13 | **G** | | Isa. 2. 12–end<br>Matt. ch. 3 | Dan. 3. 1–18<br>Rev. 3. 1–13 |
| Ps. 137; 138; ***143***<br>*alt.* Ps. 35<br>Dan. 3. 19–end<br>Rev. 3. 14–end | **G** | | Isa. 3. 1–15<br>Matt. 4. 1–11 | Dan. 3. 19–end<br>Rev. 3. 14–end |
| Ps. 145<br>*alt.* Ps. 45; ***46***<br>Dan. 4. 1–18<br>Rev. ch. 4<br>**ct** | **G** | | Isa. 4.2 – 5.7<br>Matt. 4. 12–22 | Dan. 4. 1–18<br>Rev. ch. 4<br>**ct** |
| Ps. 40<br>1 Kings 3. 1–15<br>Rom. 8. 31–end<br>*Gospel:* Matt. 22. 15–22 | **G** | **THE TWENTY-THIRD SUNDAY AFTER TRINITY**<br>Isa. 11. 1–10<br>Ps. 44. 1–9<br>Phil. 3. 17–end<br>Matt. 22. 15–22 | Ps. 20; 90<br>Isa. 2. 1–5<br>James 3. 13–end | Ps. 40<br>1 Kings 3. 1–15<br>Luke 20. 27–38 |

# November 2007

| Date | Day / Colour | Commemoration | Sunday Principal Service<br>Weekday Eucharist | Third Service<br>Morning Prayer |
|---|---|---|---|---|
| **12**<br>DEL 32 | M<br>**R** *or* **G** | | Wisd. 1. 1–7<br>*or* Titus 1. 1–9<br>Ps. 139. 1–9<br>*or* Ps. 24. 1–6<br>Luke 17. 1–6 | Ps. 19; ***20***<br>*alt.* Ps. 44<br>Isa. 5. 8–24<br>Matt. 4.23 – 5.12 |
| **13** | Tu<br>**Rw** *or* **Gw** | **Charles Simeon, Priest, Evangelical Divine, 1836**<br>Com. Pastor *or*<br>*esp.* Mal. 2. 5–7<br>*also* Col. 1. 3–8<br>Luke 8. 4–8 | Wisd. 2.23 – 3.9<br>*or* Titus 2. 1–8, 11–14<br>Ps. 34. 1–6<br>*or* Ps. 37. 3–5, 30–32<br>Luke 17. 7–10 | Ps. ***21***; 24<br>*alt.* Ps. ***48***; 52<br>Isa. 5. 25–end<br>Matt. 5. 13–20 |
| **14** | W<br>**R** *or* **G** | *Samuel Seabury, first Anglican Bishop in North America, 1796* | Wisd. 6. 1–11<br>*or* Titus 3. 1–7<br>Ps. 82<br>*or* Ps. 23<br>Luke 17. 11–19 | Ps. ***23***; 25<br>*alt.* Ps. 119. 57–80<br>Isa. ch. 6<br>Matt. 5. 21–37 |
| **15** | Th<br>**R** *or* **G** | | Wisd. 7.22 – 8.1<br>*or* Philemon 7–20<br>Ps. 119. 89–96<br>*or* Ps. 146. 4–end<br>Luke 17. 20–25 | Ps. ***26***; 27<br>*alt.* Ps. 56; ***57*** (63†)<br>Isa. 7. 1–17<br>Matt. 5. 38–end |
| **16** | F<br>**Rw** *or* **Gw** | **Margaret, Queen of Scotland, Philanthropist, Reformer of the Church, 1093**<br>*Edmund Rich of Abingdon, Archbishop of Canterbury, 1240*<br>Com. Saint *or*<br>*also* Prov. 31. 10–12, 20, 26–end<br>1 Cor. 12.13 – 13.3<br>Matt. 25. 34–end | Wisd. 13. 1–9<br>*or* 2 John 4–9<br>Ps. 19. 1–4<br>*or* Ps. 119. 1–8<br>Luke 17. 26–end | Ps. 28; ***32***<br>*alt.* Ps. ***51***; 54<br>Isa. 8. 1–15<br>Matt. 6. 1–18 |
| **17** | Sa<br>**Rw** *or* **Gw** | **Hugh, Bishop of Lincoln, 1200**<br>Com. Bishop *or*<br>*also* 1 Tim. 6. 11–16 | Wisd. 18. 14–16; 19. 6–9<br>*or* 3 John 5–8<br>Ps. 105. 1–5, 35–42<br>*or* Ps. 112<br>Luke 18. 1–8 | Ps. 33<br>*alt.* Ps. 68<br>Isa. 8.16 – 9.7<br>Matt. 6. 19–end |
| **18** | **S**<br>**R** *or* **G** | **THE SECOND SUNDAY BEFORE ADVENT** | Mal. 4. 1–2a<br>Ps. 98<br>2 Thess. 3. 6–13<br>Luke 21. 5–19 | Ps. 132<br>1 Sam. 16. 1–13<br>Matt. 13. 44–52 |
| **19**<br>DEL 33 | M<br>**Rw** *or* **Gw** | **Hilda, Abbess of Whitby, 680**<br>*Mechtild, Beguine of Magdeburg, Mystic, 1280*<br>Com. Religious *or*<br>*esp.* Isa. 61.10 – 62.5 | 1 Macc. 1. 10–15, 41–43, 54–57, 62–64<br>*or* Rev. 1. 1–4; 2. 1–5<br>Ps. 79. 1–5<br>*or* Ps. 1<br>Luke 18. 35–end | Ps.46; ***47***<br>*alt.* Ps. 71<br>Isa. 9.8 – 10.4<br>Matt. 7. 1–12 |
| **20** | Tu<br>**R** *or* **Gr** | **Edmund, King of the East Angles, Martyr, 870**<br>*Priscilla Lydia Sellon, a Restorer of the Religious Life in the Church of England, 1876*<br>Com. Martyr *or*<br>*also* Prov. 20. 28; 21. 1–4, 7 | 2 Macc. 6. 18–end<br>*or* Rev. 3. 1–6, 14–31<br>Ps. 11<br>*or* Ps. 15<br>Luke 19. 1–10 | Ps. 48; ***52***<br>*alt.* Ps. 73<br>Isa. 10. 5–19<br>Matt. 7. 13–end |
| **21** | W<br>**R** *or* **G** | | 2 Macc. 7. 1, 20–31<br>*or* Rev. ch. 4<br>Ps. 116. 10–end<br>*or* Ps. 150<br>Luke 19. 11–28 | Ps. ***56***; 57<br>*alt.* Ps. 77<br>Isa. 10. 20–32<br>Matt. 8. 1–13 |

| Second Service Evening Prayer | | Calendar and Holy Communion | Morning Prayer | Evening Prayer |
|---|---|---|---|---|
| Ps. 34<br>*alt.* Ps. **47**; 49<br>Dan. 4. 19–end<br>Rev. ch. 5 | **G** | | Isa. 5. 8–24<br>Matt. 4.23 – 5.12 | Dan. 4. 19–end<br>Rev. ch. 5 |
| Ps. 36; ***40***<br>*alt.* Ps. 50<br>Dan. 5. 1–12<br>Rev. ch. 6 | **Gw** | **Britius, Bishop of Tours, 444**<br>Com. Bishop | Isa. 5. 25–end<br>Matt. 5. 13–20 | Dan. 5. 1–12<br>Rev. ch. 6 |
| Ps. 37<br>*alt.* Ps. ***59***; 60 (67)<br>Dan. 5. 13–end<br>Rev. 7. 1–4, 9–end | **G** | | Isa. ch. 6<br>Matt. 5. 21–37 | Dan. 5. 13–end<br>Rev. 7. 1–4, 9–end |
| Ps. 42; ***43***<br>*alt.* Ps. 61; ***62***; 64<br>Dan. ch. 6<br>Rev. ch. 8 | **Gw** | **Machutus, Bishop, Apostle of Brittany, c. 564**<br>Com. Bishop | Isa. 7. 1–17<br>Matt. 5. 38–end | Dan. ch. 6<br>Rev. ch. 8 |
| Ps. 31<br>*alt.* Ps. 38<br>Dan. 7. 1–14<br>Rev. 9. 1–12 | **G** | | Isa. 8. 1–15<br>Matt. 6. 1–18 | Dan. 7. 1–14<br>Rev. 9. 1–12 |
| Ps. 84; ***86***<br>*alt.* Ps. 65; ***66***<br>Dan. 7. 15–end<br>Rev. 9. 13–end<br>**ct** | **Gw** | **Hugh, Bishop of Lincoln, 1200**<br>Com. Bishop | Isa. 8.16 – 9.7<br>Matt. 6. 19–end | Dan. 7. 15–end<br>Rev. 9. 13–end<br>**ct** |
| Ps. [93] 97<br>Dan. ch. 6<br>Matt. 13. 1–9, 18–23 | **G** | **THE TWENTY-FOURTH SUNDAY AFTER TRINITY**<br>Isa. 55. 6–11<br>Ps. 85. 1–7<br>Col. 1. 3–12<br>Matt. 9. 18–26 | Ps. 132<br>1 Sam. 16. 1–13<br>Matt. 13. 44–52 | Ps. [93] 97<br>Dan. ch. 6<br>Matt. 13. 1–9, 18–23 |
| Ps. 70; ***71***<br>*alt.* Ps. ***72***; 75<br>Dan. 8. 1–14<br>Rev. ch. 10 | **G** | | Isa. 9.8 – 10.4<br>Matt. 7. 1–12 | Dan. 8. 1–14<br>Rev. ch. 10 |
| Ps. ***67***; 72<br>*alt.* Ps. 74<br>Dan. 8. 15–end<br>Rev. 11. 1–14 | **Gr** | **Edmund, King of the East Angles, Martyr, 870**<br>Com. Martyr | Isa. 10. 5–19<br>Matt. 7. 13–end | Dan. 8. 15–end<br>Rev. 11. 1–14 |
| Ps. 73<br>*alt.* Ps. 119. 81–104<br>Dan. 9. 1–19<br>Rev. 11. 15–end | **G** | | Isa. 10. 20–32<br>Matt. 8. 1–13 | Dan. 9. 1–19<br>Rev. 11. 15–end |

# November 2007

| Date | Day / Colour | Observance | Sunday Principal Service<br>Weekday Eucharist | Third Service<br>Morning Prayer |
|---|---|---|---|---|
| 22 | Th<br>**R** *or* **G** | *Cecilia, Martyr at Rome, c. 230* | I Macc. 2. 15–29<br>*or* Rev. 5. 1–10<br>Ps. 129<br>*or* Ps. 149. 1–5<br>Luke 19. 41–44 | Ps. 61; ***62***<br>Ps. 78. 1–39†<br>Isa. 10.33 – 11.9<br>Matt. 8. 14–22 |
| 23 | F<br>**R** *or* **Gr** | **Clement, Bishop of Rome, Martyr, c. 100**<br>Com. Martyr<br>*also* Phil. 3.17 – 4.3<br>Matt. 16. 13–19 | *or* I Macc. 4. 36–37, 52–59<br>*or* Rev. 10. 8–11<br>Ps. 122<br>*or* Ps. 119. 65–72<br>Luke 19. 45–48 | Ps. ***63***; 65<br>*alt.* Ps. 55<br>Isa. 11.10 – 12.end<br>Matt. 8. 23–end |
| 24 | Sa<br>**R** *or* **G** | | I Macc. 6. 1–13<br>*or* Rev. 11. 4–12<br>Ps. 124<br>*or* Ps. 144. 1–9<br>Luke 20. 27–34 | Ps. 78. 1–39<br>*alt.* Ps. ***76***; 79<br>Isa. 13. 1–13<br>Matt. 9. 1–17 |
| 25 | **S**<br>**R** *or* **W** | **CHRIST THE KING**<br>The Sunday Next Before Advent | Jer. 23. 1–6<br>Ps. 46<br>Col. 1. 11–20<br>Luke 23. 33–43 | *MP*: Ps. 29; 110<br>Zech. 6. 9–end<br>Rev. 11. 15–18 |
| 26<br>DEL 34 | M<br>**R** *or* **G** | | Dan. 1. 1–6, 8–20<br>*Canticle*: Bless the Lord<br>Luke 21. 1–4 | Ps. 92; ***96***<br>*alt.* Ps. ***80***; 82<br>Isa. 14. 3–20<br>Matt. 9. 18–34 |
| 27 | Tu<br>**R** *or* **G** | | Dan. 2. 31–45<br>*Canticle:* Benedicite 1–3<br>Luke 21. 5–11 | Ps. ***97***; 98; 100<br>*alt.* Ps. 87; ***89. 1–18***<br>Isa. ch. 17<br>Matt. 9.35 – 10.15 |
| 28 | W<br>**R** *or* **G** | | Dan. 5. 1–6, 13–14, 16–17, 23–28<br>*Canticle:* Benedicite 4–5<br>Luke 21. 12–19 | Ps. 110; 111; ***112***<br>*alt.* Ps. 119. 105–128<br>Isa. ch. 19<br>Matt. 10. 16–33 |
| 29 | Th<br>**R** *or* **G** | | Dan. 6. 12–end<br>*Canticle:* Benedicite 6–8a<br>Luke 21. 20–28 | Ps. ***125***; 126; 127; 128<br>*alt.* Ps. 90; ***92***<br>Isa. 21. 1–12<br>Matt. 10.34 – 11.1 |
| | **R** *or* **G** | *Day of Intercession and Thanksgiving for the Missionary Work of the Church* | Isa. 49. 1–6; Isa. 52. 7–10; Mic. 4. 1–5<br>Acts 17. 12–end; 2 Cor. 5.14 – 6.2; Eph. 2. 13–end<br>Ps. 2; 46; 47<br>Matt. 5. 13–16; Matt. 28. 16–end; John 17. 20–end | |
| 30 | F<br>**R** | **ANDREW THE APOSTLE** | Isa. 52. 7–10<br>Ps. 19. 1–6<br>Rom. 10. 12–18<br>Matt. 4. 18–22 | *MP*: Ps. 47; 147. 1–12<br>Ezek. 47. 1–12<br>*or* Ecclus. 14. 20–end<br>John 12. 20–32 |

| Second Service<br>Evening Prayer | | Calendar and Holy Communion | Morning Prayer | Evening Prayer |
|---|---|---|---|---|
| Ps. 74; ***76***<br>Ps. 78. 40–end†<br>Dan. 9. 20–end<br>Rev. ch. 12 | **Gr** | **Cecilia, Martyr at Rome, c. 230**<br>Com. Virgin Martyr | Isa. 10.33 – 11.9<br>Matt. 8. 14–22 | Dan. 9. 20–end<br>Rev. ch. 12 |
| Ps. 77<br>*alt.* Ps. 69<br>Dan. 10.1 – 11.1<br>Rev. 13. 1–10 | **Gr** | **Clement, Bishop of Rome, Martyr, c. 100**<br>Com. Martyr | Isa. 11.10 – 12.end<br>Matt. 8. 23–end | Dan. 10.1 – 11.1<br>Rev. 13. 1–10 |
| Ps. 78. 40–end<br>*alt.* Ps. 81; ***84***<br>Dan. ch. 12<br>Rev. 13. 11–end<br>**ct**<br>*or First EP of Christ the King*<br>Ps. 99; 100<br>Isa. 10.33 – 11.9<br>1 Tim. 6. 11–16<br>**R** *or* **W ct** | **G** | | Isa. 13. 1–13<br>Matt. 9. 1–17 | Dan. ch. 12<br>Rev. 13. 11–end<br>**ct** |
| *EP*: Ps. 72. 1–7 [8–end]<br>1 Sam. 8. 4–20<br>John 18. 33–37 | **G** | **THE SUNDAY NEXT BEFORE ADVENT**<br>To celebrate Christ the King, see *Common Worship* provision.<br>Jer. 23. 5–8<br>Ps. 85. 8–end<br>Col. 1. 13–20<br>John 6. 5–14 | Ps. 29; 110<br>Zech. 6. 9–end<br>Rev. 11. 15–18 | Ps. 72. 1–7 [8–end]<br>1 Sam. 8. 4–20<br>John 18. 33–37 |
| Ps. ***80***; 81<br>*alt.* Ps. ***85***; 86<br>Isa. 40. 1–11<br>Rev. 14. 1–13 | **G** | | Isa. 14. 3–20<br>Matt. 9. 18–34 | Isa. 40. 1–11<br>Rev. 14. 1–13 |
| Ps. 99; ***101***<br>*alt.* Ps. 89. 19–end<br>Isa. 40. 12–26<br>Rev. 14.14 – 15.end | **G** | | Isa. ch. 17<br>Matt. 9.35 – 10.15 | Isa. 40. 12–26<br>Rev. 14.14 – 15.end |
| Ps. 121; ***122***; 123; 124<br>*alt.* Ps. ***91***; 93<br>Isa. 40.27 – 41.7<br>Rev. 16. 1–11 | **G** | | Isa. ch. 19<br>Matt. 10. 16–33 | Isa. 40.27 – 41.7<br>Rev. 16. 1–11 |
| Ps. 131; 132; ***133***<br>*alt.* Ps. 94<br>Isa. 41. 8–20<br>Rev. 16. 12–end<br>*or First EP of Andrew the Apostle*<br>Ps. 48<br>Isa. 49. 1–9a<br>1 Cor. 4. 9–16<br>**R ct** | **G** | | Isa. 21. 1–12<br>Matt. 10.34 – 11.1 | Isa. 41. 8–20<br>Rev. 16. 12–end<br>*or First EP of Andrew the Apostle*<br>(Ps. 48)<br>Isa. 49. 1–9a<br>1 Cor. 4. 9–16<br>**R ct** |
| | **G** | To celebrate the Day of Intercession and Thanksgiving for the Missionary Work of the Church, see *Common Worship* provision. | | |
| *EP*: Ps. 87; 96<br>Zech. 8. 20–end<br>John 1. 35–42 | **R** | **ANDREW THE APOSTLE**<br>Zech. 8. 20–end<br>Ps. 92. 1–5<br>Rom. 10. 9–end<br>Matt. 4. 18–22 | (Ps. 47; 147. 1–12)<br>Ezek. 47. 1–12<br>*or* Ecclus. 14. 20–end<br>John 12. 20–32 | (Ps. 87; 96)<br>Isa. 52. 7–10<br>John 1. 35–42 |

# December 2007

| Date | Day | | Sunday Principal Service<br>Weekday Eucharist | Third Service<br>Morning Prayer | Colour |
|---|---|---|---|---|---|
| 1 | Sa | *Charles de Foucauld, Hermit in the Sahara, 1916* | Dan. 7. 15–27<br>*Canticle:* Benedicite 10b–end<br>Luke 21. 34–36 | Ps. 145<br>*alt.* Ps. 96; **97**; 100<br>Isa. ch. 24<br>Matt. 11. 20–end | **R** *or* **G** |
| 2 | **S** | **THE FIRST SUNDAY OF ADVENT**<br>CW Year A begins | Isa. 2. 1–5<br>Ps. 122<br>Rom. 13. 11–end<br>Matt. 24. 36–44 | Ps. 44<br>Micah 4. 1–7<br>1 Thess. 5. 1–11 | **P** |
| 3 | M | *Francis Xavier, Missionary, Apostle of the Indies, 1552*<br>Daily Eucharistic Lectionary Year 2 begins | Isa. 4. 2–end<br>Ps. 122<br>Matt. 8. 5–11 | Ps. ***50***; 54<br>*alt.* Ps. ***1***; 2; 3<br>Isa. 25. 1–9<br>Matt. 12. 1–21 | **P** |
| 4 | Tu | *John of Damascus, Monk, Teacher, c. 749; Nicholas Ferrar, Deacon, Founder of the Little Gidding Community, 1637* | Isa. 11. 1–10<br>Ps. 72. 1–4, 18–19<br>Luke 10. 21–24 | Ps. ***80***; 82<br>*alt.* Ps. ***5***; 6 (8)<br>Isa. 26. 1–13<br>Matt. 12. 22–37 | **P** |
| 5 | W | | Isa. 25. 6–10a<br>Ps. 23<br>Matt. 15. 29–37 | Ps. 5; ***7***<br>*alt.* Ps. 119. 1–32<br>Isa. 28. 1–13<br>Matt. 12. 38–end | **P** |
| 6 | Th | **Nicholas, Bishop of Myra, c. 326**<br>Com. Bishop<br>*also* Isa. 61. 1–3<br>1 Tim. 6. 6–11<br>Mark 10. 13–16 | *or* Isa. 26. 1–6<br>Ps. 118. 18–27a<br>Matt. 7. 21, 24–27 | Ps. ***42***; 43<br>*alt.* Ps. 14; ***15***; 16<br>Isa. 28. 14–end<br>Matt. 13. 1–23 | **Pw** |
| 7 | F | **Ambrose, Bishop of Milan, Teacher, 397**<br>Com. Teacher<br>*also* Isa. 41. 9b–13<br>Luke 22. 24–30 | *or* Isa. 29. 17–end<br>Ps. 27. 1–4, 16–17<br>Matt. 9. 27–31 | Ps. ***25***; 26<br>*alt.* Ps. 17; ***19***<br>Isa. 29. 1–14<br>Matt. 13. 24–43 | **Pw** |
| 8 | Sa | **The Conception of the Blessed Virgin Mary**<br>Com. BVM | *or* Isa. 30. 19–21, 23–26<br>Ps. 146. 4–9<br>Matt. 9.35 – 10.1, 6–8 | Ps. ***9*** (10)<br>*alt.* Ps. 20; 21; ***23***<br>Isa. 29. 15–end<br>Matt. 13. 44–end | **Pw** |
| 9 | **S** | **THE SECOND SUNDAY OF ADVENT** | Isa. 11. 1–10<br>Ps. 72. 1–7 [18–19]<br>Rom. 15. 4–13<br>Matt. 3. 1–12 | Ps. 80<br>Amos ch. 7<br>Luke 1. 5–20 | **P** |
| 10 | M | | Isa. ch. 35<br>Ps. 85. 7–end<br>Luke 5. 17–26 | Ps. 44<br>*alt.* Ps. 27; ***30***<br>Isa. 30. 1–18<br>Matt. 14. 1–12 | **P** |
| 11 | Tu | | Isa. 40. 1–11<br>Ps. 96. 1, 10–end<br>Matt. 18. 12–14 | Ps. ***56***; 57<br>*alt.* Ps. 32; ***36***<br>Isa. 30. 19–end<br>Matt. 14. 13–end | **P** |
| 12 | W | Ember Day* | Isa. 40. 25–end<br>Ps. 103. 8–13<br>Matt. 11. 28–end | Ps. ***62***; 63<br>*alt.* Ps. 34<br>Isa. ch. 31<br>Matt. 15. 1–20 | **P** |

| Second Service Evening Prayer | | Calendar and Holy Communion | Morning Prayer | Evening Prayer |
|---|---|---|---|---|
| Ps. 148; 149; ***150***<br>*alt.* Ps. 104<br>Isa. 42. 10–17<br>Rev. ch. 18<br>**ct** | **G** | | Isa. ch. 24<br>Matt. 11. 20–end | Isa. 42. 10–17<br>Rev. ch. 18<br>**ct** |
| Ps. 9. 1–8 [9–end]<br>Isa. 52. 1–12<br>Matt. 24. 15–28 | **P** | **THE FIRST SUNDAY IN ADVENT**<br>Advent 1 Collect until Christmas Eve<br>Mic. 4. 1–4, 6–7<br>Ps. 25. 1–9<br>Rom. 13. 8–14<br>Matt. 21. 1–13 | Ps. 44<br>Isa. 2. 1–5<br>1 Thess. 5. 1–11 | Ps. 9. 1–8 [9–end]<br>Isa. 52. 1–12<br>Matt. 24. 15–28 |
| Ps. 70; ***71***<br>*alt.* Ps. ***4***; 7<br>Isa. 42. 18–end<br>Rev. ch. 19 | **P** | | Isa. 25. 1–9<br>Matt. 12. 1–21 | Isa. 42. 18–end<br>Rev. ch. 19 |
| Ps. ***74***; 75<br>*alt.* ***9***; 10†<br>Isa. 43. 1–13<br>Rev. ch. 20 | **P** | | Isa. 26. 1–13<br>Matt. 12. 22–37 | Isa. 43. 1–13<br>Rev. ch. 20 |
| | | | | |
| Ps. ***40***; 46<br>*alt.* Ps. 18†<br>Isa. 44. 1–8<br>Rev. 21. 9–21 | **Pw** | **Nicholas, Bishop of Myra, c. 326**<br>Com. Bishop | Isa. 28. 14–end<br>Matt. 13. 1–23 | Isa. 44. 1–8<br>Rev. 21. 9–21 |
| Ps. 16; ***17***<br>*alt.* Ps. 22<br>Isa. 44. 9–23<br>Rev. 21.22 – 22.5 | **P** | | Isa. 29. 1–14<br>Matt. 13. 24–43 | Isa. 44. 9–23<br>Rev. 21.22 – 22.5 |
| Ps. ***27***; 28<br>*alt.* Ps. ***24***; 25<br>Isa. 44.24 – 45.13<br>Rev. 22. 6–end<br>**ct** | **Pw** | **The Conception of the Blessed Virgin Mary** | Isa. 29. 15–end<br>Matt. 13. 44–end | Isa. 44.24 – 45.13<br>Rev. 22. 6–end<br>**ct** |
| Ps. 11 [28]<br>1 Kings 18. 17–39<br>John 1. 19–28 | **P** | **THE SECOND SUNDAY IN ADVENT**<br>2 Kings 22. 8–10; 23. 1–3<br>Ps. 50. 1–6<br>Rom. 15. 4–13<br>Luke 21. 25–33 | Ps. 80<br>Amos ch. 7<br>Luke 1. 5–20 | Ps. 11 [28]<br>1 Kings 18. 17–39<br>Matt. 3. 1–12 |
| Ps. ***144***; 146<br>*alt.* Ps. 26; ***28***; 29<br>Isa. 45. 14–end<br>1 Thess. ch. 1 | **P** | | Isa. 30. 1–18<br>Matt. 14. 1–12 | Isa. 45. 14–end<br>1 Thess. ch. 1 |
| Ps. ***11***; 12; 13<br>*alt.* Ps. 33<br>Isa. ch. 46<br>1 Thess. 2. 1–12 | **P** | | Isa. 30. 19–end<br>Matt. 14. 13–end | Isa. ch. 46<br>1 Thess. 2. 1–12 |
| Ps. ***10***; 14<br>*alt.* Ps. 119. 33–56<br>Isa. ch. 47<br>1 Thess. 2. 13–end | **P** | | Isa. ch. 31<br>Matt. 15. 1–20 | Isa. ch. 47<br>1 Thess. 2. 13–end |

# December 2007

| Date | Day | Colour | Observance | Sunday Principal Service<br>Weekday Eucharist | Third Service<br>Morning Prayer |
|---|---|---|---|---|---|
| 13 | Th | Pr | **Lucy, Martyr at Syracuse, 304**<br>*Samuel Johnson, Moralist, 1784*<br>Com. Martyr<br>*also* Wisd. 3. 1–7<br>2 Cor. 4. 6–15 | *or* Isa. 41. 13–20<br>Ps. 145. 1, 8–13<br>Matt. 11. 11–15 | Ps. 53; ***54***; 60<br>*alt.* Ps. 37†<br>Isa. ch. 32<br>Matt. 15. 21–28 |
| 14 | F | Pw | **John of the Cross, Poet, Teacher, 1591**<br>Ember Day*<br>Com. Teacher<br>*esp.* 1 Cor. 2. 1–10<br>*also* John 14. 18–23 | *or* Isa. 48. 17–19<br>Ps. 1<br>Matt. 11. 16–19 | Ps. 85; ***86***<br>*alt.* Ps. 31<br>Isa. 33. 1–22<br>Matt. 15. 29–end |
| 15 | Sa | P | Ember Day* | Ecclus. 48. 1–4, 9–11<br>*or* 2 Kings 2. 9–12<br>Ps. 80. 1–4, 18–19<br>Matt. 17. 10–13 | Ps. 145<br>*alt.* Ps. 41; ***42***; 43<br>Isa. ch. 35<br>Matt. 16. 1–12 |
| 16 | S | P | THE THIRD SUNDAY OF ADVENT | Isa. 35. 1–10<br>Ps. 146. 4–10<br>*or Canticle:* Magnificat<br>James 5. 7–10<br>Matt. 11. 2–11 | Ps. 68. 1–19<br>Zeph. 3. 14–end<br>Phil. 4. 4–7 |
| 17 | M | P | O Sapientia<br>*Eglantyne Jebb, Social Reformer, Founder of 'Save the Children', 1928* | Gen. 49. 2, 8–10<br>Ps. 72. 1–5, 18–19<br>Matt. 1. 1–17 | Ps. 40<br>*alt.* Ps. 44<br>Isa. 38. 1–8, 21–22<br>Matt. 16. 13–end |
| 18 | Tu | P | | Jer. 23. 5–8<br>Ps. 72. 1–2, 12–13, 18–end<br>Matt. 1. 18–24 | Ps. ***70***; 74<br>*alt.* Ps. ***48***; 52<br>Isa. 38. 9–20<br>Matt. 17. 1–13 |
| 19 | W | P | | Judg. 13. 2–7, 24–end<br>Ps. 71. 3–8<br>Luke 1. 5–25 | Ps. 144; ***146***<br>Isa. ch. 39<br>Matt. 17. 14–21 |
| 20 | Th | P | | Isa. 7. 10–14<br>Ps. 24. 1–6<br>Luke 1. 26–38 | Ps. ***46***; 95<br>Zeph. 1.1 – 2.3<br>Matt. 17. 22–end |
| 21 | F** | P | | Zeph. 3. 14–18<br>Ps. 33. 1–4, 11–12, 19–end<br>Luke 1. 39–45 | Ps. ***121***; 122; 123<br>Zeph. 3. 1–13<br>Matt. 18. 1–20 |
| 22 | Sa | P | | 1 Sam. 1. 24–end<br>Ps. 113<br>Luke 1. 46–56 | Ps. ***124***; 125; 126; 127<br>Zeph. 3. 14–end<br>Matt. 18. 21–end |
| 23 | S | P | THE FOURTH SUNDAY OF ADVENT | Isa. 7. 10–16<br>Ps. 80. 1–8 [18–20]<br>Rom. 1. 1–7<br>Matt. 1. 18–end | Ps. 144<br>Micah 5. 2–5a<br>Luke 1. 26–38 |

*For Ember Day provision, see p. 13.

**Thomas the Apostle may be celebrated on 21 December instead of 3 July.

| Second Service Evening Prayer | | Calendar and Holy Communion | Morning Prayer | Evening Prayer |
|---|---|---|---|---|
| | | **Lucy, Martyr at Syracuse, 304** | | |
| Ps. 73<br>*alt.* Ps. 39; ***40***<br>Isa. 48. 1–11<br>1 Thess. ch. 3 | **Pr** | Com. Virgin Martyr | Isa. ch. 32<br>Matt. 15. 21–28 | Isa. 48. 1–11<br>1 Thess. ch. 3 |
| Ps. 82; ***90***<br>*alt.* Ps. 35<br>Isa. 48. 12–end<br>1 Thess. 4. 1–12 | **P** | | Isa. 33. 1–22<br>Matt. 15. 29–end | Isa. 48. 12–end<br>1 Thess. 4. 1–12 |
| Ps. 93; ***94***<br>*alt.* Ps. 45; ***46***<br>Isa. 49. 1–13<br>1 Thess. 4. 13–end<br>**ct** | **P** | | Isa. ch. 35<br>Matt. 16. 1–12 | Isa. 49. 1–13<br>1 Thess. 4. 13–end<br>**ct** |
| Ps. 12 [14]<br>Isa. 5. 8–end<br>Acts 13. 13–41<br>*Gospel:* John 5. 31–40 | **P** | **THE THIRD SUNDAY IN ADVENT**<br>O Sapientia<br>Isa. 35. 1–10<br>Ps. 80. 1–7<br>1 Cor. 4. 1–5<br>Matt. 11. 2–10 | Ps. 68. 1–19<br>Zeph. 3. 14–end<br>James 5. 7–10 | Ps. 12 [14]<br>Isa. 5. 8–end<br>Acts 13. 13–41 |
| Ps. 25; ***26***<br>*alt.* Ps. ***47***; 49<br>Isa. 49. 14–25<br>1 Thess. 5. 1–11 | **P** | | Isa. 38. 1–8, 21–22<br>Matt. 16. 13–end | Isa. 49. 14–25<br>1 Thess. 5. 1–11 |
| Ps. ***50***; 54<br>*alt.* Ps. 50<br>Isa. ch. 50<br>1 Thess. 5. 12–end | **P** | | Isa. 38. 9–20<br>Matt. 17. 1–13 | Isa. ch. 50<br>1 Thess. 5. 12–end |
| Ps. 10; ***57***<br>Isa. 51. 1–8<br>2 Thess. ch. 1 | **P** | Ember Day<br>Ember CEG | Isa. ch. 39<br>Matt. 17. 14–21 | Isa. 51. 1–8<br>2 Thess. ch. 1 |
| Ps. ***4***; 9<br>Isa. 51. 9–16<br>2 Thess. ch. 2 | **P** | | Zeph. 1.1 – 2.3<br>Matt. 17. 22–end | Isa. 51. 9–16<br>2 Thess. ch. 2<br>*or First EP of Thomas*<br>(Ps. 27)<br>Isa. ch. 35<br>Heb. 10.35 – 11.1<br>**R ct** |
| Ps. 80; ***84***<br>Isa. 51. 17–end<br>2 Thess. ch. 3 | **R** | **THOMAS THE APOSTLE**<br>Ember Day<br>Job 42. 1–6<br>Ps. 139. 1–11<br>Eph. 2. 19–end<br>John 20. 24–end | (Ps. 92; 146)<br>2 Sam. 15. 17–21<br>*or* Ecclus. ch. 2<br>John 11. 1–16 | (Ps. 139)<br>Hab. 2. 1–4<br>1 Pet. 1. 3–12 |
| Ps. 24; ***48***<br>Isa. 52. 1–12<br>Jude<br>**ct** | **P** | Ember Day<br>Ember CEG | Zeph. 3. 14–end<br>Matt. 18. 21–end | Isa. 52. 1–12<br>Jude<br>**ct** |
| Ps. 113 [126]<br>1 Sam 1. 1–20<br>Rev. 22. 6–end<br>*Gospel:* Luke 1. 39–45 | **P** | **THE FOURTH SUNDAY IN ADVENT**<br>Isa. 40. 1–9<br>Ps. 145. 17–end<br>Phil. 4. 4–7<br>John 1. 19–28 | Ps. 144<br>Micah 5. 2–5a<br>Luke 1. 26–38 | Ps. 113 [126]<br>1 Sam 1. 1–20<br>Rev. 22. 6–end |

# December 2007

| Date | Day | Observance | Sunday Principal Service<br>Weekday Eucharist | Third Service<br>Morning Prayer |
|---|---|---|---|---|
| **24** | M<br>**P** | **CHRISTMAS EVE** | *Morning Eucharist*<br>2 Sam. 7. 1–5, 8–11, 16<br>Ps. 89. 2, 19–27<br>Acts 13. 16–26<br>Luke 1. 67–79 | Ps. ***45***; 113<br>Mal. 1.1, 6–end<br>Matt. 19. 1–12 |
| **25** | Tu<br>𝔚 | **CHRISTMAS DAY**<br>*Any of the following sets of readings may be used on the evening of Christmas Eve and on Christmas Day. Set III should be used at some service during the celebration.* | Isa. 9. 2–7<br>Ps. 96<br>Titus 2. 11–14<br>Luke 2. 1–14 [15–20]<br>*II*<br>Isa. 62. 6–end<br>Ps. 97<br>Titus 3. 4–7<br>Luke 2. [1–7] 8–20<br>*III*<br>Isa. 52. 7–10<br>Ps. 98<br>Heb. 1. 1–4 [5–12]<br>John 1. 1–14 | *MP*: Ps. ***110***; 117<br>Isa. 62. 1–5<br>Matt. 1. 18–end |
| **26** | W<br>**R** | **STEPHEN, DEACON, FIRST MARTYR**<br>*The reading from Acts must be used as either the first or second reading at the Eucharist.* | 2 Chron. 24. 20–22<br>*or* Acts 7. 51–end<br>Ps. 119. 161–168<br>Acts 7. 51–60<br>*or* Gal. 2. 16b–20<br>Matt. 10. 17–22 | *MP*: Ps. ***13***; 31. 1–8; 150<br>Jer. 26. 12–15<br>Acts ch. 6 |
| **27** | Th<br>**W** | **JOHN, APOSTLE AND EVANGELIST** | Exod. 33. 7–11a<br>Ps. 117<br>1 John ch. 1<br>John 21. 19b–end | *MP*: Ps. ***21***; 147. 13–end<br>Exod. 33. 12–end<br>1 John 2. 1–11 |
| **28** | F<br>**R** | **THE HOLY INNOCENTS** | Jer. 31. 15–17<br>Ps. 124<br>1 Cor. 1. 26–29<br>Matt. 2. 13–18 | *MP*: Ps. ***36***; 146<br>Baruch 4. 21–27<br>*or* Gen. 37. 13–20<br>Matt. 18. 1–10 |
| **29** | Sa<br>**Wr** | **Thomas Becket, Archbishop of Canterbury, Martyr, 1170***<br>Com. Martyr<br>*esp.* Matt. 10. 28–33<br>*also* Ecclus. 51. 1–8 | *or* 1 John 2. 3–11<br>Ps. 96. 1–4<br>Luke 2. 22–35 | Ps. ***19***; 20<br>Jonah ch. 1<br>Col. 1. 1–14 |
| **30** | **S**<br>**W** | **THE FIRST SUNDAY OF CHRISTMAS** | Isa. 63. 7–9<br>Ps. 148. [1–6] 7–end<br>Heb. 2. 10–end<br>Matt. 2. 13–end | Ps. 105. 1–11<br>Isa. 35. 1–6<br>Gal. 3. 23–end |
| **31** | M<br>**W** | *John Wyclif, Reformer, 1384* | 1 John 2. 18–21<br>Ps. 96. 1, 11–end<br>John 1. 1–18 | Ps. 102<br>Jonah chs 3 and 4<br>Col. 1.24 – 2.7 |

*Thomas Becket may be celebrated on 7 July instead of 29 December.

| **Second Service Evening Prayer** | | **Calendar and Holy Communion** | **Morning Prayer** | **Evening Prayer** |
|---|---|---|---|---|
| Ps. 85<br>Zech. ch. 2<br>Rev. 1. 1–8 | P | **CHRISTMAS EVE**<br>Coll. (1) Christmas Eve<br>(2) Advent 1<br>Mic. 5. 2–5a<br>Ps. 24<br>Titus 3. 3–7<br>Luke 2. 1–14 | Ps. ***45***; 113<br>Mal. 1.1, 6–end<br>Matt. 19. 1–12 | Ps. 85<br>Zech. ch. 2<br>Rev. 1. 1–8 |
| *EP*: Ps. 8<br>Isa. 65. 17–25<br>Phil. 2. 5–11<br>*or* Luke 2. 1–20<br>*if it has not been used at the principal service of the day* | 𝕻 | **CHRISTMAS DAY**<br>Isa. 9. 2–7<br>Ps. 98<br>Heb. 1. 1–12<br>John 1. 1–14 | Ps. 110; 117<br>Isa. 62. 1–5<br>Matt. 1. 18–end | Ps. 8<br>Isa. 65. 17–25<br>Phil. 2. 5–11<br>*or* Luke 2. 1–20 |
| *EP*: Ps. 57; ***86***<br>Gen. 4. 1–10<br>Matt. 23. 34–end | R | **STEPHEN, DEACON, FIRST MARTYR**<br>Collect<br>(1) Stephen<br>(2) Christmas<br>2 Chron. 24. 20–22<br>Ps. 119. 161–168<br>Acts 7. 55–end | Matt. 23. 34–end | (Ps. 13; 31. 1–8; 150)<br>Jer. 26. 12–15<br>Acts ch. 6 |
| *EP*: Ps. 97<br>Isa. 6. 1–8<br>1 John 5. 1–12 | W | **JOHN, APOSTLE AND EVANGELIST**<br>Collect<br>(1) John<br>(2) Christmas<br>Exod. 33. 18–end<br>Ps. 92. 11–end<br>1 John ch. 1<br>John 21. 19b–end | (Ps. 21; 147. 13–end)<br>Exod. 33. 7–11a<br>1 John 2. 1–11 | (Ps. 97)<br>Isa. 6. 1–8<br>1 John 5. 1–12 |
| *EP*: Ps. 123; ***128***<br>Isa. 49. 14–25<br>Mark 10. 13–16 | R | **THE HOLY INNOCENTS**<br>Collect<br>(1) Innocents<br>(2) Christmas<br>Jer. 31. 10–17<br>Ps. 123<br>Rev. 14. 1–5<br>Matt. 2. 13–18 | (Ps. 36; 146)<br>Baruch 4. 21–27<br>*or* Gen. 37. 13–20<br>Matt. 18. 1–10 | (Ps. 124; 128)<br>Isa. 49. 14–25<br>Mark 10. 13–16 |
| Ps. 131; ***132***<br>Isa. 57. 15–end<br>John 1. 1–18 | W | CEG of Christmas | Jonah ch. 1<br>Col. 1. 1–14 | Isa. 57. 15–end<br>John 1. 1–18 |
| Ps. 132<br>Isa. 49. 7–13<br>Phil. 2. 1–11<br>*Gospel:* Luke 2. 41–52 | W | **THE SUNDAY AFTER CHRISTMAS DAY**<br>Isa. 62. 10–12<br>Ps. 45. 1–7<br>Gal. 4. 1–7<br>Matt. 1. 18–end | Ps. 105. 1–11<br>Isa. 35. 1–6<br>Gal. 3. 23–end | Ps. 132<br>Isa. 49. 7–13<br>Phil. 2. 1–11 |
| Ps. **90**; 148<br>Isa. 59. 15b–end<br>John 1. 29–34<br>*or First EP of The Naming of Jesus*<br>Ps. 148<br>Jer. 23. 1–6<br>Col. 2. 8–15<br>**ct** | W | **Silvester, Bishop of Rome, 335**<br>Com. Bishop | Jonah chs 3 and 4<br>Col. 1.24 – 2.7 | Isa. 59. 15b–end<br>John 1. 29–34<br>*or First EP of The Circumcision of Christ*<br>(Ps. 148)<br>Jer. 23. 1–6<br>Col. 2. 8–15<br>**ct** |

# CALENDAR 2007

**JANUARY**

| | | | | | | |
|---|---|---|---|---|---|---|
| Su | .. | B | $E^2$ | $E^3$ | $E^4$ | .. |
| M | 1 | 8 | 15 | 22 | 29 | .. |
| Tu | 2 | 9 | 16 | 23 | 30 | .. |
| W | 3 | 10 | 17 | 24 | 31 | .. |
| Th | 4 | 11 | 18 | 25 | .. | .. |
| F | 5 | 12 | 19 | 26 | .. | .. |
| Sa | E | 13 | 20 | 27 | .. | .. |

**FEBRUARY**

| | | | | | | |
|---|---|---|---|---|---|---|
| Su | .. | $L^{-3}$ | $L^{-2}$ | $L^{-1}$ | $L^1$ | .. |
| M | .. | 5 | 12 | 19 | 26 | .. |
| Tu | .. | 6 | 13 | 20 | 27 | .. |
| W | .. | 7 | 14 | A | 28 | .. |
| Th | 1 | 8 | 15 | 22 | .. | .. |
| F | Pr | 9 | 16 | 23 | .. | .. |
| Sa | 3 | 10 | 17 | 24 | .. | .. |

**MARCH**

| | | | | | | |
|---|---|---|---|---|---|---|
| Su | .. | $L^2$ | $L^3$ | $L^4$ | $L^5$ | .. |
| M | .. | 5 | 12 | 19 | An | .. |
| Tu | .. | 6 | 13 | 20 | 27 | .. |
| W | .. | 7 | 14 | 21 | 28 | .. |
| Th | 1 | 8 | 15 | 22 | 29 | .. |
| F | 2 | 9 | 16 | 23 | 30 | .. |
| Sa | 3 | 10 | 17 | 24 | 31 | .. |

**APRIL**

| | | | | | | |
|---|---|---|---|---|---|---|
| Su | P | E | $E^2$ | $E^3$ | $E^4$ | ... |
| M | 2 | 9 | 16 | 23 | 30 | .. |
| Tu | 3 | 10 | 17 | 24 | .. | .. |
| W | 4 | 11 | 18 | 25 | .. | .. |
| Th | M | 12 | 19 | 26 | .. | .. |
| F | G | 13 | 20 | 27 | .. | .. |
| Sa | 7 | 14 | 21 | 28 | .. | .. |

**MAY**

| | | | | | | |
|---|---|---|---|---|---|---|
| Su | .. | $E^5$ | $E^6$ | $E^7$ | W | |
| M | .. | 7 | 14 | 21 | 28 | .. |
| Tu | 1 | 8 | 15 | 22 | 29 | .. |
| W | 2 | 9 | 16 | 23 | 30 | .. |
| Th | 3 | 10 | A | 24 | 31 | .. |
| F | 4 | 11 | 18 | 25 | .. | .. |
| Sa | 5 | 12 | 19 | 26 | .. | .. |

**JUNE**

| | | | | | | |
|---|---|---|---|---|---|---|
| Su | .. | T | $T^1$ | $T^2$ | $T^3$ | .. |
| M | .. | 4 | 11 | 18 | 25 | .. |
| Tu | .. | 5 | 12 | 19 | 26 | .. |
| W | .. | 6 | 13 | 20 | 27 | .. |
| Th | .. | 7 | 14 | 21 | 28 | .. |
| F | 1 | 8 | 15 | 22 | 29 | .. |
| Sa | 2 | 9 | 16 | 23 | 30 | .. |

**JULY**

| | | | | | | |
|---|---|---|---|---|---|---|
| Su | $T^4$ | $T^5$ | $T^6$ | $T^7$ | $T^8$ | .. |
| M | 2 | 9 | 16 | 23 | 30 | .. |
| Tu | 3 | 10 | 17 | 24 | 31 | .. |
| W | 4 | 11 | 18 | 25 | .. | .. |
| Th | 5 | 12 | 19 | 26 | .. | .. |
| F | 6 | 13 | 20 | 27 | .. | .. |
| Sa | 7 | 14 | 21 | 28 | .. | .. |

**AUGUST**

| | | | | | | |
|---|---|---|---|---|---|---|
| Su | .. | $T^9$ | $T^{10}$ | $T^{11}$ | $T^{12}$ | .. |
| M | .. | 6 | 13 | 20 | 27 | .. |
| Tu | .. | 7 | 14 | 21 | 28 | .. |
| W | 1 | 8 | 15 | 22 | 29 | .. |
| Th | 2 | 9 | 16 | 23 | 30 | .. |
| F | 3 | 10 | 17 | 24 | 31 | .. |
| Sa | 4 | 11 | 18 | 25 | .. | .. |

**SEPTEMBER**

| | | | | | | |
|---|---|---|---|---|---|---|
| Su | .. | $T^{13}$ | $T^{14}$ | $T^{15}$ | $T^{16}$ | $T^{17}$ |
| M | .. | 3 | 10 | 17 | 24 | .. |
| Tu | .. | 4 | 11 | 18 | 25 | .. |
| W | .. | 5 | 12 | 19 | 26 | .. |
| Th | .. | 6 | 13 | 20 | 27 | .. |
| F | .. | 7 | 14 | 21 | 28 | .. |
| Sa | 1 | 8 | 15 | 22 | 29 | .. |

**OCTOBER**

| | | | | | | |
|---|---|---|---|---|---|---|
| Su | .. | $T^{18}$ | $T^{19}$ | $T^{20}$ | $T^L$ | .. |
| M | 1 | 8 | 15 | 22 | 29 | .. |
| Tu | 2 | 9 | 16 | 23 | 30 | .. |
| W | 3 | 10 | 17 | 24 | 31 | .. |
| Th | 4 | 11 | 18 | 25 | .. | .. |
| F | 5 | 12 | 19 | 26 | .. | .. |
| Sa | 6 | 13 | 20 | 27 | .. | .. |

**NOVEMBER**

| | | | | | | |
|---|---|---|---|---|---|---|
| Su | .. | $A^{-4}$ | $A^{-3}$ | $A^{-2}$ | $A^{-1}$ | .. |
| M | .. | 5 | 12 | 19 | 26 | .. |
| Tu | .. | 6 | 13 | 20 | 27 | .. |
| W | .. | 7 | 14 | 21 | 28 | .. |
| Th | AS | 8 | 15 | 22 | 29 | .. |
| F | 2 | 9 | 16 | 23 | 30 | .. |
| Sa | 3 | 10 | 17 | 24 | .. | .. |

**DECEMBER**

| | | | | | | |
|---|---|---|---|---|---|---|
| Su | .. | $A^1$ | $A^2$ | $A^3$ | $A^4$ | $X^1$ |
| M | .. | 3 | 10 | 17 | 24 | 31 |
| Tu | .. | 4 | 11 | 18 | X | .. |
| W | .. | 5 | 12 | 19 | 26 | .. |
| Th | .. | 6 | 13 | 20 | 27 | .. |
| F | .. | 7 | 14 | 21 | 28 | .. |
| Sa | 1 | 8 | 15 | 22 | 29 | .. |

A = Ash Wednesday, Ascension, Advent
$A^-$ = Before Advent
$A^{-1}$ = Christ the King
$A^{-4}$ = also All Saints (if trans.)
An = Annunciation
AS = All Saints
B = Baptism
E = Epiphany, Easter
$E^4$ = also Presentation (if trans.)
G = Good Friday
L = Lent
$L^-$ = Before Lent
M = Maundy Thursday
P = Palm Sunday
Pr = Presentation
T = Trinity
($T^3$ = also Birth of John the Baptist, 2007)
($T^7$ = also Mary Magdalene, 2007)
$T^L$ = Last Sunday after Trinity
($T^L$ = also Simon and Jude, 2007)
W = Pentecost (Whit Sunday)
X = Christmas

# CALENDAR 2008

### JANUARY

| | | | | | | |
|---|---|---|---|---|---|---|
| Su | .. | E | $E^{2}$ | $E^{3}$ | $E^{4}$ | .. |
| M | .. | B | 14 | 21 | 28 | .. |
| Tu | 1 | 8 | 15 | 22 | 29 | .. |
| W | 2 | 9 | 16 | 23 | 30 | .. |
| Th | 3 | 10 | 17 | 24 | 31 | .. |
| F | 4 | 11 | 18 | 25 | .. | .. |
| Sa | 5 | 12 | 19 | 26 | .. | .. |

### FEBRUARY

| | | | | | | |
|---|---|---|---|---|---|---|
| Su | .. | $L^{-1}$ | $L^{1}$ | $L^{2}$ | $L^{3}$ | .. |
| M | .. | 4 | 11 | 18 | 25 | .. |
| Tu | .. | 5 | 12 | 19 | 26 | .. |
| W | .. | A | 13 | 20 | 27 | .. |
| Th | .. | 7 | 14 | 21 | 28 | .. |
| F | 1 | 8 | 15 | 22 | 29 | .. |
| Sa | Pr | 9 | 16 | 23 | .. | .. |

### MARCH

| | | | | | | |
|---|---|---|---|---|---|---|
| Su | .. | $L^{4}$ | $L^{5}$ | P | E | $E^{2}$ |
| M | .. | 3 | 10 | 17 | 24 | An |
| Tu | .. | 4 | 11 | 18 | 25 | .. |
| W | .. | 5 | 12 | 19 | 26 | .. |
| Th | .. | 6 | 13 | M | 27 | .. |
| F | .. | 7 | 14 | G | 28 | .. |
| Sa | 1 | 8 | 15 | 22 | 29 | .. |

### APRIL

| | | | | | | |
|---|---|---|---|---|---|---|
| Su | .. | $E^{3}$ | $E^{4}$ | $E^{5}$ | $E^{6}$ | ... |
| M | .. | 7 | 14 | 21 | 28 | .. |
| Tu | 1 | 8 | 15 | 22 | 29 | .. |
| W | 2 | 9 | 16 | 23 | 30 | .. |
| Th | 3 | 10 | 17 | 24 | .. | .. |
| F | 4 | 11 | 18 | 25 | .. | .. |
| Sa | 5 | 12 | 19 | 26 | .. | .. |

### MAY

| | | | | | | |
|---|---|---|---|---|---|---|
| Su | .. | $E^{7}$ | W | T | $T^{1}$ | |
| M | .. | 5 | 12 | 19 | 26 | .. |
| Tu | .. | 6 | 13 | 20 | 27 | .. |
| W | .. | 7 | 14 | 21 | 28 | .. |
| Th | A | 8 | 15 | 22 | 29 | .. |
| F | 2 | 9 | 16 | 23 | 30 | .. |
| Sa | 3 | 10 | 17 | 24 | 31 | .. |

### JUNE

| | | | | | | |
|---|---|---|---|---|---|---|
| Su | $T^{2}$ | $T^{3}$ | $T^{4}$ | $T^{5}$ | $T^{6}$ | .. |
| M | 2 | 9 | 16 | 23 | 30 | .. |
| Tu | 3 | 10 | 17 | 24 | .. | .. |
| W | 4 | 11 | 18 | 25 | .. | .. |
| Th | 5 | 12 | 19 | 26 | .. | .. |
| F | 6 | 13 | 20 | 27 | .. | .. |
| Sa | 7 | 14 | 21 | 28 | .. | .. |

### JULY

| | | | | | | |
|---|---|---|---|---|---|---|
| Su | .. | $T^{7}$ | $T^{8}$ | $T^{9}$ | $T^{10}$ | .. |
| M | .. | 7 | 14 | 21 | 28 | .. |
| Tu | 1 | 8 | 15 | 22 | 29 | .. |
| W | 2 | 9 | 16 | 23 | 30 | .. |
| Th | 3 | 10 | 17 | 24 | 31 | .. |
| F | 4 | 11 | 18 | 25 | .. | .. |
| Sa | 5 | 12 | 19 | 26 | .. | .. |

### AUGUST

| | | | | | | |
|---|---|---|---|---|---|---|
| Su | .. | $T^{11}$ | $T^{12}$ | $T^{13}$ | $T^{14}$ | $T^{15}$ |
| M | .. | 4 | 11 | 18 | 25 | .. |
| Tu | .. | 5 | 12 | 19 | 26 | .. |
| W | .. | 6 | 13 | 20 | 27 | .. |
| Th | .. | 7 | 14 | 21 | 28 | .. |
| F | 1 | 8 | 15 | 22 | 29 | .. |
| Sa | 2 | 9 | 16 | 23 | 30 | .. |

### SEPTEMBER

| | | | | | | |
|---|---|---|---|---|---|---|
| Su | .. | $T^{16}$ | $T^{17}$ | $T^{18}$ | $T^{19}$ | .. |
| M | 1 | 8 | 15 | 22 | 29 | .. |
| Tu | 2 | 9 | 16 | 23 | 30 | .. |
| W | 3 | 10 | 17 | 24 | .. | .. |
| Th | 4 | 11 | 18 | 25 | .. | .. |
| F | 5 | 12 | 19 | 26 | .. | .. |
| Sa | 6 | 13 | 20 | 27 | .. | .. |

### OCTOBER

| | | | | | | |
|---|---|---|---|---|---|---|
| Su | .. | $T^{20}$ | $T^{21}$ | $T^{22}$ | $T^{L}$ | .. |
| M | .. | 6 | 13 | 20 | 27 | .. |
| Tu | .. | 7 | 14 | 21 | 28 | .. |
| W | 1 | 8 | 15 | 22 | 29 | .. |
| Th | 2 | 9 | 16 | 23 | 30 | .. |
| F | 3 | 10 | 17 | 24 | 31 | .. |
| Sa | 4 | 11 | 18 | 25 | .. | .. |

### NOVEMBER

| | | | | | | |
|---|---|---|---|---|---|---|
| Su | .. | $A^{-4}$ | $A^{-3}$ | $A^{-2}$ | $A^{-1}$ | $A^{1}$ |
| M | .. | 3 | 10 | 17 | 24 | .. |
| Tu | .. | 4 | 11 | 18 | 25 | .. |
| W | .. | 5 | 12 | 19 | 26 | .. |
| Th | .. | 6 | 13 | 20 | 27 | .. |
| F | .. | 7 | 14 | 21 | 28 | .. |
| Sa | AS | 8 | 15 | 22 | 29 | .. |

### DECEMBER

| | | | | | | |
|---|---|---|---|---|---|---|
| Su | .. | $A^{2}$ | $A^{3}$ | $A^{4}$ | $X^{1}$ | .. |
| M | 1 | 8 | 15 | 22 | 29 | .. |
| Tu | 2 | 9 | 16 | 23 | 30 | .. |
| W | 3 | 10 | 17 | 24 | 31 | .. |
| Th | 4 | 11 | 18 | X | .. | .. |
| F | 5 | 12 | 19 | 26 | .. | .. |
| Sa | 6 | 13 | 20 | 27 | .. | .. |

A = Ash Wednesday, Ascension, Advent
$A^{-}$ = Before Advent
$A^{-1}$ = Christ the King
$A^{-4}$ = also All Saints (if trans.)
An = Annunciation
AS = All Saints
B = Baptism
E = Epiphany, Easter

G = Good Friday
L = Lent
$L^{-}$ = Before Lent
$L^{-1}$ = also Presentation (if trans.)
M = Maundy Thursday
P = Palm Sunday
Pr = Presentation
T = Trinity
($T^{6}$ = also Peter and Paul, 2008)

($T^{14}$ = also Bartholomew, 2008)
($T^{17}$ = also Holy Cross Day, 2008)
($T^{18}$ = also Matthew, 2008)
$T^{L}$ = Last Sunday after Trinity
W = Pentecost (Whit Sunday)
X = Christmas
($X^{1}$ = also Holy Innocents, 2008)